DIALOGUES IN THE DIA

DIALOGUES IN THE DIASPORAS
ESSAYS AND CONVERSATIONS ON CULTURAL IDENTITY

NIKOS PAPASTERGIADIS

Rivers Oram Press
LONDON AND NEW YORK

First published in 1998 by
Rivers Oram Press
144 Hemingford Road, London N1 1DE

Distributed in the USA by New York University Press
Elmer Holmes Bobst Library, 70 Washington Square South
New York, NY10012-1091

Set in Sabon by NJ Design Associates, Romsey, Hants
and printed in Great Britian by
TJ International Ltd, Padstow, Cornwall

Cataloguing in Publication Data
A catalogue record for this book is available from the British Library

ISBN 1 85489 094 8 (cloth)
ISBN 1 85489 095 6 (paperback)

CONTENTS

For Heather

PREFACE

This collection of essays and interviews focuses on the problematics of situating cultural identity within a transnational framework. Although it can be seen as a record of a personal and ongoing journey between Australia and Europe, I hope it will find resonance for others working in different locations. While addressing the significance of cultural identity as a social phenomenon, it also engages with a number of new theoretical and aesthetic approaches. It is best read as a collaborative document which has embarked on diverse trajectories rather than as an anthology which surveys and maps a given field.

The aim of the book is to evaluate the issue of cultural identity. Why has it emerged as one of the dominant political forces of our time? How has contemporary theory and art responded to the current shifts? While the essays and interviews touch on a wide spectrum of disciplines from English, sociology, history of art, anthropology and media studies, these forays are also loosely guided by the complex collisions and collusions that have occurred between critical theory, feminism, cultural studies and poststructuralism in the past decade. Thus the book begins with the awareness that cultural identity is not just a race relations 'problem', and that it can no longer be represented within a discourse that presupposes purity, originality and exclusivity. However, once this essentialist discourse on identity has been rejected, and both the flux of fragmentation and generative dynamics of difference have been acknowledged, what next? Is it possible to define a cultural politics from these perspectives? My approach has been to structure the essays and interviews in the form of a loose dialogue between theory and practice.

Stuart Hall has often reminded us that the debate on cultural identity, while coeval with modernity and heightened by the processes of globilisation, has shifted from the margins to the centre of critical discourse. This shift, he notes, has only sharpened our awareness of the theoretical impasses that surround the concept of agency. In the face of the dominant debates which polarise oppositions and elide potential affinities, we must offer a more satisfying account of what is now called the process by which we come to recognise ourselves in relation to others. All too often it is perceived as the articulation of our intrinsic differences and its representations have been largely confined to the parading of badges and the bearing of scars. This process is always inflected in a context of power, hence the production and regulation of identity is always a dialogue and/or a contest with others.

Most of these essays and interviews were started either in the office of *Third Text*, which remains one of the most inspiring corridors of London, a global city, or were launched from collaborations with artists in my native Australia, a place which also has been marked deeply by its own histories of colonialism and migration. This 'shuttling' between places and the various encounters with my interlocutors have bolstered my efforts to contest the conventional models which either reduced cultural identity to an exotic commodity, or coded it within an 'us' and 'them' hierarchy. In an age of globalised cultural dissemination and the return of vicious ethno-chauvinists, we need to propose new visions of identity that go beyond the dangerous calls for purity and the outdated claims of universalism. It is for this reason that I have also included a long and painful essay on Bosnia. The ethical questions of cultural difference and the political struggles to construct multicultural modes of existence have complex histories. These are challenges which were not just born yesterday, nor are they somebody else's problem. Hence the essay on Bosnia is here, as if we need reminding, because, while the challenges of cultural difference found their sharpest moments in the context of postcolonialism, these conflicts have an ongoing history. We now confront the question of difference within the boundaries of the self, nation and home.

Towards the end of the First World War, Tristan Tzara revealed a secret: 'The thought is made in the mouth'. While I admit that these essays and conversatons have been drafted and edited, I hope that they have retained the presence of the other. In particular, the conversations are structured by the desire to discover the processes of 'thinking together'. The act of speaking to others can often tell us things about ourselves that the process of one's own reflection hides. From this perspective, my long and awkward questions are more like invitational gestures, beckoning to share space and to enquire into further possibilities. They are not predetermined requests for information. I am deeply indebted to the profound generosity shown by my friends and I apologise for my 'shuttling' across their ideas.

While such a collection could never have a proper end, the present configuration encourages me to keep pushing further, rather than the comfortable feeling that everything is now in place. This perspective is analogous to the meaning that I would give the term 'diaspora'. To be in the diaspora does not mean to be in a place which has simply transplanted the original home on to foreign soil. Diasporic culture cannot be seen in organicist terms, as if it were a seed that could be transported, and planted elsewhere. What I have tried to present here is a sense of diasporas that says more about a sensibility towards cultural transformation than designating a place of arrival and rebirth. The homeland is, for a diasporic sensibility, both absent and present.

I hope this multivocal assemblage will be read by those thinkers who are searching for new trajectories of belonging and have given attention to the 'third space' that energises the relationship between culture and identity.

INTRODUCTION
THE HOME IN MODERNITY

Home
A sort of honour, not a building site
wherever we are, when, if we chose we might
be somewhere else, but trust we have chosen right
W.H. Auden, 'In Wartime' (1942)

THE PROMISED LAND

The context for thinking about where we belong can no longer be defined according to a purely geographic notion of place and historical sense of connection. Our sense of 'who we are' and 'where we belong' has been cross-cut by a variety of global forces. The migration of peoples, the circulation of symbols and the destabilisation of the work place have all radically affected the associations with place. Although satisfying our 'feelings for belonging' may sound too abstract, today we are more like passengers in a project called modernity than we are inhabitants of a given place. Naming the project is one thing but knowing its trajectory is another. Does modernity still promise to be the home of enlightenment, progress and reason, or is it an exilic state shrouded by techno-mystification, sliding deeper into chaos, committed to inequality, a shabby justification for ecological and cultural upheaval? Modern assumptions are contradictory: on the one hand there is the belief that change makes things better, and on the other we would prefer things to stay as they are. Modernity begins with the belief in both the journey away from and the permanence of home. For all of us who are travellers on the major highways and multiple backroads of modernity there are lurking hopes. Yet, even to articulate these hopes we usually assert a different tone. This private but familiar voice is often evoked both as a plea and as a form of reassurance. I often hear it in these terms:

No matter how far we go, we can always return home.
No matter how crazy the world gets, things will always be the same back home.
No matter what they expect you to become out there, you can always be yourself at home.
No matter what they do, this is how we do things here, at home.

In these four statements we can hear the promise of return and stability that underwrites the journeys of modernity: home is where the heart lies. These 'maternal' assurances remind us that despite the geographic migrations, social upheavals, personal crises and cultural differences there is one privileged place where origin and destiny intersect, a place where security and integrity are not compromised. In the opening song to the popular American comedy *Cheers*, we hear these very assurances in the most touching way:

You wanna go where the people know
people are all the same.
You wanna go where everybody knows your name.

In a society where the domestic space is filled with trauma and insecurity, the idealised image of a 'pub' can appear as a more plausible symbol of home. Irrespective of its location home is the sacred place from which everything else is mapped. Our outward adventures are measured in relation to home. Dreams of journeys begin from home and the rest of the world extends outwardly from this radix. Mapping elsewhere is also a homing device. Our inward returns are read as confirmations of an incontrovertible dynamism. The meaning of the home has both a centrifugal and centripetal force, it combines both our inner and outer trajectories. Home is the centre of the world.

This seemingly universal belief is indifferent to any rational argument about the relativity of our particular view of home. Even if we admit that not every house is a home, we still have to acknowledge that the ideal of the home is not defined by the realities of the house. Such a concept of home is impervious to any criticism that seems to come from outside. The ideal home is not just a house which offers shelter, or a repository that contains material objects. Apart from its physical protection and market value, a home is a place where personal and social meaning are grounded. Different parts of a house may serve as the home for different members. The space of house may be defined by its material structures whereas the home is divided by symbolic boundaries. These boundaries emerge from a matrix of identification and projection and vary according to gender and age. Home is more of a symbolic space than a physical place.

The centrality of the home does not seem to be disturbed by drawing our attention to the particularity of different notions of the home, however a more fundamental challenge may now be coming from within it. We can always defend ourselves or even rebuild after the home has been attacked from outside, but how do you deal with that slow but determined process of implosion? What happens when our sense of home is filled with trauma? In contemporary Britain the discussions of home are not usually couched in terms of ontological mapping, rather they are framed by the burden of negative equity, the incessant fear of burglary, the unknown pathologies of murder and the increasingly stringent policies of asylum. Care for the elderly and disabled is administered in institutions which are euphemistically named 'homes'. The home is also now a place of ambient fears.

HOMES AND THEIR HISTORIES

In folklore the significance of the home is defined by its relation to the outside. The home may be a clearing within a forest, a camp in the middle of a desert, an island surrounded by sea. The outside space is usually perceived as dark, hostile and capricious. Beyond the clearing lies the devil. Away from the camp there are no signs of life. Out in the sea changes occur without notice. This sense of the outside as the place of threat and the unknown heightens the significance of home as the place of safety, order and even divine protection. Home is not only the place which is marked out as your own, but also the specific place in which you will be recognised by others and, most importantly, by God. To leave home is always risky.

Novalis's aphorism that 'philosophy is a homesickness of the mind' has found resonance in many great literary works which, often written from the perspective of exile, give us the most clear sighted views of home. The exile misses many things: the loss of familiar signs makes every turn problematic. Disconnected from

the place where action was guided by experience the exile is catapulted into social space where nothing can be taken for granted.
The smell of the sea, the glare of sunlight, a certain way of greet-
ing people, all these ordinary things once taken from the exile,
make the rest of living a drudgery. Exiles always complain about
the food and weather. Dante even found stairs more difficult to
climb when he was away from his native Florence. It is narcissism's
energy and the momentum drawn from the recognition by others
that is undermined by exile.

When Ovid was banished to the outposts of the Roman Empire
his judges made this punishment on the basis of two calculations:
the state would find security by establishing a distance between its
capital and this critic, but it would also find some aesthetic pleasure in silencing his 'wicked tongue'. Ovid's punishment was not
just measured by the miles he was sent out of Rome, but by the
relationship to language in this antipode. Flung out in this 'bar-bar-
ous' outpost where physical subsistence was the imperative Ovid's
communication was stripped of the excesses of language. In his
case exile was a place where the author became threatened with
silence, where one's link to the historical chain of peers, ancestors
and successors is cut.

These oppositions between home as the embodiment of culture,
order, history and exile as wilderness, chaos, oblivion are repeated
in modern literature. Through the representation of the home as
the place where it is possible to observe the expression of specific
cultural values, the development of unique traditions and the display of certain states of emotion, we are also witness to the
characteristic forms of modern identity. However, the focal point
of identity and historical consciousness shifts as it stresses a relationship between the home and the nation. The symbols and
narratives of the nation can only resonate if they are admitted into
the chamber of the home. The memory of the nation must also
inform the life-narratives of the people. The language that is spoken at home becomes the most intimate medium of a national soul.
Language, religion and nationality were envisaged by Stephen
Dedalus as a series of constrictive nets, but was not Joyce, the exile,
aiming to forge in the smithy of his soul 'the uncreated conscience
of his race'. The symbolic space of the home in modernity is
pressed up against both the traditional values of stability and
unspecified desires for transformation.

While Mircea Eliade defined the traditional home as the axis point which secured the unity between the domestic and the spiritual, a link that connected the individual vertically in time to ancestry and horizontally in space to kin, this process of ontological reconciliation is also echoed in Gaston Bachelard's reading of the metaphors of home in modern poetry.[1] The only difference between the traditional and the modern home is that the former was seen as a complete container of memories and a stable site of identification, whereas the latter is more a patchwork of silent ambitions and temporary arrangements. John Berger hints at the unstated dreams and unstable ground in modernity when he states that, 'Home is no longer a dwelling but the untold story of a life being lived.'[2]

When Georg Lukaçs developed the concept 'transcendental homelessness' he was speaking as much about the modern intellectual condition as he was about any individual's fate.[3] Hannah Arendt was one of the philosophers who escaped Nazism. After surviving the tragic crossing of the Pyrenees where Walter Benjamin took his life, she eventually arrived in New York and stayed for the rest of her life without unpacking her suitcases.[4] This figurative expression of existential homelessness is not a dismissal of the hope of home for there are only three options for an exile: to defer the homecoming to an idealised time in the future, to find a substitute home in the here and now, or madness. The exile becomes conscious of the necessary illusions of integration in the home, and the imaginary boundaries of belonging. In the brilliant and haunting fragments of *Minima Moralia*, Theodor Adorno evoked his own experiences of exile as a precarious balance between the dislocation from the past and the poisonous relations to the present.[5] Adorno becomes his own torturer, always interrogating himself about the losses of language, the betrayal of values and the destruction of an historical consciousness. 'After Auschwitz' exile is, paradoxically, a permanent condition, even as redemption is not foreclosed but deferred to an indefinite future.

MAPPING THE WORLD FROM HOME

Mapping the world starts with the primary marker of the home. The distinctions between self/other; inside/outside; order/chaos revolve around the prior constructions of the home as the position from which these values can be discerned. Home is the place where moral knots are untied and ethical patterns are stitched together. Cosmologies are significant in so far as they can address the local by differentiating it from the beyond. The primacy of the home is, however, not simply determined in a strict opposition to the space beyond. Between the inner sanctum of homely order and the outer territories of chaos lies a continuum of intermediate spaces. For the Russian semiotician of culture Yuri Lotman a variation of anti-homes are erected between the home and the state of homelessness. These anti-homes confirm the use of the home as the primary mapping mechanism because their identity is defined in relation to the ideal type of the home. The status of silence may serve as the key marker between home and anti-home. Silence signifies tranquillity in the home, whereas in the anti-home silence is filled with a deafening anguish.

Social critics who see modernity only in apocalyptic terms have not used the opportunity to classify the obvious sites of deprivation as the negation of the home. The anti-home has been identified as being located on the peripheries of the city, buried in the underground passages, raised on wheels and traversing the open roads. Brothels, for instance, wedged between the sites of all-male industrial labour, are conventionally seen as inverting the norms of domestic life. Yet, in Lotman's terms, the anti-home is not defined by inversion or deprivation, the cardboard homes of 'travellers', precariously positioned in the entrance of exclusive department stores, may commune with the principles of the ideal home: 'What distinguishes a home from an anti-home is not just dilapidation, neglect and lack of cosiness.'[6] In Lotman's account the anti-home is always riven with jealousies and rivalries. In contrast the home is where you are above suspicion and reproach, where belonging is free from the curse of evil or the burden of conflict. Or, as an Australian suburbanite once noted, 'home is a place where you can sing as you please and not care what your neighbour thinks'. In other contexts the closing of curtains does not announce the beginnings of intimacy and freedom but the concealment of shame. The private is always subject to scrutiny for the public.

The identification of home as a place of personal and familial development is, as David Morgan has observed, a phenomenon which is neither a permanent nor universal feature of social life. The value given to home can only be understood in its variations. Morgan's discussion of the home highlights two important relationships, first, its inscription in a series of strategies of surveillance; second, as a gendered space.[7] When the concept of home is confined to domesticity this space is usually identified as maternal or feminine. However, not all of the home belongs to women. The division of labour, say from the kitchen to the garage, constructs gendered boundaries that differentiate the spaces within the home. The performance of banal tasks, such as who takes out the rubbish, may highlight both the contingency and the continuity of boundaries between inside and outside. As the outside world is characterised as dangerous and impersonal the home becomes a privileged space for nurturing intimacy. The Australian suburbanite may harbour the fantasy of freedom in his home, but this freedom is in turn dependent on a broader social stability. In a world where trust has been thoroughly eviscerated, the watchful eye of the neighbourhood extends from the maintenance of taste to protection against crime and also includes the monitoring of sexual and childhood abuse. Thus the sanctity of privacy at home is far from assured.

MOVING ON WITH MODERNITY

The concept of home is not safe in modernity. One of the clear objectives of modernism is to move out of the old home but the precise shape and location of the new home of modernity is never specified. The old home needs to be left behind because from the modernist's perspective it is locked into the frozen time of the past: bound to unchangeable customs; restricted to pure members; ruled by strict authoritarian father figures; stifled by superstitious beliefs. In short the old home represents closed traditions. To stay there is to atrophy. In contrast, modernity promises a sense of the present which is open, encourages mobility over stability, promotes difference as the stimulus for novelty, suggests that decision making should be participatory, and recognises that reason bows to no God. The spirit of modernity is defined by the dynamism for change; the significance of place is always secondary in this revolution against the rooted practices of being and belonging.

Modernity sought to sweep away the remnants of tradition, yet it actually displayed a degree of 'dialectical hesitancy'[8] when it came up against the home. For if modernity swept away the past, it also had to invent a new mode of living in the present. The forms of individualism that are expressive of this new age emphasise that identity is not bound to a specific past or a particular place. The 'self-made man' of modernity needed a new home, yet the modern home could also be read as the greatest oxymoron of our age. For if the home nested in traditions which were by definition incompatible with modernity, then the modern home could only, and at best, be the white cubic spaces divested of any crannies in which traces of the past may lurk, or a crowded museum in which kitsch orders memory. The concept of home haunts modernity. In an age where moving out of home is the first sign of independence, and yet when there is no definite sense of where to go, the prospects of finding the ideal home seem constantly threatened by a looming fear of living in a state of permanent homelessness. Modernity may be fully committed to a process of detraditionalisation but it either balks at pursuing its central target or only partially achieves its own goal by hollowing out any value in the prize. What many of the modernists, like Baron Hausmann who saw space as either a neutral stage or an impediment to utopian grids, failed to appreciate, was that the semantic richness in the experience of the home was also inextricably linked to an historically elliptical and unconscious process of ontological mapping.

The significance of traditions was found in the extent that they enable individuals to connect their identity within a time-space continuum. Traditions are forms for the articulation of memory and meaning. The technocratic assumption that traditions can be dispensed with, presumes that after a change of season they are as superfluous as the snake's winter skin. This analogy overlooks the resilience of traditions: they return like the next layer of skin. Yet this rhetorical oversight is repeated throughout the discourses of modernity. When Marx gave us that insight into the drive of modernity with the iconic phrase: "all that is solid melts into air", this was also a prophecy of the perils of detraditionalisation. This ambivalence towards tradition in modernity is compulsively reiterated by the founding fathers of classical social theory. These great bearers of the enlightenment felt deeply opposed to tradition, they saw it as a source of mystification, an enemy to reason and an obstacle against progress. Yet it is tradition which offered the necessary interpretative framework and safety net for social meaning. The moral deficit that is expressed in Weber's phrase 'the iron cage of disenchantment', and Durkheim's account of vertiginous 'anomie' is nowhere felt so painfully as it is in the modern home.

Despite the contemporary anxiety over the status of the home, with responses varying from the extreme sterilisation of domesticity in the radiant plans of Le Corbusier,[9] to the bulimic display of homeliness in the 'cyburbian' pastiche of American cities that has been described by Sorkin and others;[10] either way, it is unlikely that the concept of the home will disappear in modernity. The search for home is neither a nostalgic retreat to a familiar past nor a defensive reaction against the brutalities of the present. The meaning of home is now found in the future-oriented projects of constructing a sense of belonging in a context of change and displacement.

Lazlo Maholy-Nagy was one of the few artists and critics to understand that the problem of housing was far too important to be left to the specialists. Throughout his writing there is the suggestion that our relationship to space is never neutral but expressive of all the broader contradictions that affect the intensity and clarity of living in a modern context. This aspiration to shape the space which we inhabit positively is, he notes, totally alien to architects and builders. 'Yet, beyond the satisfaction of his eliminatory bodily needs, man must also experience space in his home — at least, he must learn to experience it. The home must not be allowed to be an escape from space but a living-in-space, an honest relationship with it.'[11]

The question of belonging in modernity requires a fundamental rethinking of our relationship to space. In classical social theory the predominant understanding of this relationship proceeded from a strict polarity which stressed that the traditional home was a place of integration and conformity whereas the modern home is a place of self-expression and freedom. The shift from one position to the other can be heard in every teenager's demand: 'I need my own space'. It is indicative of the limited frameworks for understanding change in our culture that the space of the past is considered as embedded within a closed territory. This is evident in the classical definitions of community which stressed unity of purpose and the occupation of a given place. The idea that community is formed out of the sharing not only of particular interests by a group of people but a common and universal framework 'wide enough and complete enough to include their lives' is looking increasingly remote.[12] Such a view on the question of belonging is now bending to a perspective which stresses that the consequences of industrialisation and global migration have generated looser social affiliations and more hybrid cultural formations. Anthony Giddens has argued that one of the characteristic features of modernity is the destruction of fixed attachments to place. The dynamic of modernity is towards fragmentation and dispersal and therefore all identifications with place are invariably contingent and partial, and inevitably disruptive of the embedded character of traditional social relations. Giddens argues that,

> In traditional societies, the past is honoured and symbols are valued because they contain and perpetuate the experience of generations. Tradition is a means of handling time and space, which inserts any particular activity or experience within the continuity of past, present and future, these in turn being structured by recurrent social practices.[13]

Modern identity is no longer confirmed by an exclusive and autonomous linkage between time and space. The question 'Who am I?' can no longer be answered by identifying our place of origin and the time of living there. Even the most local identities are now influenced by global processes. The disjunctive processes of globalisation and even the defensive strategies of localisation are both defined by a framework of 'time-space distanciation'. Modernity increasingly tears space away from place, and Giddens describes this process of lifting out relationships from local contexts as the disembedding of the social system.[14] Perhaps this ambivalence with the concepts of home and community is expressive of an unresolved yearning for domesticity in an age of excessive mobility.[15]

Modern nostalgia is not a wish to return to the mother's womb. The answer to the dilemmas of the migrant experience is not just to pack up and go home. Few who have left their native village and headed to the foreign city retain the illusion of a triumphal return. It is not just the chilling thought that their place of origin will have changed, leaving them with the sense that they are still out of place, but there is also the wish to claim something for themselves within the new city. Since I grew up in the migrant neighbourhoods of Melbourne, I have become conscious of how the home is the archetypal test-tube of modernity. Greek migrants were obsessed with home-ownership. Not only were loans repaid with record speed and at great personal sacrifice but the structures of these homes became symbols of their journey. The space for the suburban garden was redrawn to accommodate a mini vegetable patch. Neo-classical columns were knocked down and replaced with the smooth 'Roman' arches. Tomatoes and chili peppers on one side, ferns and gum trees on the other, the sweeping concrete driveway with its impeccable straight borders was not only an expression of cleanliness but also an incorporation of the order of modern geometries. Whenever I read Homi Bhabha's discussion of the 'double frame'[16] of the diasporic aesthetic I think of one of my neighbours who had painted images from his Aegean island within the six inset panels of his front door. Whenever he returned home he, would resee the scenes that were visible from the porch of his father's house: small boats in the harbour and a lighthouse on the cliffs. These 'hand painted postcards', like windows on this old Victorian door evoke another world which exists simultaneously in the mind's eye of this householder. This world keeps moving and the current occupants, a family of refugees from Vietnam, when returning home to this door face at least three worlds. Migration is best described as a series of waves. The migrant desires repetition and difference. The migrant home always combines the sensual experience of novelty and familiarity.

A sense of the 'great transformation' ushered in by modernity has often been mapped out in terms of the shift from the 'knowable community' to 'imagined communities'. Traditional communities were considered 'knowable' because most social relations were conducted on a face-to-face basis. Knowledge of others was often determined on the basis of physical and proximate relations or through oral forms of storytelling. By contrast modern societies, as Benedict Anderson pointed out, construct a sense of community out of a much broader social space. The characteristic form of unity in the modern nation is not defined by the 'vertical' development of a local and intimate relation but is an imaginary horizontal association with other members.

It is imagined because the members of even the smallest nations will never know most of their fellow members, meet them, or even hear of them, yet in the minds of each lives the image of their communion.[17]

How this sense of communion is transmitted in order to consolidate these abstract forms of social bonding is a key question in contemporary thought. Anderson has stressed the importance of the print media and the utilisation of symbols and traditions in the origins of nationalism. Few social theorists have extended this idea to the importance of camera-based media in reconstructing identity in modern society. John Thompson has recently theorised the practice of conducting significant relationships through mediatised technologies as part of the 'remooring of tradition'. 'With the development of the media ... individuals were able to experience events, observe others and, in general, learn about worlds — both real and imaginary — that extended well beyond the sphere of day-to-day encounters.'[18] Mediatised encounters which have scant regard to distance are the ascendant forms of social interaction. The symbolic content in these new forms of communication is in itself expressive of a new relationship to place. Paul Virilio has gone one step further and noted that the impact of new camera-based technologies has fundamentally altered our relationship between perception and agency.

Everything I see is in principle within my reach, at least within reach of my sight, is marked on the map of the 'I can'. In this important formulation Merleau-Ponty pinpoints precisely what will eventually find itself ruined by the banalisation of a certain teletopology. The bulk of what I see is, in fact and in principle, no longer within my reach. And even if it lies within reach of my sight, it is no longer necessarily inscribed on the maps of the 'I can'. The logistics of perception in fact destroys what earlier modes of representation preserved of this original, ideally human happiness, the 'I can' of sight, which kept art from being obscene.[19]

From Virilio's insight into the transformation of the connection between vision and experience we gain an understanding of both the prevailing blasé attitude in everyday life towards the televisual display of other people's pain, suffering and drama, as well as a hint at the cost of privileging sight as the dominant medium for the linkages of power and knowledge. The enlightenment's elevation of the sense of sight as the ultimate beholder of authority had its limits, and modernity unceasingly pushed itself towards these boundaries. The eye of the enlightenment, with its forward-looking fixation, was not entirely detached from the consumerist body of modern culture that both devoured and scorned all signs of backwardness.[20] The presumption that the past was a closed space or that tradition could be reduced either to a manipulable commodity or to a reified spectacle that could be inserted within the consumption industry, was symptomatic of the enlightenment view of history as the linear march of progress. Traditions have to be seen as the principles with which a society interprets its place in the world. The construction of tradition as the antonym of modernity was an all too convenient marker for the grand narratives of progress through change. Traditions have become disembedded, or rather the gaps between belief and practice and the fluidity in the formation of traditions have become all the more accentuated.

LEAVING HOME

> You won't find a new country, won't find another shore.
> This city will always pursue you.
> You'll walk the same streets, grow old
> in the same neighbourhoods, turn grey in the same houses.
> You'll always end in this city. ...
> Cavafy

I would like to end by considering the question 'Can we ever leave home?', from the perspective of another question; 'What kind of commitments should we give to the home?' Cavafy's poem is a caustic slap against the modern myth that one can escape the past by leaving home. A haunting sense of repetition pumps through the body of the man, who thought that he could leave his old self behind. The dread of eternal return freezes him as if his veins were filled with cold blood. It is a poem that castigates the man who thought he would resolve things by drifting away from the source as it reminds him that the source is always carried within himself. The home is never left behind.

Yet the dream of escaping is a powerful one in our age. From the promiscuous view 'wherever I lay my hat that's my home', to the categorical declaration 'that you will never see me back home', there is the conviction that one can break with the past and develop new attachments elsewhere. Roger Palmer's photographic installation explicitly sets out to investigate how one responds to a city in which you live but do not belong. The work involved twenty-one close-up photographs which show castings of Glasgow's coat of arms. The choice of symbol is far from accidental. With a degree of both fondness and sadness Palmer successively stages the decaying spirit of civic pride. Originally each casting had an identical sense of fortitude, but now each is in a different state of blistered, corroded or over-painted transmutation. The signature of the city ages variously according to the strength of local economies. Yet each of these images gives no indication of their location. Place is totally bracketed out from these signs.

Why should these images speak for an artist who has lived for over a decade in Glasgow and who states that 'I can be as happy living here as I can be in Cape Town, and feel as strange in both these places as I do when I return to the place where I grew up'. Palmer must position himself like a flâneur whose sense of attachment to place is perhaps confined to a form of vision that lightly passes over the surfaces of a city without aiming to disrupt the space. This is neither a boastful cosmopolitanism nor an expression of alienation, nevertheless the haunting air of detachment is unmistakable. Palmer does not give us any insight into what sort of space and timeframe he engages with in this city. There is just a slow but abstract display of anonymity in the signage of place. Does the city mirror back this sense of growing old, being forgotten and leaving without any trace of recognition. Sartre said 'Hell is other people' but, while they continue to speak of you death and oblivion will not quite engulf you. The only way we can break with the past is to pretend that we live in an absolute present. To confine movement to the present is one way of bypassing commitments to space. But as my mother always complained, 'Your home is not a hotel'.

REFERENCE NOTES

1. Gaston Bachelard, *The Poetics of Space*, tr. M. Jolas, Beacon Press, Boston, 1969.
2. John Berger, *And Our Faces, My Heart, Brief as Photos*, Writers and Readers, London, 1984, p.64.
3. Georg Lukaçs, *The Theory of the Novel*, tr. A. Bostock, Merlin, London, 1971.
4. This account of Hannah Arendt's life, proposed by Richard Sennett, clearly exaggerates the asceticism of exile and, while it is contradicted by her biographer, it is still revealing of the image of a spiritual homelessness.
5. Theodor Adorno, *Minima Moralia*, tr. E. Jephcott, Verso, London, 1974.
6. Yuri Lotman, *The Universe of the Mind*, tr. Ann Shukman, I.B. Tauris, London, 1991.
7. David Morgan, *Family Connections*, Polity Press, Cambridge, 1996, p.179.
8. To use George Steiner's phrase from *Extraterritorial*, Faber & Faber, London, 1972.
9. Le Corbusier, *The Radiant City*, Faber & Faber, London, 1967.
10. Michael Sorkin, ed., *Variations on a Theme Park*, Hill & Wang, New York, 1992.
11. Lazlo Maholy-Nagy, 'Man and his House', *Maholy-Nagy*, K. Passuth, tr. E. Grunz, Thames & Hudson, London, 1985, p.309.
12. I.. MacIver, *Society: Its Structure and Changes,* quoted in Margaret Wood, *The Stranger: A Study in Social Relationships*, Columbia University Press, New York, 1934, p.53.
13. Anthony Giddens, *The Consequences of Modernity*, Polity Press, Cambridge, 1990, p.37.
14. In a parallel vein but with different tones, Nestor Garcia Canclini argues that the traditions which shape contemporary communities are not only no longer bound to specific locales, but that social theorists over-emphasised the way tradition was fixed to a specific place, mired in atavistic rituals and enclosed within specific kinship networks.
15. Cf. 'what we suffer most from these days is an excess of domesticity and a nostalgia from mobility', Guillermo Santamarina, 'Recodifying a Non-Existent Field', *Global Visions*, ed., Jean Fisher, Kala Press, London, 1995, p.23.
16. See Homi Bhabha, *The Location of Culture*, Routledge, London, 1995.
17. Benedict Anderson, *Imagined Communities*, Verso, London, 1983, p.15.
18. John B. Thompson, *The Media and Modernity*, Polity Press, Cambridge, 1995, p.180.
19. Paul Virilio, *The Vision Machine*, Indiana University Press, Bloomington, 1994, p.7.
20. For a remarkable study of the ubiquity of visual technologies and their effects in the displacements of modernity, see Scott McQuire, *Vision and Modernity*, Sage, London, forthcoming.

1.
THE ACT OF APPROACHING
A CONVERSATION WITH JOHN BERGER

John Berger was born in London in 1926 and began his writing career as the art critic for the *New Statesman* in 1951. The essays he wrote in the following decade were a constant exercise in opening up the relationship between art and politics. These controversial essays which often ignited spirited debates were the seeds for his popular film programmes and most influential book, *Ways of Seeing*, published in 1972. His first novel, *A Painter of Our Time*, 1958, which sensitively explored the hopes and struggles of an artist in exile, was met with a savage attack by the right and was withdrawn from the bookshops by his publisher. In the early seventies, while researching for *A Seventh Man*, 1975, his social documentary of the migrant experience, he visited a number of peasant villages in the French Alps. This experience reinforced a deeply held respect for the courage and resilience of the peasantry. For over twenty-five years he has lived and worked there. This has also provided the starting-point for a trilogy called *Into Their Labour*, which comprises two collections of short stories, *Pig Earth*, 1979 and *Once in Europa*, 1987, as well as a novel *Lilac and Flag*, 1990. This work chronicles the complex transitions from traditional rural to contemporary urban society.

Throughout his life, Berger has pushed himself into new frontiers of thought, straddled disciplines and media, and with every step expanded our 'ways of seeing'. His novel *G* was awarded the Booker prize in 1972, and his essays on art are amongst the most profound and exciting statements on modern culture. Berger is also a painter, playwright, poet and the author of numerous screenplays. All his work is an encounter with the journeys of other people's lives. In this epoch, which he has rightly characterised as the 'century of banishment', it is a constant struggle to narrate 'the bricolage of the soul'. He has remained an intensely political writer, never losing sight of the subtle needs and the glimmers of hope in everyday life. Storytelling, in his hands, has been sculpted into a form of communion which gives pleasure as it prompts resistance.

Nikos Papastergiadis Now that your trilogy *Into Their Labour* is complete, it might be an opportunity to ask you to tell a few stories about storytelling. In particular I would like to focus on the space of the other in the project of writing. Perhaps we can investigate the presence of a borderline between the self and the other in the writing process.

John Berger Is it a borderline, or is it a process of osmosis? As soon as you begin to think of writing about another human being you begin to efface that border. You might then ask, where does the energy come from for the effacement of that border? I think it comes from what one has already lived. That which has become part of one's own experience and life is already other people. If one wants to put it in a rather cheap aphorism: the self is already collective. That collective is made of all those people with whom one has interacted positively or negatively, it is made up of pain and pleasure, of hope and fear, of security and risk. Think, for example, of how we dream of people, either of people who are dead but whom we knew, or people who we once knew and are still alive. We say that they come back to us in our dreams, but what it means is that they are already within in us. Writing about other people at the most primary and deep level is writing about those who are already inside us. I'll give an example which says something about the area which we are trying to approach. About ten days ago I was in the Swiss mountains, high up, about two hours' walk from the nearest road and there was one of these small alpine lakes. I was fascinated by this lake and I wrote a page about it. If you like I could read it to you?

I am an alpine lake. I measure 750 metres by fifty metres. I am about seventy metres deep. One of my neighbours to the west is an alpage called Annely. I am called Falin. I reflect with my eyes shut. When I do this indiscriminately, you, you see dark green, nothing else. In my depth are arctic fish and a current that never stops. Men take photos but they never work because I keep my eyes shut. On my surface, flat stone, when well thrown, ricochet. And, whenever I am touched, ripples of sensation are visible. The snows melt in May and June. In August when the sun is hot, Hunstein pours cool sand down my spine. The sun is high enough to reach me only in the summer. And every summer Schlafberg and his rockfaces tell the same story: it is the kind of story which is told when a crowd of people are drunk. According to this story I was once a fountain in a bath parlour, a haman. After being massaged, men came to play dice on low round stone tables arranged around me, sometimes they brought women to me. They gambled for whatever good they could see on this earth. One day a man lost everything he had and might have. He was a god, and it is dangerous to let gods lose. We've always known that. In his terror he lifted up the haman and threw it on its side. The gambling-tables rolled through the walls like millstones and have stayed there vertical ever since. Everybody fled. Nobody returned. The edge of the table cracked and crumbled. Grass grew where the dice once rolled. But in the summer, when the sun is in the right position, one can still see the round gambling tables and the shepherds call them Hunstein. When I reflect indiscriminately with my eyes shut, the dark green you see may change in mid-afternoon to turquoise, and at dusk when the trout leap through my lids the turquoise become slate. In August kids row the length of me. But at other moments, concentrated by the pain of memory, eyes still shut, I reflect with discrimination. I reflect shadows, light, stone, sky, goat, pine, cows, rowing boat, man, face, moustache, ear-ring, linen shirt, Hunstein diving, Schlafberg floating on his back, grass, grass, grass, stars, a boy's zizi. People try to buy me in jewels, but I am never there, nor my sister Zamtisa. About her I cannot sing. But it happens to me that sometimes, I open my eyes, when I do it you fall into me, helpless.

After several readings of this piece, I realised that it is actually the story of Narcissus seen from the other point of view. Even more precisely it is the Narcissus painted by Caravaggio. You see how myths are inside us. For a while I thought I was writing about a lake which was out there, I was writing actually about something which was already inside me, although I was not writing about myself. I suppose it is worth remembering that the myth of Narcissus is one of somebody who cannot escape the self. By telling the story from the point of view of the lake, and lending a kind of intentionality to the lake, I reverse the story. Suddenly it isn't that Narcissus can't escape himself, on the contrary it is that he answers a call. We could go further, we could say that Narcissus looks at his own reflection and falls in love with *its* life. In looking at himself he looks at something outside himself.

NP Let's move back and talk about your art criticism in the fifties. Despite the constraints of the genre, each critical essay is written like a story. I marvel at the elegance of each story and the clarity of every portrayal of a character. If the vibrancy and authority of each article seems to emerge from experience, then how is it that one person can be the author of so many images?

JB Let's begin with something very simple. When you are writing for a newspaper, the first thing that you know is that you only have so many inches, and you have to arrange what you have to say within that space. If you don't, then your copy will be edited and therefore distorted. The elegance that you talk about, if there is an elegance, comes from the need to seize that space and to arrange it exactly as you arrange furniture in a room. Before I started writing I would have in my mind a small number of key metaphors which were the principal bits of furniture. I would arrange them to fit that space, and to make that space as hospitable as possible. Then I would write. Maybe I would write badly and I would change things, because I always change an enormous amount, I still do when writing. It could take all day to write 250 words. But I would change always trying to get closer, as close as possible to that first ground plan of the given space. Then, if we continue with the image of the room or the house, you might ask whose room, whose house? In a sense it was my room in my house, because it was I who was arranging it, but the way that I arranged it was to make it a room for the work of the artist I was writing about. That would be true of about nine-tenths of what I wrote, and it was true even if I was negatively critical of a work or an artist. The one-tenth when it wasn't true was when I wanted to attack something ferociously. Then, probably, the room belonged to my own anger and the result was not very good writing, because anger, although sometimes justified, has within it its own spiral of egocentricity.

NP This metaphor of arranging the imaginary room of the other explains the sense of a visit that I experienced while reading your

criticism. There was the sense of a revelation of a unique ordering process and a journeying towards an unknown space. Your
criticism was never an evaluation of the consequences of an
artist's achievement but a rumination on how an artist works,
or an estimation of aspirations.

JB Yes, I think that is true, and that was quite conscious at the
time. It only occurs to me at this moment that this is parallel to
what a painter does within a canvas, or what a sculptor does
within a space. Wait, this can be very easily misunderstood. The
point of this parallelism between my writing about painting, and
the painting of a painting, is that what interested me was not
what the painter had made but the making of it. Christian
Bobin, a French writer I admire very much, said: 'When you are
reading a book you are writing it'. Similarly, when you are really
looking at a painting you are painting it. A more commonplace
example is, when you are listening to a singer, you find yourself
singing.

NP I can see now a possible rationale for the self-conscious role of
storytelling that your writing has taken, and the move away
from the modernist experimentation with the multiplication of
perspective which was crucial in your novel G. I think the
emphasis in your recent fiction is more on trying to allure and
draw the reader in, rather than self-consciously to play with the
elements of a text which can distance and ironise everything.

JB Yes, the style of much criticism and much reading today is a
refusal to receive what is there.

NP This brings us to thinking about the seductive role of the storyteller, but then again I am not satisfied with that metaphor.

JB Better than the seduction metaphor, is the metaphor of hospitality. And maybe that touches your preoccupation with exile,
because we know that the duty, awareness and need of hospitality is at its most intense amongst nomads. The more sedentary
and fixed abodes become, the more formal and the less spontaneous hospitality often becomes. A banal example of this can be
glimpsed on quite ordinary train journeys. The way people start
an acquaintance, the way they open to and receive one another,
is also a form of hospitality, but it takes a travelling train to
bring it about.

NP In the critical attention that your work received, there is something that has struck me as a little odd. When critics respond to

your work positively, they seem to take it in order to fly faster to somewhere that they seemed to be already going. Over the years the number of destinations has been as diverse as the social fashions and the political commitments to which each critic subscribes. Whereas the negative criticism always reads as if it were written by the same person. The repetition was stunning and, at first, I wondered whether there is something in the content of your work which solicits this response. But now I have come to the realisation that, more than anything else, it is a knee-jerk reaction against the position you assume.

JB What is this position?

NP First, there is a consistent resentment against the explicit giving of advice, even when expressed in the most sympathetic tone and, to be able to dismiss it they equate it with political or moral dogma. This is another way of saying we don't need to go to where Berger is taking us, or to say that the place he writes of does not exist. Along with this is a rejection of the position of one who has voluntarily left his/her place of origin. The ambivalence of your social location seems to launch the same set of cultural projections regularly.

JB I am sure that these questions of house, place, this ground between travelling and being fixed, and this question as to whether one is at home or not, are deeply embedded in my imagination and in my writing. But it is difficult for me to say very much about it. I can say simple things. I don't own a house and I have no wish to. This predisposition in myself — it is almost a repugnance — perhaps served me well in my relationship with the peasants who were my neighbours. Because when a foreigner buys a house, to everybody, and even perhaps to the man who sold it, it is felt as the illegitimate taking of something that belonged to them! My friend Louis, with whom I make the hay every summer, always calls me *le comédien*, which, in a certain sense, means the bohemian, but also the wandering player.

NP What do you call him?

JB *Le patron*, the one who decides, the one who is in charge. And, of course, he plays with me like a king plays with a comedian or a clown. For example, during haymaking it is always a gamble about the weather. There's always the question: what is the weather going to be today, what are the signs for tomorrow? And Louis forces me to decide. If, as often happens, I am wrong and it rains, he always has the comeback: 'Hah! You're just a comedian'. If it turns out to be okay, he assumes that it was he who decided anyway!

Another example, one which is completely different. I live in a house which he owns, and for which I pay a small rent. A few years ago the chimney caught fire and the house almost burnt down. It was a question of two minutes. Had it not been for all the neighbours who came with water, the whole thing would have gone. Fortunately the damage was not very great. Knowing that Louis would hear about it very quickly via the bush telegraph, I immediately went to tell him. His reply was: 'Well as long as you are fine, it's all right'. A couple of months later I went around to pay the rent and he refused to accept it. 'No I don't want the money. You use it to buy the things of yours that were burnt.'

NP Such stories about relationships of trust gained through work and proximity brings us to one of the persistent themes in your work: the distinction between modern and traditional, urban and rural. Many of your stories from village life express a sense of compassion which is not bound to a prescribed code of behaviour. Whereas much of the inhumanity and barbarism in modern society is not only a consequence of the transgression of laws but also the intransigence of laws which conflict with a sense of social justice. There is often a conflict between justice and legality. One of the strongest lessons we can draw from your work is a critique of the wholesale disavowal of traditionalism in modernity, and the understanding that the possibilities within the present are partly shaped by our continuous imaginings of the past and the future. The question of destiny and history is always open at both ends. I wonder if this is also related to what you've said in *Pig Earth* and in *A Seventh Man* concerning the relative space for secrecy within the village and the city. Perhaps the cruelty of the city is in the attempt to regulate the infinity of secrets that it contains, whereas in the village, the absence of a central law, but the presence of a shared past, facilitates a greater flexibility in the realm of ethics.

JB Yes, but I think this comes about not through any intrinsic virtue which implies that rural life is purer or nobler than urban life, of course not. Rather, it comes about for quite pragmatic reasons, to do with experience. If you are continually dealing with nature, with all its unpredictability and with all its constant secrets, then the rigid application of rules is the surest road to catastrophe! You have to continuously weigh one thing against another and then guess.

NP Is this guessing another metaphor for your writing process?

JB Perhaps I should adjust the word guess, for, yes, guess, but what is this guessing? It is actually a kind of listening. It isn't that one projects a guess as a solution, it is rather that one listens and something comes as a solution. Weighing one thing against another and then listening, I suppose you might say that is how I try to narrate and guess.

NP How does it relate to the earlier metaphor of arranging that you used to describe criticism?

JB In storytelling the space is arranged in a somewhat similar way, but there's another dimension which is the waiting for the voice of the story. You know the story which is called *Once in Europa*? Well, for many years, I had the idea of writing this story and I tried writing it but it never came. It was never right. I knew all about the setting of the story. I knew the factory very well, I had spent nights in it, smuggled in by my friends. The kind of woman the story was centred on was also there in my mind. But I couldn't find what I call the voice of the story, so I abandoned it. Then one day I met a woman who was a peasant and whom I knew quite well. She said to me, 'You'll never guess what I did last week, John.'

'What did you do?'

'I flew.'

'Where to?'

'No, no not in a plane, I flew!'

At that time, hang-gliders jumped off the mountain at a point near her chalet in the alpage. A young man, seeing this lady with her goats, had said jokingly, 'If you like, you can have a ride with me.'

And, I am sure to his great surprise, she said, 'Yes, all right, tomorrow.'

So he took this woman who was nearly sixty at the time. They circled for half an hour over the mountain and landed on the village below. When she told me this, I saw that my story had to be told by a woman whilst she was hang gliding with her son. Which is actually how *Once in Europa* is now told.

I'll give another example, this time concerning the story of *The Three Lives of Lucie Cabrol*. In real life there was such a woman, although she wasn't called Lucie Cabrol, who was in fact murdered. Again, this was a story that I tried to write on many occasions but couldn't, until I realised that the story should be told by a man who had once loved her when she was young. As soon as I found, invented, this man, I was able to write the story of Lucie Cabrol. The voice came.

NP What these stories have in common is that the 'voice of the story' came after you discovered a position for the narrator. I wonder if we can use this to lever us back into the distinction between storytelling and criticism. For me, the distinction implies that criticism begins when I know where something is going, but in storytelling you are already there: encircling your subject. But then your book, *And Our Faces, My Heart, Brief as Photos*, seems to collapse this distinction.

JB That's right, the story of starting to write that book is also interesting. For a long time I wanted to write a kind of essay about time. I had done an enormous amount of reading and thinking around the subject. But it wouldn't come. Then one day I had the idea, no it was a compulsion, to write what I had to say in the form of letters to Nella. She gave me an extraordinary book with brown pages, like wrapping paper, a little shiny. It was when she gave me this book, that I decided to write those letters to her. That's how the idea came.

NP Storytelling as a response to the gifts of a lover?

JB Yes, and brown paper for gifts!

NP This returns us to the early questions of empathy and identification, which the social sciences invariably reduce to regressive and passive forms of understanding. However, the position that you repeatedly describe is a more vigorous and critical form of identification. It is a sort of oscillation between distance and intimacy. A passage from the introduction in *Pig Earth* is illustrative of the relationship between an author and his or her subject, but perhaps it can also serve as a guide to the reader.

To approach experience, however, is not like approaching a house. 'Life', as the Russian proverb says, 'is not a walk across an open field.' Experience is indivisible and continuous, at least within a single lifetime and perhaps over many lifetimes. I never have the impression that my experience is entirely my own, and it often

seems to me that it preceded me. In any case experience folds
upon itself, refers backwards and forwards to itself through the
referents of hope and fear; and, by the use of metaphor, which is
at the origin of language, it is continually comparing like with
unlike, what is small with what is large, what is near with what is
distant. And so the act of approaching a given moment of experience involves both a scrutiny (closeness) and the capacity to
connect (distance). The movement of writing resembles that of a
shuttle on a loom: repeatedly it approaches and withdraws, closes
in and takes its distance. Unlike a shuttle, however, it is not fixed
to a static frame. As the movement of writing repeats itself, its
intimacy with the experience increases. Finally, if one is fortunate
meaning is the fruit of intimacy.

JB If you remember listening to stories as a child, you will remember the pleasure of hearing a story repeated many times, and you
will also remember that while you were listening you became
three people! A strange fusion! You become the storyteller, you
become the protagonist and you remain yourself, listening to the
story. You are all three. This is one of the advantages of having
heard the story before. The fusion is something, which is intrinsic to storytelling at its most primitive and, therefore, at its most
profound.

NP In *Lilac and Flag*, the choice of the old woman as the narrator
was intriguing for a number of reasons, some of which are quite
personal. It provides a sort of haunting bridge to facilitate the
traffic between the worlds which the protagonists belong to and
struggle to reconcile. In one sense, the village then becomes more
than the conventional site for nostalgia in the story of migration.
Locating the narrator there also adds a paradoxical twist, for
she receives the experiences of the protagonists without wit-
nessing them, and she receives them in an incredibly
compassionate and knowing way. This prescience reminds me
of all those proverbs my mother would drop like aspirins into
my despair. What always impressed me was not only their
uncanny contemporaneity, but also the fact that she had so
many in store, for each new experience which seemed to be
beyond her reach there was yet another little proverb, and it
always seemed to come from a place of which I didn't know.

JB There was a woman, who is dead now, called Angeline. She was
the inspiration, not in the sense that I told myself that the story

of *Lilac and Flag* would be told by Angeline, but when thinking of the old woman I would nevertheless think of Angeline. When she was alive I would refer to her as 'Ma', as a joke. She was a mother figure, but always more complicated than that. She was an extraordinary woman, never lost for repartee. She was funny, sad and incredibly compassionate. The connections with your mother, Nikos, are very strange, because Angeline used to say to me: 'Huh! Yes, well you're a writer and all writers are liars. There are no bigger liars in the world than writers. That's what you do, you go into that room and write down lies, don't you?'

She talked about her death through a local expression. Instead of saying, 'When I die', she said: 'When I shut my umbrella.' The last time I saw her was when she was in hospital. She was talking to her son about her father, as I entered she said. 'And now you come in, the Holy Ghost!' That was almost the last thing she said. Although it is nearly two years since she died, whenever I go near the house, I forget, and I say 'Angeline'. It is always a shock. I've already said the name before I remember that Angeline is dead. Now I think she's in *Lilac and Flag*.

In Germany a critic, instead of saying, as a lot of people have said, that *Lilac and Flag* is a very synthetic book, not proper narrative etc., said that the whole book was actually composed of voices, and these voices were interrelated as in a requiem. All that is left out, that which makes people think it's synthetic, has to be left out for a requiem.

NP I can see why the other critics have seen *Lilac and Flag* as synthetic, because they are describing what you describe, whereas the German critic describes what you made. Troy, the city in *Lilac and Flag,* is a patchwork of desperation and love, ambition and nostalgia, but your book is not a map of Troy.

JB The book, *Tales from the Garbage Hills*, by the Turkish writer Latiffe Tekin, which she wrote ten years ago, was very important to me in writing *Lilac and Flag*. I owe a lot to her. It is about a shanty town outside Istanbul, where she was born and spent her childhood. It is made up entirely of rumours and full of incredible inventions. It is not a novel in the ordinary sense, because how can you write a novel about a shanty town? It would be a contradiction in terms because, for a novel in the classical sense, a minimum of security is necessary. Here in the shanty-town everything is makeshift, nothing is controllable, everything is inexplicable, the only voice is the voice of rumour. Rumour is one kind of collection of voices. A requiem is another. They are different but they still have something in common. She has shown how it is possible to write about this shifting world of the poor in a big city. There are shanty towns in other books, but only as decor, or as a moral and political problem. Latiffe Tekin makes it possible to see how such a place can be seen as the centre of the world, somewhere between earth and sky.

I know what I would like to do now by way of an end. As you were talking about the theme of hospitality and forgiveness, I thought of some pages which I've just written. Not fiction, but a true story, told to me by Tonio. He has been a friend of mine for forty years.

To know how to weep that's a real test for a man. I've seen Antonin the shepherd cry three times. The last was when his wife died at the age of fifty. He didn't see much of her, shepherds are like sailors in this respect. But Antonin loved his wife in his way. The second time was when he learnt at the hospital that she had cancer. I tried to tell him something but what can you say? The first time was more mysterious and surprised us both.

On the three occasions when Tonio saw Antonin the shepherd weep, the two men where in the valley of El Requenco, just north of Madrid, they never met elsewhere. On a large-scale ordnance map of the area you can find a building marked on the southern slope of the valley and beneath the little square are printed the words 'Casa Tonio'. Tonio took three years building it. It's not really a house, more like a cabin. Perched at an altitude of 1000 metres on a mountain side of broken boulders and ilex trees, perched there like a leaning tomb, like a man sitting there at a corner of a table. When Tonio gets out of his Fiat van lower down the slope and starts the slow climb up to his cabin he walks exactly like a Saint Gerome, he has hermit legs, long and thin with inexplicably rounded knees. Around the cabin there is a dry stone wall four metres high, forming a kind of coralle which was built long ago to protect an apiary. Every year in May a lorry loaded with hives came along the dust road and men carried the hives to place them in the coralle. For two months the bees made honey there. Otherwise it is a place only for sheep, goats or lizards.

'In May the gilo's in flower', says Tonio.

The gilo is an ugly shrub but its white blossoms everywhere like snow, no, like manna from heaven.

Since he has had his pension Tonio has taken to drawing. He draws the smashed rocks, the ilax, the sparse turf, the dry beds of torrents. Large black drawings in which he fits everything together as if the coiled surface of the earth at El Requenco was the shell of an immense and ancient tortoise. High above the vultures circle, as he draws he can hear their faint cries, cries which imitate as if to encourage the last moans of some animal victim. In El Requenco bovids need shepherds. Antonin is short and square. On his feet he wears sandals cut out of old lorry tyres. Tyres which have been driven through a lot of goat shit. Antonin never learnt to read and had his own way of speaking.

'By the gaet waters', he refers to the torrential rain provoked by frequent thunderstorms. He wears a black hat with the same pride as Solomon wore a crown. After days alone in the valley with his herd, the 'Casa Tonio', is for Antonin when he spots it, like a photograph in a frame: a solemn reminder of otherwise forgotten occasions. Both men alone in the valley defend themselves fiercely against encroaching intimacy. A cigarette sitting on one of the terraces where the hives used to stand, a glass to drink while they recount what they've seen on the mountainside during the last week, nothing more. And often when they sit looking down the valley they swear.

One day Antonin came by when Tonio was preparing a meal—potatoes with bacon. Tonio invited the shepherd to join him. The idea came to him without any reflection. He pronounced the invitation as if recounting a simple fact, like, 'last night I saw the badger'. Antonin indicated his acceptance by taking off his hat and lowering his head. Tonio made a sign to suggest that the two dogs should stay outside. When, however, the shepherd crossed the threshold and into the single room of the casa, something unforeseen occurred, one knew his way about blindfolded and the other did not. Tonio laid plates on the table, placed knives, forks and glasses beside them, fetched a flask of black wine, brought out the bread. Antonin leant back in his chair, speaking a sentence or two from time to time, talking of torrents, coralles, of names which were unfamiliar to Tonio, but mostly he sat silent, smiling, like a man having his hair cut in a café on a Sunday morning. Tonio cut up tomatoes and trickled olive oil over them. The dogs outside found a place in the shade beneath a rock. When the two men were at last seated Antonin poured wine into their glasses. But otherwise it was Tonio who served his guest. Both ate with gusto. Sometimes they'd lean back to talk. When they finished eating they went on drinking the black wine. Finally, Antonin put on his hat and after fumbling for some minutes in his pocket, he drew out a 1000 peseta note which he slipped discretely on to the table.

'You can't do that!' Tonio remonstrated. 'You can't! It was my pleasure.'

'No man before in my life has ever served me at table,' declared Antonin. 'It was like a great restaurant.'

'Pick it up!' shouted Tonio. 'You are spitting on my pleasure.'

'Not horses ...' began Antonin.

But the other with a shaking hand held out the note across the table. Antonin stood up, hid the money in his pocket, took off his hat, and then he stood there, his two arms a little apart from his square body. Between the fingers of his left hand he held an unlit cigarette, with his right he held a hat. He stood there motionless in the cabin and down his cheeks rolled tears. Seeing Antonin, Tonio began to weep himself. Neither hid anything. The dogs watched their master with his back to the door and the other man on his feet as if turned to salt. For many minutes neither moved, then they slowly raised their arms and embraced. Such was the first time.

WORKS CITED
JOHN BERGER

A Painter of Our Time, London, Secker & Warburg, 1958

G: A Novel, London, Weidenfeld & Nicolson, 1972

Ways of Seeing (with S. Blomberg, M. Dibb and R. Hells), Harmondsworth, Penguin, 1975

Pig Earth, London, Writers & Readers, 1979

And Our Faces, My Heart, Brief as Photos, London, Writers & Readers, 1984

Once in Europa, London, Writers & Readers, 1987

Lilac and Flag, New York, Pantheon, 1990

A Seventh Man (with J. Mohr), London, Writers & Readers, 1975.

2.
AMBIVALENCE IN IDENTITY
HOMI BHABHA AND CULTURAL THEORY

Both the left and the right are anxious about identity politics. Gay activists, feminists, anti-racists, eco-militants are all calling for the right to be recognised, and in many cases they argue that recognition not only requires attention to their specific needs but also a transformation of the existing political framework. The backlash against 'political correctness' by the right, and the trepidation over 'minority rights' by the left are symptomatic of a more profound uncertainty over — 'what it is that is being negotiated?', 'how far can you go?', and 'who is entitled to be included within the boundaries of identity politics?' The problem for the left and for the right is that it is not clear what identity means, and what sort of politics it entails.

Ever since modern society underwent the radical upheaval whereby people's attachment to communities were broken either by migration or new labour patterns, and people's social horizons were altered either by emancipatory political movements or by consumerist media culture (all of which placed far greater emphasis on individual choice), we can observe the emergence of conditions that promoted a form of identity politics. The destruction of traditional bonds that linked people to specific place and imbued their cultures with unique values is the source of many of the anxieties that motivate identity politics.

The transformations that have so powerfully altered modern society have also heightened our understanding of the basis on which identity is formed. Identity is no longer perceived as natural, exclusive or fixed. It is always formed in relation to others. 'Our' identity is defined as it is differentiated from 'their' identity. Or, to use Eric Hobsbawn's lucid phrase in his account of the ascendance of identity politics, 'Without outsiders there are no insiders'.[1] Thus identity is to be seen as being formed out of historical processes rather than being a divine essence or a supernatural spirit that is selectively bestowed to a 'chosen few'. All identities are subject to change. The social context in which people are situated will invariably influence the priorities, responses and shifts that shape their identity. The form of this identity is therefore always specific and dynamic rather than coded by a prior set of psychic dispositions and immutable cultural biases.

Identity politics is born from the realisation that certain social and historical circumstances have effectively marginalised or negated the representation of their identity: the primary struggle is against self-negation. To reclaim, or to invent an identity which was previously prohibited, is a confrontation with the structures of power that privileged one form of identity over all others. It is this process of rethinking the relationship between the personal and the political which is disturbing. It raises questions concerning the construction of the categories for self-definition and the way they constrain choices and possibilities. It introduces an awareness of the way identity is always a performative process and how identity is constructed across difference. It highlights the role of institutions for the establishment of roles and functions that affirm certain forms of identity.

This understanding of how identity is constructed is rarely perceived as threatening to the established political order. What is disturbing is the way the appreciation of specificity has been translated into a politics of division and competition. The politics of multiple identities, for instance, is often perceived as the collapse of the political because it is considered impossible to reconcile solidarity with difference. Where there was once a hope of identifying the commonality amongst the oppressed, there is now little more than the negotiation of particular interests and the tactical alliances against a common enemy. The front of resistance has fragmented. Communities are more isolated and new social movements are mobilised for the advance or defence of increasingly limited goals. Identity politics is now seen as one of the causes, not a symptom, of the narrowing of political horizons. For Eric Hobsbawn, the problem of identity politics is twofold; first, it lacks a universalist philosophy or an all-inclusive framework for connecting various movements together; and second, it constrains the very subject it seeks to promote. Identity, once defined around one aspect of social life, whether this be sexual orientation, cultural background, or ecological awareness, confines the very possibility of understanding the multiple ways our identity is enfolded in the lives of others.

If identity politics deepens the crisis of modernity, then what is the way out? The promise that the questions of identity would be resolved after the more urgent social division of class was addressed no longer seems sustainable. Identity politics have become ascendant precisely because the old universalist agenda failed to be perceived as all-inclusive and this failure cannot now be overcome by repeating the invitation to 'join hands'. This frustration with the traditional discourses on solidarity should now serve as a spur for fresh thinking on the forms of unity and commonality in contemporary politics. The question of identity will be central in these new debates and it is imperative that we proceed from the premise that identity and collectivity need to be addressed conjuncturally rather than assume that identity would be cleared up after collectivity was secured. For as Judith Butler argues:

> it is no longer clear that feminist theory ought to try and settle the question of primary identity in order to get on with the task of politics. Instead, we ought to ask, what political possibilities are the consequence of a radical critique of the categories of identity?[2]

Within the fields of feminism and postcolonialism the inter-relationship between identity and culture, agency and power have been debated rigorously in the past decade. From this perspective one of the most significant contemporary critics is Homi Bhabha, and a closer examination of his writings on cultural difference may illuminate new trajectories of critical thought. On one level, Bhabha's work has involved an analysis of texts which explicitly displayed the authority and power of colonial regimes. Yet on close reading what Bhabha reveals is that this disclosure of power is riven with contradiction and uncertainty. The authorial voice which seeks to assert itself in unequivocal tones and with clear objectives is shown to be undercut by whispers of doubt and ambiguity. These gaps and hesitations are, Bhabha argues, anticipated and manipulated by the colonised. This setting which highlights the 'ambivalence' in colonial discourse and the 'sly civility' practised by the colonised challenges the presumption that colonialism was exclusively an exercise in absolute power and coerced submission. By shifting attention to the more subtle forms of resistance and identifying the ruptures in colonial authority Bhabha helps to also address the ways opposing groups are interdependent upon each other and to reveal how Western discourses on identity are formed out of the encounter with the non-Western other.

To unpack this complex history Bhabha has devised a number of concepts which are themselves partly derived from social, psychoanalytic and literary theory. Ambivalence is the central concept that stretches across all the contexts that Bhabha discusses. It is first used to describe the unstable characterisations made by the coloniser in their attempt to represent and control the colonised. Ambivalence refers not only to the emotional oscillation from desire to disgust, but also to the very difficulty a stranger has in understanding the identity of others. It is this difficulty in naming the other and being able to name one's own relationship to the other that first exposes the limitations of the available codes and conceptual frameworks. Thus the confrontation with the other creates a crisis of representation. Conventional language seems inadequate to either satisfactorily accommodate or precisely differentiate between the foreign and the familiar.

This crisis of signification cuts across all encounters with otherness. Bhabha argues, that while colonialism provides the extreme points of the disjuncture between the available signs for communication and the actual experience, this uneasiness of language is also to be found throughout modernity. Ambivalence thus becomes a concept for identifying the tensions, contradictions and slippage between signs and the ideas, images or experiences to which they are supposed to refer. By further situating ambivalence within a dialogical theory of subjectivity Bhabha proceeds to argue that the fundamental concepts of identity, community and nation must also be radicalised. This presents us with the opportunity to assess the theoretical frameworks for understanding the self-other relationship and the theories of the nation which are often referred to but rarely critiqued within identity politics.

FROM THE MARGINS OF THE NATION

A convenient starting-point for this investigation is Homi Bhabha's essay 'Dissemination: Time, Narrative and the Margins of the Modern Nation'[3] which addresses the logic of political affiliation and the structures of ideological negotiation that is exercised in the margins of national culture. It is an attempt to understand the encounters of both colonialism and postcolonialism as both continuous and discontinuous with the overall project of modernity. For we cannot claim that urbanisation is integral to modernity and then declare the arrival of the migrant as the signifier of the pre-modern. As Etienne Balibar has argued, racism is neither a hangover from pre-modern fantasies, nor a transportation of archaic modes of bigotry and prejudice, but is the perverse composition of disavowal and projection that arises from a modern aggressivity against cultural difference.[4]

Bhabha's overriding concern with the presence of cultural difference, is primarily directed at the discourse on modernity and consequently — although often only by implication — the structures of modernisation. His investigations whether in the domain of the colonial encounter or the 'migrant metaphors' of the nation, also aim to test the conceptual and political limits of liberal pluralism. At what level does this questioning proceed? It primarily deals with texts. The subject is not strictly speaking the representation of 'raw' experience. The attention is with the tropes by which social meanings and personal experiences are articulated. While drawing from the studies on nationalism within the discipline of sociology and history, he looks to poststructuralism for most of his theoretical components and from there traverses the relatively new field of cultural studies. However, Bhabha's acute awareness of the problems within historicity, while alerting him to the dangers of merging the event with the idea, has not yet led to a satisfactory reformulation of the divide between theory and history, or sufficiently addressed the problematical opposition between critical distance and empathy.

Working very much on the side of theory, rather than repeating the humanist rhetoric on victimage, or stockpiling empirical evidence on social inequality, Bhabha has patiently constructed a 'new' set of terms which are partly dextrous derivations and partly necessary modifications of the current critical concepts. These conceptual devices are used to re-examine the 'correlation' between liberalism and modernisation, and the more particular need of differentiating between the subject position, and the appropriate narrative form, for the subaltern in the colony and the migrant within the metropolis. An assessment of Bhabha's perspective on cultural difference is further illuminated as it is set against the mainstream response to the phenomenon of migration within the sociological tradition. It is my contention that as Bhabha reveals the limitations of liberalism through its simultaneous approach and retreat from the question of cultural difference. One can also identify the parallel way in which social theory has also foreclosed and bypassed one of the crucial questions of the modern age: ontological homelessness. Consequently, I see in Bhabha's theory of ambivalence and hybridity not just an attempt to understand the perplexity of cultural difference, but also a way of redefining the process of identification and the praxis of agency in modernity.

In the early sociological accounts the depiction of the migrant condition had been a subset of the debates concerned with the disfunctions of the state. Migrants and racial minorities have been the subject of many empirical studies which have demonstrated the injustices, hypocrisy and negligence of the welfare system. The critique that is often generated from such accounts is framed by a legalistic or ethical demand for compensation and equality. Despite the intensity of polemic against the discrimination within the state, critical attention is invariably confined to functional discrepancies, the gaps between theory and practice. In short, the insistence is simply for the state to 'normalise', not alter, it practices.

Is multiculturalism merely another reminder of the need to regulate the state's resources on a more egalitarian basis? Or can its 'brief' go beyond the confines of political access and into the structural reformation of the polity? For when migrants have entered these debates, with their cumulative suspicions of both the benign and the malignant face of liberalism, they have always expressed a certain discontent against the construction of their claims for recognition purely on the grounds of moral justice. From the various histories of contestation within the nation state two general projects can be identified; a critique of the models of social integration, and the emergence of the modern crisis of signification. While attention to the complicity between the structures of domination and the institutionalisation of racism productively reveal the contradictions and repressions of a national culture, and assign a counter set of values and meanings to the submerged histories, Bhabha claims that 'in the heat of political argument the 'doubling' of the sign can often be stilled'.[5] The conventional representation of the process of contestation, by polarising the accents of difference, tends to underestimate both the relation to otherness which is internal to all symbol forming activities and the complexities of social affiliation.

The Foucauldian principle that power operates through a network of multifarious aggregates, and that domination produces a state of unstable equilibrium, can serve as a useful reference point to examine Bhabha's representations of authority and resistance. For instance, the nation state is not envisaged as an object which is exterior to the lives of 'the people'. Bhabha argues that 'the people' do not live under the state, for the modern notion of 'the people' is itself coeval with the formation and the internalisation of the nation state. To imagine the nation state one also needs a corresponding but not necessarily equivalent image of 'the people'. The one oscillating within, but not conforming to, the measurements of the other. In this sense literature, and particularly the literature of minorities, provides the appropriate reference points, because as Simon During argues: 'Being embedded within a society, it assumes and works on a set of social connections rather than promotes a national character.'[6] Bhabha utilises minority discourse not to demonstrate the discordant conditions of subjectification, but to investigate the socio-psychic determinants that disturb the 'fit' between the ideology and the legitimacy of the nation state. His concern is with the ambivalent process of identification which sustains the authority of the nation and colonial discourse as objects of 'desire and derision'.[7]

At its best, Bhabha's method invokes a sort of Frankfurtian dialectic that renders a methodology through the articulation of the subject. For instance, the concept 'displacement' signifies both the positioning of the subject and the textual strategies of criticism. It is also a methodology whereby 'hybridity' can serve as both the concept for examining the structure of social affiliation and the name for the genre of his work. Theoretical abstractions and historical sources constantly rebound against each other until the authority of the former and the transparency of the latter begins to appear more questionable. Bhabha describes minority discourse as emerging from the '*in between* of image and sign, the accumulative and the adjunct, presence and proxy'.[8] Similarly, his own position and voice performs a negotiation *between*, rather than asserts an imperious negation of the preconstituted critiques of genealogical origin, cultural supremacy and historical priority. For instance, both the tautness of his style and the polyvalency of his argument can be measured by a single paragraph in which he compresses together statements from Benedict Anderson, Michael Oakeshott, Hannah Arendt and Tom Nairn, until the 'modern Janus' surfaces as the only suitably double-edged metaphor for the incommensurability within the nation's 'coming-into-being'.[9]

Bhabha's attempt to define the transitional space of modernity is guided by two methodological convictions: the utility of psychoanalytic and deconstructive strategies, and the prophetic testaments of the marginalised. The writings of Franz Fanon serve not only as the most lucid chronicle of the cataclysms of modernity, but also as the paradigmatic example of what Said call's the need to give 'the nonsequential energy of lived historical memory and subjectivity its appropriate narrative authority'.[10] Bhabha proposes to extend the investigation of the margin by following the social strategies and textual tropes of chiasmus and displacement, supplementarity and repetition. With small but carefully selected steps his method appropriates as it colludes with the subversive intent of his subject.

STRANGERS IN THE METROPOLIS

The subject position of the subaltern in the colony and the postcolonial migrant in the metropolis are not isomorphic. Hence, the theoretical advances that Bhabha proposes for the former are not automatically transferable to the latter.[11] However, the theme that links Bhabha's reading of colonial discourse and the postcolonial narratives of migration is the questioning of the dominant Western assumption that the road to modernisation is paved by liberalism. As noted earlier, Bhabha's strategy has been to interpret the effect of encounters rather than to mythologise the structure of the journey. Before turning to a closer examination of Bhabha's conceptual advances, I wish to situate it against various responses to the phenomenon of migration within the sociological tradition. This initial contrast will thereby illuminate the necessity to overcome the entrenched ethnocentric dispositions and to expand our theoretical frameworks.

In *The Fall of Public Man*, Richard Sennett rightly argues that the city is a congregation of strangers. Yet in his attempt to define the expansion of the city through the increasing number of immigrants, Sennett proposes that there are two types of strangers. There is the stranger who is culturally, linguistically or racially distinct and is thus immediately recognisable as an outsider, and a stranger who carries no explicit signs of difference but who is nevertheless unfamiliar and unknown. Modern New York serves as the paradigmatic city of outsiders. Whereas the swelling of eighteenth-century London and Paris is attributed not to the arrival of 'outsiders' but to the migration which is a consequence of the ruptures and displacements within the borders of the nation. The identity of the outsider carries with it an a priori exclusion: a relation of non-relation. Whereas the stranger possesses an identity which is internalisable but unlocatable. The outsider's identity is one of non-identity, an untranscendable stigma, whereas the ambiguity of the stranger's identity has the potential to blur the categories of identification. The strangers Sennett describes were people who came from the provinces but who were no longer provincial but not quite urbane. Their ascendancy in the metropolis challenged the rigid language of the prevailing social hierarchies as they inserted themselves between the 'us' and 'them', 'insider' and 'outsider' and 'above' and 'below'. Consequently, he argued that their inclusion was an intervention, rather than an addition to the very structure of the city:

> Increases in population usually instigate a reorganisation of the whole ecology of a city; cities have to be thought of in terms of crystals which re-form their structures each time more substance of which the crystal is composed is introduced.[12]

Ironically, this principle which established a nexus between migration, urbanisation and social transformation is not extended to New York. The modernity of its ethnic subgroups is denied as their use of space is compared to 'medieval and Renaissance use of squares'.[13] The mingling of different languages in New York is shorn of the productive dissonance of cultural exchange and reduced to primary signifiers of exclusive and static ghettoes: 'In

American cities strangers were interpreted through ethnic stereotypes, rejected as unfit or dangerous to know because of the
negative connotations involved.'[14] Significantly this statement
remains unsubstantiated. This is a crucial omission for his whole
argument on the modernity of social space is premised on a polarisation between identity and originality, which in turn prescribes a
limit on the possibilities for integrating strangers within the
metropolis.

In Fichte's writing, which is one of the earliest formulations of
the relationship between an individual and the nation state, one
sees a metaphorical linkage which is to recur throughout the sociological tradition, identity is the result of the integration of the part
of the whole:

> Between the isolated man and the citizen, there is the same
> relation as between raw and organised matter. ... In an organised
> body, each part continuously maintains the whole, and in
> maintaining it, maintains itself. Similarly, the citizen with regard
> to the state.[15]

Such metaphors are popular even in the contemporary debates on
civil rights and national rights. Within liberalism the conventional
response to the demands for the public recognition of cultural difference is to privatise them, that is to preserve them purely within
the personal space. When individuals seek to make this as the basis
of their public and political self-image, then liberalism is faced with
a dilemma. The public sphere, in a liberal democracy provides min-
imal space for heterogeneity, and therefore the politics of difference
become equated with the threat of fragmentation. The nation state
has always been poised over a precarious paradox: it has sought
to defend the rights of minorities and to preserve the right to dissent, while at the same time insisting that the nation must be
inspired by unifying themes. The nation, is seen as a container
whose centrist institutions must not be challenged even while it
continues to evolve through the incorporation of differences. From
this perspective, if diversity can only be secured and affirmed
within a broader unity, then multiculturalism is no more than a
slight extension to the prior politics of assimilation.

Genealogies of the nation state which are structured to suggest
that it is the ultimate stage of political maturity, or to signify the
sense of historical arrival, invariably presuppose the immaturity or

the belatedness of other administrative units. Such theories which mutually derive the conceptual space of the nation state and the process of identification from analogies to organic development and the enlightenment concept of progress, are for Bhabha a political and a theoretical point of departure. In contrast to the binarisms proposed in such theories, he claims that the 'cultural temporality of the nation' constitutes an 'ambivalent emergence ... a much more transitional social reality'.[16] He argues that the nation state — with all its administrative structures of belonging, its powers of political affiliation, its determination of the institutional conditions of everyday life, its codified sense of social order and justice — is produced by the incessant crossing of borders.

Critiques of the essentialism of functional organicism, and the dualism of conflictual hierarchies are commonplace in the contemporary debates on multiculturalism, but this leaves the liberal position and the division of social hierarchies according to segmented interest groups in a dubiously neutral position. This model has often served as the safehouse for both the apolitical relativists and the radicals who have not quite fathomed the complexities of cultural difference. Shils's metaphor for the composition of a society with neither a centre nor a periphery but comprising of a succession of overlapping but separate 'onion leaves' is most illustrative of the liberal pluralist perspective. However, by foregrounding the 'disjunctive time' and the 'internal liminality' of modernity, Bhabha would argue that even such a model would assume too much homogeneity, for it merely multiplies the principle of organicism. Shils's schema validates identity as it presumes both a commensurability between components and a consensus over the perimeter of inclusion and exclusion, whereas for Bhabha identity is problematised through the negotiation over incommensurable units and the perception of the border as a zone of oscillation.

From this perspective one can see more clearly the need to radicalise our understanding of the polarities of estrangement and belonging from fixed opposites to positions that are bound by relative degrees of familiarity and foreignness. For just as the modern notion of globality has redefined the relationship between centre and periphery, similarly the foreignness of the stranger now oscillates between a fixed sense of difference and an ambiguous form of similitude. The edges of xenophobia in contemporary London and New York are not necessarily hardened by, but superimposed with linguistic and racial heterogeneity. Sennett's distinction collapses because it presupposes that the stranger's unknown qualities can be measured against the known qualities of those who purportedly belong to the city and already have a place in the national imaginary.

Yet Sennett's distinction is also a brilliant illustration of the limits of liberalism, for it argues that the dynamism of the city presupposes the stranger's disavowal of the past and the place of origin as an ongoing reference point. This apparently, is the failure of the immigrants in New York, having arrived in clusters they organised themselves in tight exclusive ghettoes, and thus the city was condemned to mutually exclusive segments. Having come without a vision for the future they simply imitated what they left behind. Sennett reinforces the stereotype of the migrant experience by arguing that survival dictated either a forgetting of the past, or a wholesale reproduction of it. He offers no attempt to engage with the stranger's experience of new places, he examines only the similitude within consequences without any attention to the subtle changes of occasion or context. By seeing the past as a closed model rather than as open-ended metaphor that informs the present he fails to see how a journey may not be either denial or retrieval but a form of repetition that includes both. Consequently, he underestimates the tensions in the migrant's attempt to negotiate the difference between past and present, and ignores the spillovers between and the transformations within these zones of dispersal and assemblage.

THE TIME AND SPACE OF CULTURAL DIFFERENCE

The patchwork of cross-cultural signs that dominates the modern cityscape often triggers two responses, either the lament for the loss of authenticity, or the eulogy for the conquest over forbidden territory. However, between the fall and the ascent is the business of survival: the bridging of distances and the mixing of differences. John Berger calls this more humble form of construction through negotiation, the 'bricolage of the soul'. And it is this phenomenon which demands further scrutiny. For this would require us to recognise that the migrant's relationship to the past is at best metaphorical rather than a rigid translation. The attempt to bring near what is distant is not an example of treating space as the tabula rasa upon which predetermined desires or retroactive nostalgia are fulfilled, but is an exercise in forging a sense of continuity and meaning out of discontinuous fragments. Consequently, the attention that is given to the engagement with space should include an appreciation of how space functions as an active surface that provokes an attitude in which nostalgia and desire occurs concurrently. Space cannot be dismissed as an inert entity, existing somehow prior to the force of history. Space is not a passive vector which time occupies and sediments itself in.[17] The dissonance produced by the confrontation with 'new' horizons and the repetition of 'old' compulsions are neither negligible, nor reducible to the inherent tendencies within the original, but are crucial to the 'catalytic' dynamism of modernity. Simmel understood the perplexity of spatial disjunction within the modern crisis of signification.[18] He represented the identity of the stranger through a schema that constantly oscillated the moment of identification between the dual axioms of proximity and distance.

While the politics of identity formation and racism are no longer bound by quasi-scientific and colonial categories the processes of discrimination are still perceived as operating with an aggressive binarism. Codified by practice and prejudice rather than by mandate, spheres and zones are defined by racial terms. Once internalised, stigma is no less potent even if it isn't overtly imposed. This hierarchical internalisation of difference detaches people from their past by primarily reducing all non-modern cultures to objects that can be dispensed to either the historical dustbin or the museum. However, the current options are not staked between redeeming the cultures that modernity has sundered, and claiming the 'centrality' of the 'margin', but also includes the need to focus on the paradoxes of synthesis and the tensions that emerge as cultures jostle within modernity. Hence a critical study of modernity must contest the paens to uniformity and examine what Guillermo Gomez-Pena calls the 'borderisation' of the world.[19]

Throughout Bhabha's writing there is a consistent attempt to formulate the hybridity and ambivalence within self-identity and political culture. It is here that Bhabha signals his departure from the folkloric versions of multiculturalism which privilege the past and the place of origin as provider of cultural autonomy, his concern is with the tensions of presence rather than the hypostatisation of absence. For Bhabha cultural difference does not presuppose a primordial or fixed cultural identity, it is not a legacy of the premodern past, but is located in the ever present frontier between the intermittent time and interstitial space of modernity. The central question is, how does a culture that is under foreign stars map itself, and does this remapping shift the very co-ordinates by which we conventionally understand the meanings of culture. Cultural difference does not offer the opportunity for travelling back in time, but poses the question of how we interpret the juxtaposition of times within the present culture. It is not adequate to know the historical meaning of cultural signs but to see how the shifting of signs across time can split the moment of revelation in the present.[20] Thus Bhaba's concern with the phenomenon of cultural difference is not in its excavation of a repressed object or the realisation of an alter ego, but in its formulation of a qualitatively different but not totally new object: the hybrid.

If there is a polemic in 'Dissemination' it is against the invisible racism which constructs the borders of the nation's imaginary space as it identifies the enemies within and beyond. It is the racism which underwrites the linkage between cultural homogeneity and political stability. Its subject is the process by which the acceptability of difference is defined and how it is either repressed, marginalised, assimilated or incorporated. 'So long as a firm boundary is maintained between the territories, and the narcissistic wounded is contained, the aggressivity will be projected on to the Other or the Outside.'[21] Bhabha is here emphasising that slogans like 'unity in diversity' are not just a reminder of the nation's need to focus on common goals, but also serve as a shield to protect 'the people' from the return of projections that can split them from the desire for cohesion.[22] Coterminously, the supplementarity of the minority discourse 'interrupts the successive seriality of the narrative of plurals and pluralism',[23] for the asymmetry of its insertion is both a rearticulation of the mode of addressing the 'national community', and a revelation of the ruptures within the totalising discourse on nationhood. For Bhabha cultural difference is not bound to the demands of integration or assimilation, but emerges from the tension of the supplement: that appendage which questions the unity of the object to which it is attached. It is those bits and pieces which hang over and on to the hegemonic edges of modernity that announce the location of cultural difference, and it is by virtue of this adjacency and its 'untranslatability' that cultural difference operates as a critique of the principles of progress, homogeneity and cultural organicism.[24]

Thus, the identity of the other is defined through the unresolved tensions within dominant discourse. Similarly, the position of the periphery is not defined by its autonomous oppositionality, but through the incommensurability of its cultural location and production. This marks a departure from the three conventional perspectives on social crisis; the Marxist model of dialectical conflict between centre and periphery, the liberal strategy for 'organic' integration via appropriation or delegation, and the Romantic vision of redemption through the consumption of the idealised periphery. By drawing attention to the shift in the meaning of signs articulated in alien contexts Bhabha is compelled to redefine the relationship between centre and periphery and produce a new configuration for the self-other dynamic.

AMBIVALENCE AND AGENCY

Bhabha claims that the arrival of the other not only signifies a rupture within the hierarchical forms of rationality, but also initiates both the emergence of an 'other' people and the double temporality of modernity. To represent the space/time of transition within the nation's cohering, and to articulate the 'indeterminacy' of modernity Bhabha mobilises the term 'liminality' in an original way.[25] First, it is related to Raymond Williams's distinction between residual and emergent practices in oppositional cultures, which signifies both the interjacency of the planes that constitute identity and the interdependency between transformational power and historical displacement. Second, it is connected to Foucault's claim, that the alterity of the modern state's rationality is revealed in the heterogeneity and the 'perpetual movement of the 'marginal integration of individuals'.[26] In this sense, the concept of liminality comes to signify both the process of identity formation in the experience of transition and the empowering perspective that results from the tension between the dominant culture's inability to recognise the aspirations of the margin. The modification that he brings to terms such as fetish, mimicry, hybridity, stereotyping and liminality marks a beginning of a new perspective that will radically expand our interpretation of the documents that chronicle the emergence of the 'other' people in modernity. Bhabha is preparing clues that will lead to a more complex understanding of both the traumas and the potency that results from people crossing paths.

For Bhabha the identity of the subject is represented through its relationship with the Other:

> It is constituted through the locus of the Other which suggests both that the object of identification is ambivalent, and, more significantly, that the agency of identification is never pure or holistic but always constituted in a process of substitution, displacement or projection.[27]

This anti-essentialist model of subjectivity (which, as it foregrounds the process of mimicry, stereotyping and fetishism, highlights the hybridity of identity) has prompted both confusion and resistance.

Some critics have taken this as an example of the celebration of fragmentation that vindicates the worst excesses of postmodernism, while others have argued that this model is Eurocentric in that it repeats the very structures of violence that fracture and dissipate the knowledge system of non-Western cultures. In other words, this model has been perceived as echoing the specific self-image of postmodernity rather than articulating the general processes of identification. Vivek Dhareshwar, for instance, has criticised Homi Bhabha's theory because it 'unwittingly' leads him to represent colonial discourse as the 'unconscious of metropolitan discourse'.[28] Dhareshwar challenges Homi Bhabha's model of identity by arguing that the 'alloy' of colonial subjectivity was not a product of the ambivalence of colonial discourse. Subaltern subjectivity, he argues, contained a combination of distinct elements which not only predated colonialism and inspired the resistance against it, but also guaranteed the survival of a 'native idiom'. In Dhareshwar's account there is an emphasis on both the intactness of pre-colonial subjectivity and the qualitative difference in the experience of power by the oppressor and the oppressed. He argues that the strength of Bhabha's model lies in its ability to highlight the equivocation within the production of knowledge systems whereas its weakness is revealed by an inability to discriminate between the asymmetrical experiences of what Foucault called the 'governmental technologies'. Manthia Diawara has also taken a similar line of argument in his critique of Homi Bhabha's preface to Fanon's *Black Skins, White Masks*. He too has argued that Bhabha's account of the quest for identification relinquishes the notion of an autonomous identity that precedes colonialism, and that his reading of splitting confines the colonised subject to the position of lack and thereby reaffirms the sovereignty of the white subject.[29]

Such critiques fail to see how Bhabha's writing seeks to challenge rather than perpetuate the antagonistic opposition between the dominant self and the subordinate other. Without underestimating the discrepancies in power Bhabha attempts to demonstrate the emergence of agency in the twixt of displacement. It is not a form of agency which is either free floating in a state of transcendence or whose autonomy abstracts and attenuates the very points of conflict, but one which is effected by and grounded in the mobility, contingency and partiality of resistance and negotiation. It is a form of agency which is sustained and generated by the continuous and discontinuous tensions of resilience, but not in the terms of a liberal pragmatism that would both advance ethnocentric limits against cultural hybridity and retreat from the agonism in identification. To dismiss this model on the ground that it disempowers the subjectivity of the colonised is to both caricature the liminal moment of identification and to bypass its critique that all cultures lack a self-sustaining unity either in origin or in apogee.

These criticisms point to but fail to address adequately the necessity to turn to psychoanalytic and discourse theory in order to explain agency and power. The critical task that Bhabha brings to colonial discourse is not merely to pay homage to the resistance in the colonial context, but to ask whether such practices can challenge the very terms by which we understand cultural survival. However, as Robert Young argues the weakness in Bhabha's theory of identification is in the link between ideology and psychoanalysis, for while it reveals a psychic process that entwines the coloniser with the colonised, it fails to disclose the asymmetry in their relationship. Paradoxically, the closer it gets to revealing this asymmetry, 'the less need there is for his psychoanalytic schema of fantasy and desire, narcissism and paranoia'.[30] Psychoanalytic theory has always seemed uncomfortable when confronted with the apparatus of power and the expressions of resistance by the powerless. But then, how else can one fully elaborate the process of motivation and conviction without some account of projection and disavowal?

Bhabha's work is part of a shift in the New Left's scrutiny of resistance, a step away from the binary opposition that separated the objective apparatus of domination from the subjective processes of power. It was in response to Edward Said's *Orientalism* that Homi Bhabha first used the concept of ambivalence to explore the dissonance between liberal civility and colonialism as a symptom of the alterity within Western knowledge. Here he attempted to take Said's argument a step further by revealing that the knowledge which defined both the 'non-identity' and the 'identity' of the other, was not simply a matter that could be reduced to the binarism of power and powerlessness, but followed the process of recognition and disavowal: 'colonial discourse produces the colonised as a fixed reality which is at once an 'other' and yet entirely knowable and visible.'[31]

Bhabha's reading of the strategies and practices by the coloniser and the colonised always revolves around the mis-takes between knowledge and power. Bhabha argues that ambivalence disrupts the narcissistic demand for wholeness and essential difference, that justified the colonial hierarchies of identification. By highlighting the role of unconscious determinants Bhabha parts company with those crude adherents to Marxism who reduce ambivalence to ideological duplicity. And by extending the strategic value of ambivalence beyond the liberal terms of crisis management he is able to open up the paradoxical constituents of modern authority. Ambivalence is not to be confused with a negative component within identity, that is, as an instance of moral cowardice and intellectual vacillation. Ambivalence refers to a broader social framework where divergent cultural signs interact, intersect but fail to coincide with each other. Ambivalence also addresses the form of transformation in meaning that is initiated by the presence of an 'other'. Hence, it is from this position that he can argue that in the colonial context authority was always articulated through a process of displacement; inserted as both difference and repetition; recognisable in both its atavism and its modernity.

Bhabha's elaboration of the four key concepts — fetish, stereo-type, mimicry and splitting — is not a validation of the pathos arising from the gap between the acquired and the desired identity, but a demonstration of the crisis of signification within the 'double time' and 'contested space' of modern culture. In his first essay Bhabha proposed that we consider the construction of colonial discourse as 'a complex articulation of the tropes of fetishism'.[32] This proposal was subsequently elaborated through a closer study of the role of stereotype which he argues is a 'form of knowledge and identification that vacillates between what is already "in place", already known, and something that must be repeated'.[33] Similarly, mimicry is not just an example of imitation but serves as a metaphor for the 'excess' and 'slippage' that 'becomes transformed into an uncertainty which fixes the colonial subject as a 'partial presence'. By 'partial' I mean both 'incomplete' and 'virtual'.[34] Consequently it is the elusive and mercurial space between image and identification, between mask and identity, which Bhabha suggests creates a crisis in the schematisation of authority as it displaces the unitarian system of identity, 'where the self apprehends itself: it is always the split screen of the self and its doubling, the hybrid'.[35]

Drawing from Fanon's statement that the 'colonial subject is always overdetermined from without', Bhabha argues that alienation is positioned in all the configurations of identity. Identity is, no more but no less, than a constant process of negotiation between image and fantasy, in which there is no pre-alienated self which can be redeemed, but rather the 'Otherness of the Self' is what is 'inscribed in the perverse palimpsest of colonial identity'.[36] The condition of the colonial subject explicitly opens up the splitting within the processual forms of imaging an identity, and to extend an understanding of both this condition, and these two part identities which imbricate the self in the other, Bhabha adopts the psychoanalytic concept of identification. In a later essay he clarifies his position, that is, his intervention into the psychological, anthropological and philosophical discourse which presuppose the stability of the ego:

> The postmodern perspective insists that the question of identity
> can never be seen 'beyond representation', as a psychological
> problem of personality or even an ethical problem of personhood

.... We are no longer confronted with an ontological problem of
being but with a discursive strategy of the 'moment' of interroga-
tion; a moment in which the demand for identification becomes,
primarily, a response to other questions of signification and desire,
culture and politics ... it is the priority (and play) of the signifier
that reveals the Third Space of absence or lack or doubling (not
depth) which is the very principle of discourse.[37]

The non-equivalence between image and identity is also the key
theme in his exploration of cultural difference in the discourse of
the nation. Note again how Bhabha's attention to the aleatoric destiny of the sign in modernity and the slippage between signification
and meaning in the migrant's negotiations with the metropolis
leads him at first, to praise Benedict Anderson's claim that the
nation, as a 'homogenous horizontal community', is coeval with
the notion of the 'arbitrariness of the sign'. However, Bhabha then
goes on to argue that, by stressing that the collective voice for the
imagined community of the nation is located in the homogenous
time of the realist narrative, and by giving primacy to unisonance
as the discourse of public identification, Anderson has failed to
acknowledge the profound ambivalence — 'the alienating and iter-
ative time of the sign' — that runs through the narrative of
modernity. Bhabha takes Anderson's historicism to task as he
argues that the emergence of the problematic of signification
occurs not in 'a synchrony but a break, not simultaneity but a spatial disjunction'.[38] Thus, Anderson's account of the very rupture
which opened up both the 'anonymity' and the 'anomie' of the people is resealed, without inserting the specificity or acknowledging
the disjunctive potential of those who occupy the margins of
national culture.

To restore the problematic position of non-hegemonic signification in the imagined space of the nation, Bhabha turns back to
Renan's famous formulation of the necessity for selective amnesia
in the formation of a will to nationhood:

It is this forgetting —— a minus in the origin — that constitutes the
beginning of the nation's narrative ... that the problematic identification of national becomes visible.[39]

Bhabha's account of identification is thus interwoven with an
account of the epochal forms of social crisis: colonialism and the

postcolonial experience of migration. He argues that the lesson from both these experiences forces us to rethink the paradigms by which we understand both identity and culture. By foregrounding the incommensurability of cultural difference Bhabha has shifted the attention to culture away from being an ethnographic object that facilitates modernity's understanding of its other, to being a discursive and enactive process in the ethnography of modernity. This also constitutes a significant departure from both the assimilationist perspective and the integrative 'ethics' of liberal tolerance which generates the hegemonic terms of reference for the management of cultural diversity. Bhabha's approach is not aimed at isolating the boundaries of cultural difference for the purposes of separation or containment, but rather attempts to follow the already existing criss-crossing patterns of cultural interjacency. His interest is in the formation of identity and culture that occurs within the process of dispersal. His focus is on the nature of a claim that emerges between the recognition of exclusion and the demand for inclusion. His concern with the transformation of culture is not expressed in the digestive metaphors which prescribe the faecal destiny of foreign entrants, but is located in an examination of the presence of indigestible fragments that not only assert their right for representation but also question the forms of signification.

In this essay, I have tried to demonstrate how Bhabha's theory of cultural difference offers a more dynamic understanding of the self-other relationship. The consequences of this argument goes beyond the claim that modernity seeks moral rejuvenation through a tradition of selective synthesis. With regard to the narratives of the nation, it implies that within the very notion of the nation there are already other nations. It also suggests that the task that lies before us is not simply a recuperative one, for there is no original object that can be recovered without the opening of yet another story of origin. In the absence of resolute criteria for identification we recoup through invention.

REFERENCE NOTES

1. Eric Hobsbawn, 'Identity Politics and the Left', *New Left Review*, No.217, May/June, 1996, p.40.
2. Judith Butler, *Gender Trouble: Feminism and the Subversion of Identity*, Routledge, London, 1990, p.xi.

3. Homi K. Bhabha, 'Dissemination: Time, Narrative and the Margins of the Modern Nation', *Nation and Narration*, Routledge, London, 1990.

4. Etienne Balibar differentiates between bigotry and racism as he demonstrates the centrality of racism in the formation of the modern state. See '*Es Gibt Keinen Stadt in Europa*: Racism and Politics in Europe Today', *New Left Review*, No.186, March/April, 1991.

5. Homi K. Bhabha, op.cit., p.3. However, we should also not underestimate the extent to which the 'doubling' of the sign can also be stilled by the 'coolness' of academic argument.

6. Ibid., p.144

7. Bhabha's theoretical framework in *Nation and Narration* emerges from his prior essays on colonial discourse and here I am making use of Bhabha's formulation of the process of subjectification and identification that he set out in his essay 'The Other Question', *Screen*, Vol.24, Dec. 1983. A useful essay that can serve as bridge between the essays on colonial discourse and 'DissemiNation' is his 'Commitment to Theory', *New Formations* 5, 1988, pp.5-23.

8. *Nation and Narration*, op.cit., p.307.

9. Ibid., p.2.

10. Ibid., p.298.

11. The immediate difference in the two projects is apparent in the use of texts which function as representations of particular positions. For instance, in the colonial context, Bhabha relies on documents by the colonisers, missionaries etc. and through them he can explore the dissonance between the official world-view of the ruler and the native order of the ruled. However, in the context of the nation state, the sources do not proceed from such polarities. While Bhabha's strategy is once again to explore the shifts in meaning, the ruptures in this instance are far more problematical because they are already internalised, hence he draws on literary and theoretical material whose location within metropolitan culture is ambivalent.

12. R. Sennett, *The Fall of Public Man*, Faber & Faber, London, 1977, p.53.

13. Ibid., p.60

14. Ibid., p.52.

15. Fichte quoted in E. Kedourie, *Nationalism*, Hutchinson University Library, London, 1960, p.40.

16. *Nation and Narration*, op.cit., p.1.

17. Here I am drawing on the marvellous conclusion that Paul Carter puts forward in *The Road to Botany Bay*, Faber & Faber, London, 1987, and the proposition made by Foucault in 'The Eye of Power', *Knowledge/Power: Selected Interviews and Other Writings 1972-1977*, ed. C. Gordon, Pantheon, New York, 1980, p.149.

18. G. Simmel, *The Philosophy of Money*, Routledge and Kegan Paul, London, 1978, p.69. See also 'The Stranger', *The Sociology of Georg Simmel*, translated and edited by Kurt H. Wolff, Free Press, New York, 1950, pp 403-8.

19. Quoted in R. Bartra, 'Mexican Oficio; The Splendors and the Miseries of Culture', *Third Text*, Vol.14, Spring, 1991, p.15.

20. In this sense the time of cultural difference is very close to Walter Benjamin's notion of Jetztzeit, see 'Theses on the Philosophy of History' in Walter Benjamin, *Illuminations*, translated by Harry Zohn, Schocken, New York, 1969.

21. *Nation and Narration*, op.cit., p.300. See for instance, the European, May 10–12, 1991 a weekly publication which calls itself 'Europe's first national newspaper', and which chose to celebrate its first birthday with the following front-page headline: 'Europe Braced for Migrant Invasion'.

22. Stuart Hall's attempt to decouple the concept of ethnicity from an exclusive linkage to nation and race, and to realign it to a new sense of identity which asserts the specificity of cultural experience is a parallel project to Bhabha's differentiation between cultural diversity and cultural difference. Both are contesting the truncation of cultural difference into an exotic commodity that merely serves the tourist industry. See Stuart Hall, 'New Ethnicities', in *Black Film, British Cinema*, ed. K. Mercer, Institute of Contemporary Arts, No.7, London, 1988.

23. *Nation and Narration*, op.cit., p.305.

24. For a crystal clear account of the dual process of displacement and correspondence in the act of translation see Homi K. Bhabha, 'The Third Space', in *Identity*, ed. Jonathan Rutherford, Lawrence & Wishart, London, 1990, pp.209–10.

25. To be distinguished from the anthropological sense that involves the inversion of two or more stable but very different points, or a passage of initiation which is an irreversible process. See A. Van Gennep, *The Rites of Passage*, translated by M.B. Vizeden and G.L. Caffee, Routledge & Kegan Paul, London, 1960.

26. *Nation and Narration*, op.cit., p.300.

27. *Ibid.*, p.313.

28. V. Dhareshwar, 'Mimicry and/as Identity: Cultural Poetics of the Colonial Habitus', *Mapping Colonialism*, Group for the Study of Colonialism, University of California, Berkeley, 1988, p.58.

29. M. Diawara, 'The Nature of Mother in Dreaming Rivers', *Third Text*, Vol.13, Winter 1990-1, p.80.

30. R.J. Young, *White Mythologies*, London, Routledge, 1990, p.151.

31. 'The Other Question', op.cit., p.23.

32. 'Difference, Discrimination, and the Discourse of Colonialism', in *The Politics of Theory*, ed. F. Barker et al., University of Essex, Colchester, 1983, p.204.

33. 'The Other Question', op.cit., p.18.

34. 'Of Man and Mimicry: The Ambivalence of Colonial Discourse', *October*, Vol.28, Spring, 1984, p.127.

35. 'Signs Taken for Wonders: Questions of Ambivalence and Authority under a Tree Outside Delhi, May 1817', *Critical Inquiry*, Vol.12, Autumn 1985, p.148.

36. 'What Does the Black Man Want?', *New Formations*, No.1, Spring, 1987, p.119.

37. 'Interrogating Identity', in Lisa Appignanesi (ed.), *Identity*, Institute of Contemporary Arts, London, Documents, No.6, 1987, pp. 6–7.

38. *Nation and Narration*, op.cit., p.309.

39. Ibid., p.310.

3.

IDENTITY AND ALTERITY

A CONVERSATION WITH
GAYATRI CHAKRAVORTY SPIVAK

Gayatri Chakravorty Spivak is a critic who works across the fields of feminism, deconstructionism and Marxism. She is Professor of English and Comparative Literature at Columbia University in New York, and spends a considerable period of her time working at grass-roots level in India, as well as teaching at various academic institutions throughout the world. Her translation and introduction to Derrida's *Of Grammatology* not only gained international acclaim but more importantly presaged the crucial influence of Derrida's work. Spivak is cognisant of the fact that the world is full of 'massive brutality, exploitation and sexual oppression', and her writings are politically motivated, treating deconstruction as an intellectual ethic rather than just an academic method for interpreting texts.

Although trained in literary criticism, Spivak has been tracking the relationship between the levels of consciousness in a text and the various contexts and class interests that are also in play. A persistent theme, from her early work on Yeats to the collaboration with the Subaltern Group in India, is the anti-foundationalist critique of colonialism and nationalism. Her first collection of essays, *In Other Worlds* presents us with a deconstruction of the coloniser / colonised dichotomy as well as pointing to Eurocentric tendencies within the feminist movement. More recently she has turned her attention to the responsibilities and pitfalls of an interdisciplinary intellectual practice with global aspirations. Many of the essays in *Outside in the Teaching Machine* are not only brilliantly theorise the interconnections that are made possible in the field of cultural studies, but also give sharp warnings against the unearned privileges of Western globality.

The essay and the dialogical form of interview is particularly suited to Spivak's intellectual practice. Each encounter, as is evidenced in the collection of interviews in *The Post Colonial Critic*, is a lesson in critical thinking. Throughout her work there is no singular totalising model, rather she combines the theoretical and political insights of Marxism, feminism and deconstruction into a unique and syncretic method. Forever on the move and thinking through the historical and institutional structures of her position, as either First World critic, diasporic intellectual, or Indian woman, she rigorously refuses to be bound to any singular position. Shuttling between these locations she turns again and again to the problem of representation and the constitution of the subject.

Nikos Papastergiadis Your essays regularly end with questions but, in a peculiar way, they always return to the mechanisms of shuttling, the never-fixed process through which identity is negotiated, inscribed and contested. This process seems to have particular implications for the disenfranchised, the subaltern.

Gayatri Chakravorty Spivak Yes, in a robust sense we diasporic intellectuals are always shuttling. It is not a message of despair. We are shuttling between Narcissus and Echo: fixating upon the pre-fixed image, a pre-fixed staging, saying to other women within the culture that is how we should be identified. On the other hand, the construction of ourselves as counter-echo to Western dominance, we cannot in fact be confined to behaving as we have been defined. Where there is a moment of slippage there is also a robust aporetic position, rather than being either the self-righteous continuist narcissism in the name of identity, or the message of despair of nothing but Echo.

NP The Romantic notion of shuttling is always dressed with privilege, but the way you talk about shuttling has nothing to do with travelling to the idealised place and everything to do with negotiating claims in everyday politics. It also draws attention to the dynamic tension within the gaps between self-image and identity.

GCS I am glad you picked this up. If I have learnt anything from within the context of tribal groupings in India or in Algeria, it is through having seen this shuttling within the totally disenfranchised women. This is the other face of Janus, which falls back on the narcissist position and flies forward into the position of an interlocutor, an Echo which is not quite an echo. Consider this remark by an urban proletarian Algerian woman on the eve of the municipal elections that brought in the Islamic party: 'Why should I vote for the Islamic party? I am a Muslim. I don't have to vote for a Muslim government. I don't need a Muslim government.' Both the invocation of the narcissus position: iste ego sum — I am a Muslim, the face looking at its own image, and therefore, I don't have to give back an echo to the fundamentalist candidates. This particularly neat example can be found all over the place, whereby it is a clinging to the tradition and strategically recognising that other holds have to be found. I could give one thousand examples. This could become a storytelling session.

NP A theory composed of nothing but examples.

GCS Yes, if in fact we had what one does have in disenfranchised situations, talk sessions not magazines.

NP Can we then turn to talking about the problematic of representing the subaltern?

GCS Let me first of all make a small point about 'isms'. I think that one should beware of claiming 'isms' these days. Postmodernism, for instance, manages the crisis of postmodernity, similarly the quick claims of postcolonial liberals are attempts to manage the crisis of postcoloniality. There is nothing called neo-coloniality there is only neo-colonialism, and there is nothing called decoloniality, only decolonisation. These words are not unimportant because each points at a discontinuous process. Subalternism relates to official historiography. The subalternist historians are indeed questioning official historiography, but their relationship to subalternity is the relationship of the investigator to that which is investigated. Therefore we are not talking about the same thing when we are talking about subalternity and subalternism.

NP Isn't the point of subalternism, as a method, that it also challenges some of the principles of investigation, and that a certain complicitous relationship is defined between the strategies of the investigator and the investigated?

GCS Yes, but it doesn't work the other way. It is not a two-way street.

NP Then how does the subalternist avoid the pitfalls of appropriation through representation?

GCS It marks an attempt to clean the house of history, but not the house of subalternity. There is a very poignant article by one of the subalternists which attempts to narrativise violence. He went into some of the areas where the greatest fundamentalist violence was taking place in India, and one of the questions he asked is: 'How am I to write as a historian about this violence?' Then there is also the fact that his presence made the subalterns think that he could do something for them, and so he was faced with the problematic of how to keep the line between subalternist and activist clear. We should not be too quick to identify this form of investigation with something that does something for the subalterns in the immediate run.

NP Do you think that some of their methodology can be applied to issues within the diaspora?

GCS A book that I am quoting all over the place is Jack D. Forbes: *Black Africans and Native Americans*. This is the case presented by a Native-American historian who is really trying to uncover the Native-American movement within the history of the last 1000 years. In that book there is no attempt to restore subaltern consciousness because he is dealing with such an extraordinary variety of Indian nations, black Africans. In a sense the title is a misnomer because he is also dealing with the so-called Moors and the Spanish Empire. The extraordinary heterogeneity of his field doesn't allow him to speak of restoring consciousness. He is also showing, without even citing a single deconstructive source, that the field of identity is completely textual. He goes behind words like Moors, Mulatto, Mestizo. He gets behind dictionaries, to show how dictionaries work in the interests of rationalisation and the interests of eighteenth-century Linnaean systemisation. He goes against the grain of the accepted research of people like Winthrop Jordan which tends to make the Native-American disappear and Africanises the US context. He argues that the only way you can find anything there is by looking through words, not just the accounts of slaves but how these words are being used so that they finally secure a context in post civil-war America. He recognises that the African-American struggle very importantly claims colour as black, but then he situates it historically.

That kind of an effort is an expanded subalternism which is without some of the problems of the subaltern studies group. Its amazing that Forbes, working completely as an empirical historian on this problem, has given corroboration to some of the basic ideas of deconstruction on identity. You will also find a similar achievement in Patricia Williams's book on race. There are some items which overlap with subaltern studies, yet it is also clear that Forbes proceeds without talking about restoring consciousness or having an axe to grind over the question of nationalism. Instead, he defines identity through intertextuality. To me the subalternist work that is done outside the collective is more interesting now, for here is the example of no national identity out of which one can speak. If there were to be full-scale subaltern studies on tribality in India I hope they will follow the lead of Forbes, for he also shows how difficult it would be to apply a genuine Foucauldian analysis outside the unified European context. It is a daunting project to do *pouvoir savoir* — that is to say, how one can know, not *power/knowledge* — involving all those African and American nations with their different languages and cultures, with the absences of contact, with the non-exchange of languages et cetera. It is that awareness of the historical complexity that energises me when I read Forbes.

NP Looking at it from this perspective one sees the inextricable locality of *pouvoir savoir* and, indeed it is worth pointing out that the profundity of Foucault's project rests on the specificity. He did not, for instance, attempt to write the history of prisons in all of Europe.

GCS Even for the great polymaths of the European tradition that would be hard. But it is not comparable to the enormity of the task that would confront a researcher attempting to embrace the heterogeneity of the Native-American and African nations because there simply isn't the disciplinary university structure to support it. One can imagine the expansion of the Foucauldian method within the European context, but it is impossible to imagine it beyond. People like Todorov are always claiming globality for the European, but in fact that globality is spurious. The whole point of a genuine investigation is that the subaltern is not dominant, the emphasis must remain local not global.

And again Forbes's work is exemplary in the way he traces both the absorption of the Native-American and the African nations and the emergence of two new 'races': the Eastern Neo-American and the Western Neo-American. (American for him means Native-American.) The Western Neo-American is American dominant and the Eastern Neo-American is African dominant. He reinscribes the cartography of the region and computes the emergence of new identities by setting up the Greater Caribbean as the identifiable space with the outlying areas being North and South America.

NP Going back to the role of identity in the struggle against colonialism, there is a common assumption that what both inspires the resistance and secures the survival of a 'native' idiom is the identity that preceded the contact with the coloniser. Within this schema there is little sympathy for psychoanalytic concepts. One critic has gone so far as to argue that Homi Bhabha's use of the concept of identification relegates the other to the unconscious of the metropolis.

GCS I would contest this in only one way. The unconscious is an important category in psychoanalysis, and I think that it is the investigation of the unconscious that keeps psychoanalysis going. In a position where all the emphasis falls upon the metropolis, the unconscious is not investigated, the unconscious is not seen as that which is rewritten in the metropolis. So it is only if you take a precritical view of the word 'unconscious', as that which is not conscious, that the analogy holds. I agree with the sentiments of the critic but I don't accept the formulation. I say it in cruder terms. I say that if one keeps the metropolitan situation as the important arena, the decolonised spaces within subalternity just drop off. They are perhaps engulfed but they just drop off. Within psychoanalysis the rupture between the unconscious and the subject's history is investigated over and over again. No such thing happens when the metropolis is seen as the important space. Even in Jameson's *Political Unconscious* it is the unconscious that is the most important area, that is the basic subtext which gets laid out in a displaced and condensed form in the narrative of the West. But in an analysis which lays the emphasis on the metropolitan migrant, that subtext is not investigated in any kind of detail. There is no particular knowledge of the subtext, and here the analogy breaks down between the metropolis and its unconscious, for it can only hold if one takes unconscious in its colloquial sense.

NP Such accounts would also seek to emphasise the intact nature of the pre-colonial constituents to identity and distance themselves from concepts such as 'mimicry' and 'catachresis'.

GCS The subaltern in the 'native' space may also lead to nostalgia. The subaltern lives in a state; the subaltern votes and, if the subaltern doesn't vote the job of the native activist is to make damn sure that the subaltern does vote, hence the subaltern is inserted into citizenship. So let's not get nostalgic about the 'native' space by thinking it is outside mimicry. The question that I ask when I am with disenfranchised people is: 'What is it to vote?', for quite often there is no clue as to what this voting means. But the point there is not to just let it remain like that but to allow, through activism, for the subaltern to catachretise parliamentary democracy.

NP Can you explain what you mean by catachresis?

GCS Catachresis is a metaphor for which there is no literal referent. Of course nativists will come forth and say that there is a tradition of democracy in the native culture, which is fine as gesture politics. You can usefully talk about the primitive Communism of the tribals. But this is not fine in the production of knowledge because then that leads to what I have called 'the invocation of narcissism': you look at your own image in the water and assume that it will give you enough of everything. But, in fact, it is not the native tradition of parliamentary democracy that one is using. Rather, one is trying to insert the subaltern in terms of citizenship and in terms of a constitution that is built on the enlightenment model. Although I would honour the terms of campaigning — establishing the possibilities of activism — the gesture politics of finding models within the 'native' traditions seems to me to be a very different practice from simply talking about it in the house of knowledge. What I mean by catachretising parliamentary democracy is the insertion and the reinscription of something which does not refer literally to the correct narrative of the emergence of parliamentary democracy. One must not either get nostalgic about or take away the cultural good of the native space, but I am talking politics and the activist's job is to make damn sure that the dominant classes are not the only ones with access to the state.

NP Within the Anglo-Saxon milieu, feminists have often rejected Lacanian and deconstructive strategies because they argue that it reproduces rather than critiques the binary oppositions of plenitude and lack. Do you think that a similar criticism is often made against the utility of deconstruction in subaltern studies?

GCS I don't really think that the subaltern is always relegated to the position of lack. The subaltern is placed in the position of the uninvestigated. As for the polemic against deconstruction, what would be the alternative to this model?

NP It seems that deconstructive strategies, which to me seek to draw attention to the intertextuality of identity and culture and thereby highlight the violence with which identities and knowledge systems have been selectively truncated and reinscribed are, nevertheless, often accused of being complicit with rather than critical of the violence done to the subaltern.

GCS But they are also critical of the dominant subject, and this is the gift, for the metropolitan has never questioned its own identity. So isn't that a significant difference? And, being a practical person, I ask myself what is the alternative? What is the other side proposing?

NP Shall we move on then to discuss the relationship between subaltern studies and minority discourse and the influence of deconstructive strategies?

GCS Subaltern and minority are not interchangeable terms and here we need examples to clarify these differences.

NP Could you, then, relate the work on, say, Asian communities in Britain to subaltern studies?

GCS The basic difference that arises is that a migrant minority has a stake within the metropolitan nation, whereas what stake does the subaltern have in decolonised space? The relationship to the state and the access to the political structures of representation are different. If one only emphasises the situation of the relationship between an Asian dominant and an Asian minority in a metropolitan state, one simply obliterates the fact that the real subalternist effort has always been in terms of decolonised states and that the subalterns are without much access to the culture of imperialism. It seems to me that we have to keep these two situations distinct. Owing to the specificity of the insertion of the subaltern into citizenship, which is the national activist's programme, the activist has no choice but to be deconstructive there because the questions of national identity have not embraced the subalterns, and if one stays mired within subaltern identity there is no way that they are going to emerge into the state. So it seems to me that the quickshift from subaltern studies into the question of migrant minority is a mistake. Let's keep subaltern studies where they belong.

NP In my own work I use the term exile to signify not just physical displacement but also to describe the process of negotiating the discordant elements within cultural dislocation. I think we need to give more attention to this process if we are attempting to explain the modern manifestations of identity rather than retrieving paradigms which either lament the losses or praise the gains.

GCS Moving away from the rural and the landless, let us look at a slightly more privileged but not a privileged class, to the pre-scene of migration, to the visa room of the British High Commission in New Delhi. It is an extremely racist staging. The High Commission is a palatial building except for the visa room, where of course most of the people who are looking for visas are Sikh who are themselves getting a bad deal in India. They are obliged to stand in the merciless Delhi sun in the summertime, and move slowly toward a tiny room with one fan placed as a joke in the corner. As the queue moves very slowly there is a moment when you get the fan.

It is this tiny, overfilled room with people wanting a visa, wanting to go to Britain, wanting to go and so they wait. As we are waiting one of the women says: 'It is this difficult to get to England'. We are sitting there hour after hour, waiting for our names to be called, and in that situation, if you try to fit it into the narcissus scene, it will be a hard order but it can be done. In that situation one woman asks me: 'Who is there?' You see, because they all have someone, their husbands, and they are trying to get there. It is only afterwards that there comes the counter-echo; when they are in Britain perhaps. So I say: 'No one'. She says: 'You are trying for it alone?' And I say: 'Yes, for six weeks'. Immediately, class difference is established when she says: 'You are going on tour?' I said: 'No I have work'. She replies: 'Business?' I say something that is regrettable perhaps but 'business' hit me in another way: 'No a salaried job of the intelligence!'

In this context, if you really want to do a close reading of this racist staging of independent India, within the capital city, of how much the disenfranchised want to go to the metropolis, to stage it in the worst possible way, you really are like a supplicant in that situation. Within that appalling context of the visa office, you take the two parties: the ones seeking short term visas and those wanting permanent visas. And, then, if you do a close reading in terms of the figuration of Narcissus and Echo, and then you shift the scene towards the new migrants in Britain, you will see that what I am talking about is much less in the detail being politically theorised than in the mere invocation of a narcissistic, self-fixated, collective identity without any consideration of the institution at the origin.

NP This is a very useful story because it shows the imbrication of the migrant's aspirations and the institutionalisation of racism. The poignancy of this story is that it suggests that displacement begins in institutions rather than in aeroplanes. And, of course, there are institutions of migration that precede the visa office.

GCS That is where you have to consider various historical scenarios that cannot be dismissed as mere infinite regression which is often interpreted as the institution of origin: paralysis, nihilism, you can't do anything out of it. For, if you take it not as a formula but as a case, as examples, as the histories of lives, then you have to consider the historical script, the palimpsestic rememoration in a much more heavyweight way, and this distinction between diaspora and nostalgia begins to become vacant.

NP Here again this distinction between diaspora and nostalgia is often inserted to mark the regressive mind set of the migrant. What I would want to see is a case of the nostalgia that precedes migration.

GCS But, remember, most of these people in the visa room were women, and remember that the women asked me: 'Who do you have over there?', and I was saying: 'No one'. What I lose is the inscription of the woman as Echo: there is Narcissus over there, but that Narcissus is in fact not the West but 'My man in Britain'. That is the division, and I lose that particular inscription, but then what I was trying to point out in my response is that I become a kind of Echo of another kind of echo, of the salaried position in the West. That brings us back to Amin's remark in *Unequal Development* that we cannot take as examples the figures who become competitive on the other side. I reminded my fellow Indian woman that I was not in the same place as she was; I was competitive on the other side. To my chagrin I immediately reclaimed for myself a place as counter-echo because the thing that knocked me was that she had thought that I was in 'business abroad'. The text is complicated but there are also only these two positions within which we shuttle.

NP In that case, how would you shift into migrant studies?

GCS I have not interested myself much with migrant studies. I live in the United States and the situation of the migrant there has always seemed to me rather different from the situation in post-imperial countries. The continuist tradition of Native-American and African-American insurgency and its constitutive presence is a fact. The US is also an immigrant country. There have been waves of white immigrants who had themselves carved out certain kinds of hegemonies. Their way of relating to the African-American and Native-American is now behind us. After the 1980s and the computerisation of the stock exchanges, the situation of the new immigrants is completely different. Because of this historical spectrum, certain kinds of historical situations are developing which I call 'the absence of a spectral vision'. Here the idea of postcolonial studies goes against the problems on the ground, and we cannot focus on the term 'postcolonial' very usefully in the US because it refers to another narrative altogether: the disbanding of the colonies. In the US nothing has been disbanded. The US is a neo-imperial power, and while its economic hegemony is threatened by the emergence of the US of Europe and Japan, it is fighting tooth and nail to contain the crisis of its economic disadvantage by using this very long tradition of the management of migrancy through neo-colonial cultural projects, a kind of hegemonic multiculturalism. In that context I am very concerned with the problem of how to think cultural studies in the US without becoming politically empty. But that really doesn't relate much to the problems in postcolonial countries where there has been large scale migration since the disbanding of Empire.

NP So we have at least three categories to deal with: the postcolonial migrant in the metropolitan space, the subaltern in the decolonised space, and what you call the management of migrancy in the neo-imperialist space. I can see how, in places like Australia, the second generation of migrants are being inserted into that category.

GCS Again, you put me in a place where I would have to imagine more than analyse. I am extremely confined by what I try to learn because, if there is one thing that truly frightens me, it is general-isation on the basis of stereotypes. The use of the term subaltern to describe any disenfranchised group anywhere in the world gives me a great problem, as also does the term postcolonial. I first started using that term to describe specific places like Algeria and India which were postcolonial in a certain sense but, before you know what's what, it becomes a buzzword to talk about anything that involves the Third World. Australia is obviously a very dif-ferent case and I don't think that one can transfer the solutions that one supposedly finds in a small place like Britain with its totally imperialist past. The model of Britain is not something that can offer any theory on what to do with migrants. To assume that it can is a case of intellectual neo-colonialism.

The subaltern languishes as a group when we focus our atten-tion on the discontinuous migration that constitute the nation state. Discontinuous migration, for it to be a migration in the first place, is already insertable into class discourse. If one wants to consider the subalternist argument then one has to think about the disappearance of peoples and the strategic exclusion of the peoples who are not inserted into class discourse. I think that perhaps this needs to be applied to the Australian case. I really do not see any benefit in the universalisation of the term subaltern as if it were another word for minorities or the recip-ients of racism. This would diminish both its intellectual clarity and its political usefulness.

NP Are there similar problems with the term postcolonialism?

GCS For me postcolonialism doesn't exist. Postcolonialism assumes that decolonisation has taken place. A more appropri-ate question is who decolonises? The basic, conservative, historical situation was that decolonisation was supposed to take place on the part of the imperial authorities as they dis-mantled their machinery on departure, and the people who take authority in the new nation then use some of this dismantled machinery to create new structures in order to construct a new state. This is supposed to be decolonisation. Well, clearly, this is not sufficient for our purposes. If we are to take Ngugi's extremely important idea of the decolonising of the mind, or Foucault's idea of the practice of liberty after the fact of nego-tiated independence, then those kinds of ideas keep the question of decolonisation open. The claim to postcolonialism is a way of closing that question and is utterly premature. In the context of nations that strictly speaking were not colonies, there is no such concept of postcoloniality and, if there is, then we must look at how the situation of postcolonialism has changed.

There is also the interesting question of how a postcolonial nation can, in economic terms, enter the game of neo-colonialism. For example, Hong Kong is both; it is one of the major players in neo-colonialism, but it is also by fiat a postcolonial place.

NP I don't know why we even need such generalised terms. Isn't it more important to figure out what is happening rather than looking towards a regularising language? And in this spirit can you say something more about the process of invagination and its relation to shuttling?

GCS Well, it is not really a process but a structural description, that the two things are both separate from each other but share a common space. The example I come back to is that little eye-shaped space in Venn diagrams where you are opposed to each other in terms of a certain characteristic, but you are also together because you share another characteristic. The space in between is the space which is invaginated. What is important to me is the recognition of the alliances that form within invagination. That is why, when I talk of global feminism, I mention we are touched by the culture of imperialism. So that in academic culture, the opposed groups, male and female, share a space, so that they can talk to each other, rather than only between themselves. That's the area that is neither inside nor outside, and that's what is interesting. In the space that you and I inhabit, is a space that asserts critical intimacy rather than critical distance. The recognition of invagination is an acceptance that the useful critique takes place from within the inaccessibly intimate, rather than the objectively distant. Imperialism and global feminism are invaginated. Let the space of invagination become the space of sabotage.

WORKS CITED
GAYATRI CHAKRAVORTY SPIVAK

In Other Worlds, Methuen, London, 1987.
The Post Colonial Critic, Routledge, London, 1990.
Outside in the Teaching Machine, Routledge, London, 1993.

4.

METAPHOR

THE ENERGY FOR BEGINNING

Diego Reboredo Ferrari was born in Argentina and has lived in Barcelona and London. The body of work that he has produced fascinates me not simply because of the mastery of his practice or by the exceptionality of his journey. This essay is not a comment on achievements, interventions and arrival. It is about the dynamism of beginnings. What could best represent these interminable starting-points? The colour blue for both of us, and in different ways, signifies both home and horizon. Growing up beside the ocean, he facing the Atlantic and I the Pacific, made us both aware of the slender collision between two shades of blue as sky and sea meet. This alluring but unreachable division of blues suggested the awe of distance and the light by which we define our position in the world. The blue used in Renaissance paintings as background, to heighten the outline of a subject, is taken by Diego Reboredo Ferrari and transposed on to the surface of his installations. The background steps forward, carrying within it the suggested androgyny of the Renaissance subject while also beckoning the sublime. Meditations on beginnings are less involved with the identification of an original location than they are an engagement with the practice of mediation and assemblage. To find the beginning is as much an invention as it is an excavation. In this sense discovery is not a return journey, but the forward search of an initiation point. The power of discovery is thus found in the confirmation of knowing how to continue. Beginnings are sources of energy.

The dispatching of starting-points and the cross-dressing of impasses are predicaments that are shared by many artists from

Latin-America. Home and exile have many forms. Juan Davila left Santiago and moved to Melbourne. Shifting from one periphery to another, perhaps this dislocation sharpened his attention to the loss of language and history, a loss which a nationalist iconography would rather gloss. Davila's reply to exile, the condition of isolation and fragmentation is found in his transvesting of itinerancy. Eugenio Dittborn has made the art of mailing his work from Chile to elsewhere, as both the conceptual grid for its construction, and as a message that gives resonance to the positions of distance and proximity implicit in the act of sending and receiving. It was not just the physicality of restraint and freedom that compels the questioning of borders. Which language and what skin will reveal presence? A still from a video shows Tunga holding a model brain in his palm. With the pressure of Gabriel Orozco's fingers on a ball of brick clay, followed by a clean release, a heart is revealed. The open palm is the gesture of offerings. Both Tunga's *The Silver Nerve*, 1986, and Gabriel Orozco's *My Hand is the Memory of Space*, 1991, are bafflingly simple. Yet the resonance that is activated through the twin axioms of absence and presence slightly jolts the fragile walls of our self-understanding. How will history speak and geography map delicate gestures and continental shifts? *Mestizaje*: the metaphor for the 'hysterical' syncretism at every level of being between the Americas, Australia and Europe. There is no straight continuum which co-ordinates origins and destinies.

The difficulty of starting-points is to be found in the contradictions between production and validation. It is in the gap between the dynamism of living cultures and the static terms of institutions which either cover the vastness of other civilisations with flimsy clichès or turn their back to the enigmas of new formations. The paradoxes of location and orientation, posed by Guy Brett in the exhibition *Transcontinental*, 1990, have alerted us to a peculiar figuration of surplus and lack in the resourcing and referencing of Latin-American cultural identities.[1]

To consider the complex patterns of influence and projection I would like to interweave a number of stories that Diego Reboredo Ferrari recounted to me. The first story is concerned with growing up in the Argentinean pampas. It is as significant to his self-understanding as are the stories that outline his response to the work of other artists. The central concern of Diego Ferrari's work has been an examination of the position of the spectator. The philosophical question of alienation and the physical experience of integration by a spectator have been addressed in his work in relation to particular responses to light and space.

Diego Reboredo Ferrari's fascination with the qualities of the horizon is clearly linked to childhood experiences in the pampas. The horizon, or what Waltercio Caldas called 'the line that's nowhere',[2] presents us with the instance in which it is possible both to visualise and contemplate the border between absence and presence. This possibility is particularly heightened by two features: a road and the sunset. As a child Ferrari would stare down the straight roads leading into the pampas as if he were looking into the barrel of infinity. Similarly, when the sun seemed to dissolve into the flatness of the pampas and the day merged into night, the expansiveness of earth and sky found new proportions at the cusp of mutual penetration. The solitariness, not solitude, of a figure framed within the immensity of elements, presented to Diego Reboredo Ferrari's attention, the experience of the relationship between background and foreground and the oscillation between near and far. Against this setting there are three figures — Michelangelo, Saenredam and Durham — which can be proposed as markers in Ferrari's practice. Each figure serves as a station through which he passes, enhancing the beginnings and clarifying the multiple crossroads of a modern myth. With each arrival, the examination of one question becomes all the more restless, how does the work of art communicate the potentialities of competing realities? The ambivalent sensations of open and closed, light and dark, are the constant axioms in Ferrari's installations.

To recount this journey, let us commence with Michelangelo and the story of the eye. This is a familiar starting-point. We all know that Michelangelo was commissioned to paint the story of creation and, what we admire today, more than the technical virtuosity, is the incorporation of meanings and values which were previously excluded from the genre of painting. This was a titanic struggle between individual will and institutional dogma, which centred on the determination of the 'diameter' of interpretation. Michelangelo challenged the code which excluded the possibility of ambivalence. 'Look into the way he painted the eyes of the prophet Jeremiah,' declares Ferrari. 'How could we overlook the sense that the benign gaze may also hold evil?' Folkloric wisdom does not deny the existence of such contradictions. Protection from the evil eye is not a defence from the external enemy. It is rather, an acknowledgment that the look of admiration can also carry the harm of envy. Embracing such contradictions and displaying ambivalence is the deepest threat to an institution founded on dogma. Within the enclosed world of dogma there is no space for the underdetermined or polyvalent signs. Dogma demands fixity. Boundaries are made rigid and meanings inflexible. Michelangelo's refusal to comply with the rules of codification, and the portrayal of ambivalence in the structure of vision and interpretation, present Ferrari with a number of salient starting-points.

The concern with the ambivalence of vision was developed in the installations, *Reflection*, 1991, and *The Split Personality of Light*, 1993. Both installations construct a scenario in which the spectator's perception of the space is time-bound. The positioning of walls in both installations serves partially to filter the natural light and to stress the relationship between darkness and shadow. At the centre of *Reflection* is a reproduction of Michelangelo's Jeremiah; our focus is directed to his eye, which in turn is the source of the electrical cable which supplies the light for three discs positioned outside the room, seemingly hovering on a pavement below. At night these discs glow with the same blue that washes the interior of the installation. The fluidity of light as it is transmitted between private and public space is the subject of *The Split Personality of Light*. The resulting images and the experience of time and space are substantially affected by the location of floating walls, the projection of light and the position of the spectator. The interaction between light and position is always intensified by the 'competition' between internal (artificial light) and external (sunlight). In the case of *Reflection* this 'competition' affects the perception of the central image of the eyes of Jeremiah, whereas in *The Split Personality of Light*, it affects the projection of the spectator's shadow from the internal wall to the dark exterior. In the latter work, this play with exteriority simultaneously opens up the philosophical dimensions of transmission and absorption as well as exposing the subject to threat of being cast into the psychological abyss of non-reflection.

Apart from the thematic continuities between the two installations there is also a significant development. The ambivalence of vision and the opposition between objectivity and subjectivity are balanced in different ways. In *Reflections*, the two eyes are also the surfaces on, and through which light is most delicately or force-fully filtered. This staging of the source is also cast with specific values. One eye narrows and turns inward: it withholds or ban-ishes communication. The other eye looks outward with an inviting gesture towards possible dialogue. The axis is divided and the spectator is forced to negotiate this uncertain gaze. Art critic Jean Fisher astutely observed that an echo of this dual message is established by positioning three discs which seeming to float over fluorescent lights outside the room:

> The ambivalent surface of the solar film as both penetrable and
> reflective, and the light halo around the discs at night — each
> moment functioning as an immaterial interval between states. This
> interval or border is a limit that cannot be said to be either 'inside'
> or 'outside', but an indeterminable and vacillating interface
> between two different spatial dimensions or fields. As such, it may
> be said to function as a metaphor of the artist's self as the 'gap'
> which separates and conjoins two geographical spaces.[3]

This 'gap' is posed more radically in The Split Personality of Light, where the projection of artificial light passes through a small hole from the back wall that divided the kitchen and the living-room. Upon entering the dematerialised living-room, the spectator has taken a position within the frame. The absence or presence of a shadow on to the facing window is determined purely by the rota-tions of sun. The reflection of the spectator's self-image is thus bordered by the horizon formed between two sources of light: external sunlight and internal projected artificial light. Within this installation the splitting of forms is also a convergence, the site of ambivalence and the ambivalence of sight is further locked together.

From the rebel, whose struggle is to expand the terms of refer-encing, to the reactionary, whose motivation for acting is directed towards establishing a strict equivalence between signification and meaning, Ferrari turns to consider the figure of Pieter Saenredam. Saenredam's painting De Groote Kerk, Haarlem, was, for Ferrari, an example of the contradiction in the construction of an idealised field of vision within the terms of the Renaissance. This painting also provoked a collaboration with artist/critic/architect Mark Pimlott. For both Pimlott and Ferrari, it is the presence of a dark spot, within an almost transparent interior, that produces a disturbing tension. The linear gaze into this expansive interior is arrested and then absorbed within the dark painting that is positioned inside Saenredam's painting. Their response suggests that the presence of the dark painting hung on the white columns within this painting contradicts the principles of optical certainty.

> The painting within the painting denotes representation: it is flag, token and icon; its temporal, historical and commemorative; it is *memento mori* and subjective; it is obscure; it is subject. Its conventions and knowledge conflict with those of the depicted interior, which present themselves as rational, ahistorical, illuminated and objective. The internalised discontinuity of the painting calls attention to its status as representation, as exposed and troubled artifice. It shatters its own initial claim to a vision of objectivity, by opening up its own ambiguity, its place between knowledge, between object and subject. The rational is thus revealed as representation; the representation as presence. The painting as subject (as an inversion of optical confirmation) interrupts the agreement between viewer as subject and painting as object. An empathy is demanded, as boundaries of otherness collapse.

Ferrari's concern with the interaction between the position of the spectator and the embodiment of vision finds a tantalising twist in this project. By identifying the tension between the different levels of image, and the contrary uses of light, he directs attention to the repositioning of the spectator, away from a fixed exterior vantage point, to an exilic shuttling between the inside and the outside of the frame. The perspective is decentred and the hierarchy of interpretation is destabilised. The Enlightenment's promise of integrating the scopic drives of vision and knowledge appears to negate itself within its own framework. It is in this project that the multi-dimensional conception of exile becomes apparent in Ferrari's work. Exile is perceived not just as an experience of physical displacement but is also linked to the semantic ruptures in representation. Exile is inserted as a conceptual process that heightens the metaphorical mode of carrying difference into critical thinking. It alerts attention not only to the difference between things but also to the connectivity of the space between them. Space is no longer seen as a neutral stage, but an active field constituted by dynamic forces. Situating the body of the spectator in this field undoes the Renaissance's certitudes that grant the unity and clarity of insight, as they abstract and neutralise the concept of space. This exilic perspective is seen as the counter to the vision proposed by the Enlightenment. However, this is not to be confused with an embrace of boundless relativism and disunity. The exilic perspective is the product and the process of shuttling from one position to another; if it appears loose and open-ended, this is not because it is unstructured but because it is structured without a centre.

If we imagine the struggle for interpretation in Michelangelo, in terms of a contestation over the range of possible meanings, an opening of valves that expand the flow of interpretation, then, despite Saenredam's intended code, the presence of the black painting within *De Groote Kerk, Haarlem* represents the impossibility of the return to orthodoxy. The constriction of the potentiality of meaning is prevented from arriving at a singular point of intersection. The dark spot undermines dogma's demand for an absolute and predetermined fit between the sign and its interpretation. The power of this absolute fit colludes with the promises that truths and errors are always fixed. Reassuring as it may be, the security of this symmetry ultimately rests on an unacknowledged set of denials and exclusions. The relationship between an image and the eternal can only be stable if the metaphoric mode of interpretation is confined to a codification of symbols. The multiple connectiveness in the tissues of thought are striated and hardened into linear veins which singularise the suggestions of a glance into the tyranny of the stare.

The position of the spectator and the politics of representation have been brought to the surface of many debates within the transnational art world. Some of the best-informed critics and most celebrated artists have not always succeeded in creating a critically engaged perspective and interpretation. Gayatri Chakravorty Spivak and Alfredo Jaar, in *One or Two Things I Know About Them*, 1991, set out to question the stereotypes of the other and reflect on their own subject positions as they represented the intimate realities of a Bangladeshi community in East London. Neither, the division of labour between theorist/critic and photographer/artist, nor their practice of quasi-fieldworking succeeded in finding a tone that affirmed the identity, let alone gained the trust of their subjects. The resulting exhibition which publicly played on the disjunction between the text of people's life stories and images

taken from their everyday life aroused protest and anger by the very
girls who had been photographed. The collaboration backfired,
exposing that the pedagogy of the investigative camera and the
dialectics of the gaze are easily turned against each other. Translating
the truth of a quick glance is hard earned.

The meeting of eyes can be the precursor of communication, the
invitation for exchange, the first breath of dialogue; it can be as
full as the horizons of silence that surround speech. I am reminded
of Pantelis Voulgaris's film *Stone Years*, 1985, which depicts the
horror of political repression and the persecution of the opponents
to the junta in Greece most powerfully in those vital moments
when emotion is necessarily withheld. There is a haunting scene
where two condemned lovers face each other across the bridge of
the ship that was carrying them to exile, and for fear of further retribution they dare not even weep. Any expression of recognition
could only intensify their suffering and endanger clandestine networks. The space between them stings with denial. The lovers were
bonded by history. They felt as if the choice of a conventional life
with open expressions of love did not exist. All aspects of their time
together were also a struggle against the times in which they lived.
Entwined like this they dared not speak of their love. Their solidarity required no verbal testimony. Understanding the lexicon of
eyes implies profound intimacy. In other situations the understate-
ment is part of the violence of silence as it rebounds between the
mirrors of misrecognition.

When we look into distant eyes what do we discover about ourselves and about the other? There is a tendency which recurs
throughout the history of Western art which seeks a transcendence
from the limits of the self via an incorporation of the other. The
aim usually involves the combination of two perspectives in the
construction of a new single image. This romantic escape rarely
produces the intended result. The utilisation of other subjects and
codes also requires a questioning of the methods of interpretation
and the definition of perspective. The colonial hierarchy of vision
and interpretation was ironically the structure which secured the
strategy of the appropriation of the other for the benefit of the self.
Latin-America was being reinscribed by the terms of Europe. The
dilemma that is born from the dissatisfaction with one code of representation is only compounded as the desire to reach a universal
synthesis flounders on the rocks of repetition: the inevitable return

to the dominant code. There is no break, at best an extension through incorporation, there is just the oscillation within the binarism of a romantic idealisation of the other and the acknowledgment of the other as the same. To confront other traditions as if they were static and timeless, is to see the artefact and lose sight of the methods for *working through*. The complexity of *working with* another way of seeing is blocked by the blindness to the inflections of power in culture.

We seem to have passed through the trinity of rebellion, reaction and appropriation without a sense of resolution. Perhaps the fourth stage will be the place where a reconciliation of opposites can be found? Yet the moment the name Jimmie Durham is announced as a present-future source I smile, prepared for further complexity. The insight that Durham's work offers is one which follows directly from the realisation of the blindness in appropriation. Durham's work consistently follows two trajectories, an attack of the exploitative thematic of non-reciprocity, and a mockery of the codes of misrecognition. Ferrari has grasped Durham's perception of the absences within the dominant language and barriers between competing codes. This knowledge induces a melancholy, a tragic awareness of the inevitability of alienation, yet the irony of this sadness is heightened as Durham plays it out, for instance through the desirous eyes of two lovers, Malinche and Cortez. What bonding could entwine these strangers? I wonder about those exchanges before she learnt to speak his language. What dreams were held in the cusp of Malinche's desire as she became the bridge between two worlds? She presaged the destruction of her culture as she translated his desires. The conqueror remained in his language. The asymmetry and the vilification of her body has spawned its own complex, but we end with her name not as a symbol of betrayal but as metaphor for ambivalence.

Commenting on Jimmie Durham's installation *Ama*, 1992, Jean Fisher observed the etymological dissonance within the title. In Spanish it is the imperative 'love me!', but in Cherokee it means 'salt' or 'water', serving as a metaphor for the asymmetry of gift exchange that define colonial relations. Durham's reoffering of vessels begs the question, what is Malinche? Jean Fisher answers:

> One might think at first that, by 'collaborating' with the invaders in the destruction of her culture, she is no more than a con-

temptible symbol of the submission and 'feminisation' of the Americas to European machismo. And yet, was she not already a gift — a form of currency circulating within the symbolic system of inter-cultural exchange amongst the Mesoamericans? Again, as lover and interpreter to Cortez, Malinche's body becomes the site of a linguistic transcription across which coloniser and colonised trace out the contradictions of their relations. For Durham, she is 'water'; bearing an almost infinite capacity of absorption, she will eventually dissolve salt — that crystalline form which, in any case, contains its aqueous other. Her reality is, then, as it always was: resilient, and ionisable on contact with salt, whereupon it transforms into a power unrealised, undreamt.[4]

The dialogue between these two artists/writers is most resonant for Ferrari. Who is the interpreter? What worlds are beings exchanged/translated in these acts? Here we see an exchange where the status of the writer is not regarded as subordinate to the artist. The two forms oscillate in a state of unstable equilibrium. Writing and sculpting is not the materialisation for exclusive ideas. Both Durham and Fisher move across these boundaries. They both take the responsibility of representation, and in that gesture there is also a sacrifice. One does not follow the other like the shadow behind the body. First World and Third World, polarities and nomenclatures which sustain Eurocentric hierarchies, are repeatedly transgressed. The plurality of the Americas yields a surplus that does not conform to the history of the self as either primitive or exotic. In a text called 'Here at the Centre of the World', Durham asserts: 'Until tomorrow, the culture and the cultural history of what is incorrectly called "Latin-America" is nothing more or less than a backwater of European culture.'[5]

These propositions and gestures which call the West to take account of itself in the terms it projected to the other, do not offer any resolute conclusions, they are all intimations for new beginnings. The melancholic beckoning of each practice outlined in this essay emanates from the desire to hold contrary worlds in one language. Given Ferrari's predicament, such an impossible gravity is not only alluring but also axiomatic in the itinerary of his own practice. The starting-point of work includes the bitter-sweet consciousness of partial translations, the gap between absence and presence in every exchange. It is the ambivalence within language, vision and interpretation which is his field. The forms of the aesthetic utterances in Ferrari's practice is not motivated by an act of integration or alienation but an investigation of the space that activates the gap between them. Philosopher/sociologist Georg Simmel, while meditating on the transformations of space — the bridge as unification and the door as separation — articulated these metaphorical dynamics that dominate everyday life.

> Because the human being is the connecting creature who must always separate and cannot connect without separating — that is why we must first conceive intellectually of the merely indifferent existence of two river banks as something separated in order to connect them by means of a bridge. And the human being is likewise the bordering creature who has no border. The enclosure of his or her domestic being by the door means, to be sure, that they have separated out a piece from the uninterrupted unity of natural being. But just as the formless limitation takes on a shape, its limitedness finds its significance and dignity only in that which the mobility of the door illustrates: in the possibility at any moment of stepping out of this limitation into freedom.[6]

REFERENCE NOTES

1. Guy Brett, *Transcontinental: Nine Latin-American Artists*, Verso, London, in association with Ikon Gallery, Birmingham and Cornerhouse, Manchester, 1990.
2. Ibid., p.71.
3. Jean Fisher, 'Border Patrols: Art Criticism and the Margins of Art', *Memoria Catàloga*, Feria de Arte Contemporànio, Guadalajara, 1992, pp.3–7.
4. Jean Fisher, 'The Savage Gift: Jimmie Durham's Ama', *Third Text*, No.21, Winter 1992-3, p.25.
5. Jimmie Durham, 'Here at the Centre of the World', *Third Text*, No.5, Winter 1988-9, p.22.
6. Georg Simmel, 'Bridge and Door', *Theory, Culture & Society*, Vol.11, No.1, February 1994, p.10.

LANGUAGES FOR LANDSCAPE
A CONVERSATION WITH DAVID MALOUF

David Malouf was born in Brisbane of Lebanese and English parents. He has written eight books of fiction, nine books of poetry, a play and three libretti. Amidst this broad corpus of writing are the image of the journey and the figure of exile, recur both in a substantive form and as a metaphorical mode. *Johnno*, 1975, Malouf's first novel, focused on the experience of self-imposed exile. A sort of Cavafian tale of escape and repetition of how the past persists within everyday practices. This oscillation between departure and return resonates through the series of images which established a relationship between the body, memories, maps, lines and scars. In one passage, the protagonist Johnno, tells the narrator Dante, a fellow writer, that if after every six years the body replaces all the tissue, then he has expelled Australia from his own body, he has excreted every archipelago and every little island. The body seemingly has been shed by exile. However, while it constantly changes, old scars and features are reproduced. The map of Australia is marked by lines that trace the rivers rarely, if ever, filled. And at the end of the novel, it is one of these rivers that raises itself to claim and drown Johnno.

An Imaginary Life, 1978, Malouf's most acclaimed novel, is based on the banishment of Ovid from Rome to an austere frontier village. The sting in the punishment is not just the exclusion from home but also the necessity to define a different relationship to language. Ovid's crime is after all, in his exorbitant and rather decadent use of language. Being sent to this remote outpost of the Roman world, not only removed him from his context, thereby denying him of an audience, but it also sentences him to a place where language is a sort of scarce commodity. Denied the opportunity to perform his sophistry and confined to a level of subsistence communication, his tongue has been cut, metaphorically speaking. Ovid's response to this banishment is an ecstatic fusion with the landscape which is mediated by wild boy/guide who leads him further into nature. Like that of all exiles, Ovid's identity is reordered as much by the initial severance as it is by the projection of an imaginary salvation.

Since the 1980s, Malouf has lived both in Italy and Australia. The focus of this interview is his novel, *Remembering Babylon*, 1993, which was shortlisted for the Booker Prize and the inaugural winner of the world's most valuable literary award, the Impac Prize. The story is about a young boy called Gemmie who grows up as a streetchild in London, finds himself aboard a ship bound for Australia where he is cast overboard and rescued by an Aboriginal community. Eventually, he 'returns' to a frontier white settlement in Northern Queensland; it is so remote that 'even the Syrian peddlar did not trouble to come so far'. Through this encounter between Gemmie and the settlers Malouf explores the fears and hopes that crystallise around a stranger. *Remembering Babylon* is about the relationship between historical consciousness and the perception of space, the stutters between language and silence, the jump cuts between possession and dispossession. These burning themes are dramatically staged by those historical words with which Gemmie greets the white settlers: 'Do not shoot. I am a BBBBBritish object.'

Nikos Papastergiadis Could you describe the role of landscape in your fiction?

David Malouf One of the things that goes back to something that I was interested in *An Imaginary Life* is the idea of landscape itself. Landscapes have been shaped either to our practical uses or they've been shaped to our recreational uses. Landscapes reflect back and tell us how human we are and how powerful we are because we have made them.

When those early European settlers came to confront the Australian landscape, it wasn't the hostility of extreme drought and rain that was most frightening to them, rather it was the sense that the landscape reflected nothing back of their own humanity. They would look at it and it would remain as something quite separate. It had not been shaped by them and so they could not see their humanity in it. That in itself is a very frightening thing, to be faced with an entirely unmade landscape when the very notion we have of landscape is of something made.

What the settlers in this book can't see is that the continent had already been completely humanised by the people who lived there. The indigenous peoples had created a culture which read that landscape and filled it with meanings, but we couldn't see the meanings so what we saw was the landscape that was completely meaningless and we saw people living there who were incapable of placing meaning on the landscape. We have changed our idea of that now, we understand that Australia already had a culture, it didn't need us to come along to bring human culture, it already had one, but it was one we couldn't recognise.

In *Remembering Babylon* I wanted to face the conflict between the white settlers and the black communities from the perspective of somebody who has gone into that black world, who has entered that landscape, has been reborn into that landscape and reshaped by it. My story begins with the return of this person to the white community and their perception that he has been changed in some kind of way. He represents a kind of pioneer spirit of what that landscape and that continent might do to you if you really and completely committed yourself to it. So he is a figure that they know as white but they can't smell him as white and they can't even feel him as white, and that element of undecidability throws up to them the dubious quality of their own whiteness. When it is said in the book, 'what if you can lose it', what is meant is not losing the language, for what he seems to have lost is his Europeanness, his whiteness. This is what they are afraid of.

This is the challenge of Australia, for if you stay there long enough your very nature as a migrant, your very consciousness, might in the end be changed. Australians can't believe that the European notions of culture are either essential or universal because they have to live side by side with people who do it in a completely different way. And you know, once you've admitted that's a human way and not a primitive way, then you have to admit the way you do things is one way but not the only way. That qualifies, the whole-heartedness with which we can ever be doing, acting, as Western people. And you know, we've been changed by that.

NP Having accepted, in principle at least, that the continent wasn't simply a tabula rasa that simply awaited for the Europeans to inscribe meaning on to it, the task that lies before us is to shift from a recognition to an engagement with the prior forms of meaning and understanding. Your novel illustrates this challenge as it evokes the potential for a dynamic, or as you put it an 'electric' interconnection between land, myth and survival. Gemmie is a witness to this potential, the others hover in ambivalence.

DM If you don't see the world you're moving through as being full of meaning, then you make no connection with that land. Yet, if you are moving through a place that is absolutely alive with meaning, and that meaning may begin with your knowledge of its plants and animals which includes a sacred sense of what those things mean in terms larger than just nature, then at every point your body and your consciousness are in friction with it and that's what that creates the kind of light that Gemmie feels around himself. Whereas the other whites are, like the clergyman Mr Frazer going through it blind. When Mr Frazer and Gemmie go out botanising, Gemmie deliberately illuminates some parts of that landscape and out of a kind of a religious sense of what is proper keeps other parts of it dark. When Gemmie moves through the landscape, something happens; Mr Frazer moves through it and nothing happens. There is no interconnection yet, but there may be, and gradually what that man is doing is building up some kind of knowledge that will make those interconnections possible.

NP The botanising scenes can be contrasted with another scene where the relationship to place is saturated with meaning. On one occasion the dread of the infinite void is confronted within the closed space of a room. Here the opposition between nature and culture, or the foreign and the familiar, is marked in terms of the difference between shelter and home.

DM This book is not about a purely Australian experience. It is about an experience of landscape or a relationship to the world that is clearer in a place like Australia, or in these people's situations, because all the other kinds of explanations and comforts are taken away from them. This absence makes them ask the question, what is man's place in the world? Whereas, if you live in a little village in England or Ireland or Scotland, where you know the name of every field, where every part of the landscape has events and a story related to it, where you know every steeple on the horizon, where the churchyard has all your forebears in it going back a thousand years, then you can comfortingly tell yourself that you absolutely belong in that landscape and there is no problem, there is no metaphysical problem. Take the same people out and put them somewhere where all of those things are gone, and then, yes, they are in a kind of void. This opens up the question of what it is we need as humans to place ourselves in the world and how difficult it is to achieve that.

These people really are real pioneers, not just of another country, but pioneers of the human state. These people are not adventurers; they have gone there because they were poor and uneducated — because they had no power at home. But they are the people who have to go out and confront that metaphysical question. I am interested in their struggle.

NP In relationship to the construction of in-between spaces the role played by Mrs Hutchinson is particularly fascinating. She is a woman who has considerable cultural and economic capital and yet she shows little regard for the conventions that would be associated with her position. She somehow captures another sort of ambivalence, another sort of outsiderness, not in the sense that she's been rejected or that she is rejecting anyone, for somehow she has bypassed the norms of sociability and thereby lives outside the immediate boundary of the community. It is also worth noting that, when the community felt most threatened by Gemmie, it is the women who decided to send him to her house, as if it were safe-house for all.

DM Well I see her as a person who has the capacity for making a kind of social place that all sorts of people who can't speak elsewhere in the novel, or make contact elsewhere in the novel can come to. Her house becomes a kind of meeting place. And the people who go there see things about other people that they wouldn't see elsewhere and see things about themselves that they wouldn't see elsewhere. So I wanted that as a sort of an alternative kind of social world to the community and she does that it seems to me in a very easy kind of way by not imposing it on anybody at all, but just it being there. She creates an atmosphere of acceptance, and that is a sort of magic quality.

NP Is the novel's perspectival structure particularly conducive to the representation of experiences which are riven with ambivalence and an understanding of place which is surrounded by foreignness?

DM If you have a little society as this is, it's a little settlement of 15 families — all in the same place, all facing the same dangers, trying to make the land produce food — then they are drawn together into something that looks like a community. But all communities are extremely fragile. I wanted to introduce into such a community a kind of catalyst.

Gemmie is this catalyst because they see him as a reflection of what they fear. They are afraid for example, that he might be in contact with the blacks, and that he may be a kind of spy, an infiltrator that they've allowed into the community. Other people don't fear that, but they find him a very disturbing presence anyway because of what he tells them about the shakiness of their own securities, their very small power, which resides in their whiteness and their Europeanness. Then there are other people like the young school master who find him repulsive at first and then begin to admire his capacity to endure. The clergyman who knows that Gemmie, simply because he has lived with the aborigines for a long time has acquired this extraordinary knowledge of the land, and therefore sees him as somebody who has made the crossing to a completely different culture, and in that sense he has done something that it might take the rest of them generations to do. But there are other people there, like the children, who see him as a messenger of something else. They still believe that the world is about to reveal something miraculous to them although they don't know what that might be. It takes these two characters, Lachlan and Janet, who we follow throughout the whole of their lives, to find out what that is.

So here you have a little society in which people are different, stand in different positions in the world and see things differently. I deliberately didn't want a single point of view, because that is the opposite of what the truth of this situation

would be. You could only get to the truth of the situation by seeing it from a lot of different and contradictory points of view
that are in some ways in conflict.

NP Gemmy's status does oscillate between the internal stranger
and the external enemy. In one passage the narrator lucidly identifies the difficulty that one of the characters is experiencing:
'Gemmie, just by being there, opened a gate on to things, things
Barney couldn't specify'. This shifting perception of his true
identity is particularly evident in his relationship with Lachlan.
In what ways does this extend a persistent theme in your writing: the bonding between male characters?

DM I would have thought that was not quite true here. Gemmie
is very alert to the fact that because Lachlan is a male he sees
the world of action as his sphere. He makes use of Gemmie
when it suits him, and then drops Gemmie when it appears to
be of any kind of danger to him. Gemmie sees very clearly that
Lachlan is not to be trusted. Gemmie also notices that Lachlan
is always watching to see what the other people in the settlement
think about him. Lachlan has a very weak sense of himself and
turns to virtues that are already reinforced by that community.
While Lachlan always needs a witness to his own being, Janet
needs no witness to her being. Janet is the person with which
Gemmy shares an immediate relationship the person who sees
him as he really is. Janet has the ability of looking right into him,
and Gemmy recognises that she shares the faculty that his world
is based on.

NP By the end of the novel, have not Lachlan and Janet found a
similar reconciliation with Gemmy?

DM What Lachlan is trying to reconcile is some kind of guilt in
which he feels he has betrayed Gemmy and that is perfectly true.
Janet has never betrayed Gemmy. At the very end of the novel,
she offers a word that Lachlan could never say to himself, for
when she says to him 'we loved Gemmy' he is able to feel that
weight of guilt fall away. 'Love' is a word that belongs to her
vocabulary and not to his. I leave this word till the end of the
novel because I mean it to come as a kind of shock.

'Love' is a word I hardly ever use because it covers too many
kinds of feelings, and I'm interested in charting those feelings
which are very complex. 'Love' is not a very good word to
describe all the kinds of affection that exists between people. It

does turn up again and it's meant to be the shocking four letter word in the letter that Johnno sent to Dante after his death. People often focus on the word 'fuck', but the word love is a much more shocking word. It is a word that calls into question what kind of words we have for those feelings. This brings us to the broader question of language.

NP Yes, the question of language is often represented in your work through the boundary situation. For the boundary both separates and unites distinct fields. In this case, the frontier settlement is a place where the act of translation is most acute. One of the interesting inversions that happened in the novel is the fact that those whom we traditionally associate with the power of language aren't necessarily the ones who actually have it. Namely, the clergyman and the teacher, are in a position where their guardianship of knowledge is limited, they are seen, at best as the scribes to Gemmy's knowledge. The two real determining moments in the novel are, the first encounter between Gemmy and Lachlan, and the other one is when the rousteabout Andy sees a group of aborigines approaching and talking to Gemmy. Now these two moments are framed as encounters with a potential threat. Lachlan and Andy both seize upon the community's fear of the other and present themselves as witnesses and interpreters of the unknown. In this situation, where authority cannot be grounded on historical experience, the power of language is given to those who can either translate the signs of the unknown, or construct narratives to explain the possibility of danger.

DM The two situations you point to are quite interesting ones because the stories reveal more about the reporter's concern for power than the truth they purport to tell. The stories they have to tell are false stories.

One of the things I am interested in is the different forms of language. It's not just the forms of actual speech; dialect language, the five or seven aboriginal languages that Gemmy speaks which we never hear. But there is another kind of language which is the one I'm more interested in, and that is, the language of gesture or the language of silence that doesn't require words. Often in my books, and I suppose especially in this one, when most is happening nothing is actually been said, or not in words anyway. There are the moments in this novel in which characters break through to some kind of understanding. As a writer I have to find words to articulate this kind of sense, this reaching for understanding which doesn't come mediated through language except through the language that the writer finds for them. For example, there is the father of the children who thinks of himself as a very conventional person and whose safety, as far as he is concerned, is the fact that he is a conventional person. One of the things that happens to him progressively through the novel is that because he finds himself, at first unwillingly, as the protector of Gemmy he finds that some of the strangeness that people see in Gemmy has rubbed off on him. He doesn't like the idea that these people who have always been his mates now see him as odd in some kind of way. But at the moment when he is finally forced to recognise that oddness, what he discovers is a capacity in himself to be alone, to actually see things and open himself up to things, including landscape, in a way that he could never have opened himself up to while he was hiding in the world of the sociable.

NP The shift in the father's character from a stoic member to a critical observer has a price, he can no longer trust his own community; his relations with others are poisoned with suspicion and an increasing awareness of hypocrisy. Given the violent history of ethnocide and dispossession of the Aborigines, how do you imagine a dialogue that will reconcile the past? The Aboriginal perspective of this encounter is relatively unrepresented. For instance, you privilege Gemmy's re-entry into the English speaking world rather than his introduction into the Aboriginal world. Is there any way that you could strike a balance between these worlds?

DM I did not want to deal directly in the novel with the predicament of indigenous people, partly because I don't have the knowledge to do that, and I don't think anyone has the knowledge to do that, except those people themselves who perhaps don't have the voice or the words to do it. We can learn a certain amount from anthropology and from other things, but that still doesn't seem to be the authentic thing. I wanted to tell the story of an in-between character who would have been in contact with that culture and would be able to stand for that culture but wouldn't be speaking directly for it. His silence in the novel is their silence. He stands as an emblematic figure.

NP Are you suggesting that in the absence of satisfactory lines of communication we have to rethink the whole basis of communication?

DM Yes, for example *Harland's Half Acre* is a book about how you actually possess things, and how you possess that land. In the end, the artist in this novel realises that he can possess the land not just by becoming it, but by taking it all into his imagination, by making it continuous with his consciousness. But in some ways, that is the way in which aborigines possess that land. I mean, they don't own anything in particular, what they do is understand it. The key word in that novel is the word 'possession'.

NP In some of the semi-autobiographical essays in your book *12 Edmunston Street* you have also tackled the relationship between language and dispossession, and there is also the short story in your collection Antipodes which is called 'The Only Speaker of His Tongue', which traces the enormity of the destruction of Aboriginal culture through the reflection of one man who has been left alone, mute in a language which no one speaks. There is a very moving passage in this story which highlights the centrality of language in connecting everything, from the visceral to the cosmological:

> When I think of my tongue being no longer alive in the mouths of
> men a chill goes over me that is deeper than my own death, since
> it is the gathered death of all my kind ... O the holy dread of it!
> Of having under your tongue the first and last words of all those
> generations down there in your blood, down there in the earth,
> for whom these syllables were the magic once for calling the
> whole of creation to come striding, swaying, singing towards
> them.

DM What is lost is not just the fact that he is mute; what is also lost is the whole world as it existed in that language. The world exists in all the names in all the languages that we give it. That particular world in that language with those particular names is in his head and nowhere else, and when he's gone it will disappear for ever. We know the world by naming it. We know the world through the language we name it. The aborigines, who spoke over 300 different sets of language, gave different names for things and lay them down over the same pieces of landscape.

Each of those languages represent a different world. Language is the shape of the world as we know it.

In this book Gemmie who as a streetchild in London, had the vocabulary in English that he needed for dealing with the daily world as he knows it. It was a limited vocabulary. Yet when the objects of that world disappear the words for them disappear, and when the words and the objects disappear he has no longer any memory. His whole experiences disappear with the loss of language. When he comes back into an English speaking world, the language begins to come back, the objects of the world he has lost and the emotions and the actions that were associated with those objects come back painfully with the words. His retrieval of his past, has to do with his retrieval, by piecemeal, of the language. But, you know, this is a person who now has in his head six or seven aboriginal languages so that he knows when he sees a plant or something like that, that this exists in seven different worlds in his head, and he has to know, he has to ask himself which of those worlds he's going to let Mr Frazer glimpse by giving him the name of the plant.

NP If I could extrapolate a little bit from the scene that you have just described and if we could take Fellini's rather careless statement on the ambiguous relationship between creativity and experience, which said: 'everything and nothing that I do is autobiographical', could we draw any affinities between the multiple modes of naming and the forgetting that occur within this novel and your own history where there has also been a break with the Arabic past of your forebears?

DM Well there might be affinities, but I don't feel them strongly. I grew up in a household where nothing but English was spoken, and there was no reason why any other language should be spoken because my father spoke English and as far as I understand, no other language. Since he was the eldest son and since his mother spoke very little English, I assume he understood Arabic, but I never heard him speak a word of it or give any indication that he understood it. That was part of the painful process of turning himself into the complete Australian, so that I didn't have to do it. He did everything that an Australian should do; he was a super-Australian.

I don't feel very strongly the break of language except that I would have noticed perhaps as a small child something that you might not otherwise notice. My grandmother used different words for some common objects than I did which at least introduced me to the fact that the word I had for the object and the object itself were not absolutely related. That I suppose is a big experience.

WORKS CITED
DAVID MALOUF

An Imaginary Life, Chatto & Windus, London, 1978.
Antipodes, Penguin, Harmondsworth, 1986.
Harland's Half Acre, Chatto & Windus, London, 1984.
Johnno: A Novel, Univ. of Queensland Press, St. Lucia, 1975.
Remembering Babylon, Vintage, London, 1993.
12 Edmundstone Street, Chatto & Windus, London, 1985.

6.
ABORIGINALITY AND ITS AUDIENCE

ENTERING THE FRAME

Contemporary Aboriginal art has the paradoxical fate of bearing the scars of colonisation and genocide as it enters the international art market. Throughout the eighties acrylic paintings from the Western Desert gained international attention. Recognition and success abroad provided a plank for collectors in the state museums and private galleries at home. The commercialisation and institutionalisation of Aboriginal art often rested uncomfortably between conventional marketing opportunism and the anthropologist's salvage paradigm. The popular attraction to, for instance, the paintings from Papunya was partly generated by the suggestion that the configurations of dots were formally referencing minimalism. The representations of landscape and the portrayal of communities were similarly caught on the cleft stick of sacred nobility and squalid victimhood. However, beyond these trappings we are now witness to the emergence of a new historical perspective and aesthetic practices which involve a rethinking of the relationships between tradition, identity and belonging. What I would like to consider in this essay is how are such artworks received and represented within the international framework of modern art.

The institutions of art have recently accepted terms like hybridity and marginality with as much zeal as they previously reserved for the notions of purism and abstraction. At times there seems to be an 'about-face' against the canon which privileged the white male formalist avant garde, and a rhetorical embrace of difference. Yet in what sense are such gestures at change possible within the terms of the institution of art?[1] Is not the allegiance between the institution of art and eurocentric absolutism more like a founding principle than a tactical mistake that can be corrected with belated selections of its 'other'? What has been most palpably exposed by this turn to the 'other' are the very tensions between the context of production and the criteria for judgment.

The recent controversy over the rejection of the work by Leah King-Smith from the Cologne art fair only gives more reason to suspect that the incorporation of non-Western artists into main-stream institutions is mostly a form of crisis management. King-Smith's galleries was informed by the Cologne art committee that her cibachrome photographs were not considered as 'authentic Aboriginal art ... but contemporary art ... following in this tradition.' She was also reminded that 'folk art was not permitted at Art Cologne'. These contradictory remarks did not clarify why King-Smith's work was rejected. Was it because that she was 'Aboriginal' that she was only meant to make 'folk art'? Therefore when her work engaged with the media and forms of contemporary art she could only be judged as a fake. After an outcry in the Australian and German art world this judgment was reversed. Once the question of 'fairness' of representation was resolved it seems that the debate over this racist 'slip' did not extend to a consideration over the validity of the very criteria for authenticity and contemporaneity implied by this judgment.

TAKING THE GAP

One example of this paradigmatic shift in interpretation and evaluation between art and artefacts is to be noted in the exhibition called *ARATJARA*.[2] Demonstration of the political integrity and cultural survival of the Aboriginal peoples and the Torres Strait Islanders was high on the agenda of the curators of this exhibition. However the curators also wanted to extend the current debate on 'What are the boundaries of modern art?'. The collapse in the rigid equation that predominantly linked modernism with formalism, and a more critical understanding of the relationship between the practices of everyday life and aesthetics clearly facilitated the undoing of the colonial distinction between artefact and art. The curators of _ARATJARA_ declared all the masks, sculptures, bark and rock paintings as contemporary artworks. This is, of course, a welcome inversion of the nineteenth century perception that they 'are examples of the art of a race in a stage of intellectual infancy, and which race will certainly die before attaining manhood'.[3]

Similarly, other myths about culture and tradition need to be challenged: urbanisation can no longer be automatically interpreted as synonymous with acculturation. Being an urban Aboriginal is not a contradiction in terms. The authentic pulse of Aboriginal culture is not automatically stunted by the 'contact' with city life. What is most apparent from the contemporary urban-based artists like Gordon Bennett and Judy Watson is that the dynamism of identity was neither diluted as it was mixed, nor suspended as it was urbanised. Hybridity, as a concept for the process of cultural exchange has lost its earlier stigma, it is no longer an indicator of faked personas, declining values, or corrupted culture. Hybridity has also been the perspective with which the violent relations between cultures has been highlighted. Bennett's painting _The Nine Ricochets (Fall Down Black Fella, Jump Up White Fella)_, 1990, displays an array of complex strategies. Bennett takes the key moment in Australian history: dispossession, and cross-cuts it with reference to the work from a contemporary Australian artist, Imants Tillers. The most prominent layer of his painting is the illusory effect of geometry in bold blood red, a subtle but obtrusive gesture at deconstructing the grid of appropriation in the dominant culture. As George Petelin wryly observed, the articulation of the 'white Aborigine' issue by Imants Tiller found two powerful visual responses by Gordon Bennett and Richard Bell.[4]

CURATING AS AN INTERVENTION

In Europe there is a relative vacuum in the knowledge of Aboriginal art, yet throughout the 1980s the dominant art institutions were constantly facing the challenge of art from the margin. The ascendance of minority discourse in European and Australian cultural debates is linked to two factors. First, there have been the efforts made by artists, confronting the institutions of art with the politics of 'race' and migration. Aboriginal artists, for instance, have stressed that it was the externality of their activism which pushed against the door of the institution, rather than the internal benevolence of the gatekeepers, which was the initiating force for the inclusion of Aboriginal art into the context of museum.[5] Second, the crisis in narrating modernism has opened a space for the coding of other aesthetic representations within modernity. The intellectual debates on the relationship between primitivism in early modernism, coupled with the increasing attention to the question of authenticity in a postmodern context, have both provided a new basis for considering the value of Aboriginal art. What has emerged is a new critical discourse which has redefined the politics of representation, questioning the status of originality and appropriation, thereby revealing the dynamic instability in the distinction between high and low art. The combined energy of political and intellectual transformation has helped to remove some of the prejudices that would previously exclude Aboriginal art from the contemporary frame.

Magiciens de la Terre, Paris, 1989 like its predecessor '*Primitivism' in Twentieth Century Art*, New York, 1984, provided a peculiar starting-point for a number of other mega-exhibitions. Curators, while cautiously defending themselves against the accusation of selective incorporation and decontextualisation, were still captivated by the 'treacherously' alluring symmetry of identity and alterity; centre and margin. In the context of 'fortress Europe' and against the ghoulish backdrop of 'ethnic cleansing', almost every major art gallery has presented a large scale exhibition which has foregrounded the relationship between aesthetic practices and cultural difference for example, *Il Sud Del Mondo*, Marsala, 1991; *Documenta, Kassel*, 1992; *America, The Bride of the Sun: Latin-America, 500 Years of Cultural Exchange*, Antwerp, 1992; *Metamorphosis of the Modern: The Greek Experience*, Athens, 1992; *The Boundary Rider: 9th Biennale*, Sydney, 1992; Biennale, Venice, 1993; The Whitney Biennale, New York, 1993.

Any current exhibition which addresses the issues of Aboriginality will inevitably be seen as figuring within the broader debates on minority discourse and be aligned with the issues surrounding postcolonialism, indigenity and 'New Internationalism'.

These debates can no longer be dismissed as just sociological, they are also part of any understanding of the domain of aesthetics. To address the prior emphasis on the formal qualities of art blurred or deferred any investigation into the relationship between the history and culture within which art was produced. Any consideration of the context of contemporary Aboriginal art will have to acknowledge the history of cultural violation. Therefore the aesthetics of Aboriginality cannot be formally divorced from the politics of dispossession. The history of violation and displacement within modern culture, which has been stressed by postcolonial theory and minority discourse, is now part of the context in which contemporary art is situated. Within these debates there is a general acknowledgment of the limitations of Eurocentrism as well as a rhetorical rejection of the aggressivity in nationalism. This new consensus is both laudable and long overdue, but in what sense does this rejection signal a shift in the sensibility and practice of the art world? For if all the Biennale's of the West have accepted that the question: 'Who is the other?', can be made compatible with the question, 'What are the boundaries of modernism?', we then need to also ask, 'Who has moved out?', and 'What has changed?' What has been gained is the self-consciousness of the ideological nature of museological practice and curatorial politics. The link between the subject position and specific knowledge of the curator has become the focus of much scrutiny. What has yet to be done is a rethinking of structural questions that affect the mode of participation and the form of interpretation that is available in such a context.

Who speaks and for whom? — learning to speak in context was a question which was very high on the agenda of cultural politics in the eighties. This demanded greater specificity in the claims to represent culture, tradition and language. The problematic of representation, however, took a much broader scope, including both the formation and the articulation of knowledge/power. The form of the space was as politically charged as the content. This responsibility did not rest solely with the artist. The curator was by definition also involved in the dissemination of cultural meaning. Thus the process of collecting, classifying and staging work was never a neutral or detached methodology, but one which critically enforced particular constructions of knowledge. It is now clear that the burden of representation is partly placed on the curator's shoulders.

The most innovative strategies for the representation of Aboriginal art have been presented by the artists themselves. The work by a number of artists/critics/curators associated with Boomalli Aboriginal Artists Co-operative has demonstrated both the potentiality for a new cultural position and the articulation of a critical agenda within the art world. This vanguard role by Aboriginal artists in the representation of their own work questions the prior fear that the success of Aboriginal art within the market would simply perpetuate another form of neo-colonialism.[6]

JOINING THE BORDERS

The Western binarism between self and other helps concentrate the issue. The very distinctions between the traditional and the contemporary, the West and the Non-West which had sustained such fundamental polarities of exclusion and justified the sense of distanciation towards Aboriginality are now the subject of critique. Such categories tended to confine the image of Aboriginality as suspended in a timeless past and isolated from the flow of historical development. The philosophical dramas of a dynamic or static past are, as Brook Andrews is so palpably aware, staged on the decorative objects in the kitchens and living rooms of our dominant culture. The proverbial tea towels depicting scenes of an unspoilt and misnamed Uluru (often called Ayers Rock) and souvenir boomerangs, with instructive drawings of 'native' men leaning on their contemplative spears, are the banal 'culprits' of this fake nationalism: 'the kitsch images degraded Aboriginal culture and held it fast in a stagnant pre-white invasion representation. ... (these) images speak for the invaders and colonisers, not for Aboriginal people.'[7] It is from and against such sources that another representation of Aboriginality commences. Consider also this statement by Rea which opens the 'un'settling space between the visible and the invisible in the narratives of belonging.

> Once I asked a teacher, 'Who is that black man in the background of those Australian paintings?'
> He told me that he was a native, and that the natives used to live in Australia.
> I then asked my mother who he was and she said that 'he is one of your ancestors'.[8]

The current strategy of artists dealing with the representation of non-Western people is always at least twofold. First, there is the need to contest the iconography of a negative past, especially when this takes the idealised form of exotica or injury. Second, there is the need to devise new perspectives and practices for drawing out the links between the subject and the object in art. Jorma Puranen's installation in *Disrupted Borders* is one of the most evocative presentations of this displacement-belonging issue.[9] It is, on one level, about the complicity in the positivistic ambitions of early ethnographic and photographic practices. While visiting the vaults of the *Musee de l'Homme* in Paris, Puranen discovered a series of images of the Sami people. He was shocked to discover that some of their descendants were in fact his friends. He rephotographed these images printed them on transparencies and returned them to their place of origin. The relocation of these images — out of sterile boxes and into an open space — heightened the fragile austerity of the world as well as the curious stolidity in the people's facial expressions. The printing on to transparencies allowed not only image and landscape to overlap but provided another way of seeing this relationship. Puranen made a sort of 'homecoming' for these images.

There are certain parallels that can be drawn between Puranen's installation and the photographic practices that have been developed by a number of artists associated with the Aboriginal collective Boomalli. For these artists the determination of the subject matter, mode of representation and the subject position of the artist were issues that were charged with values which exceeded conventional aesthetic conventions. Brenda Croft's and Michael Riley's photographic portraits, for instance, were developed in response to the ethnographic and colonialist categories for representing Aboriginal people. The dominant function of photography of Aboriginal people was to document either their exoticism or their wretchedness. Such work gave little regard for the context or the subjectivity of the people being photographed. They were images which maintained patronising distance between the audience and the subject. Both Croft and Riley have countered this tendency by trying to express the trusting relationship that can be formed, foregrounding the interactive process between the photographer and those being photographed. Hence the people in their portraits are not only people they know, but these 'subjects' also participate in the determination of the setting and the construction of the frame for the image.

Embracing this sensitivity towards the person in the photograph and with an awareness of the multiple readings that photography engendered, Destiny Deacon resorts to ironising the symbolic codes of portraiture and calling herself a 'shy photographer'. The significance of these strategies is not only that the 'subject' feels 'at home' and that the resulting image will provide a heightened sense of recognition, but that they also force us to rethink our method-ological presuppositions. There is a perspectival shift from critical distance to critical intimacy, helping us to move out of the stulti-fying polarities of either naive identification on the one hand, or clinical detachment on the other. The role and position of the pho-tographer also shifts. The photographer is no longer the conventional outsider figure who simply captures the image and conveys it to an anonymous audience. Instead there is the emer-gence of what Scott McQuire astutely describes as 'collaborative documentary' whereby the relationship between the context of the subject and the critical response of the audience is mediated via more specific circuits of knowledge.[10] This is the beginning of a far more sympathetic interaction between the medium of art and the required knowledge of a specific culture. When there is an imbal-ance in this relationship it should not surprise us that the interpretations will also be limited.

At the beginning of this century European artists stretched the boundaries of modernism as they incorporated and experimented with non-European art forms. As the century comes to a close we observe a different level of fascination. The focus has moved from the artefact to the art practice; from the static object to the mar-ginalised strategies of the colonised or the diasporised. There is now a heightened consciousness of borders and limits. Art pro-duction seems more preoccupied with the paradoxes of content; a renegotiation of the local and the global, rather than the determi-nation of the 'progressive' path towards the universal.

NAMING THE SILENCE

The unsuitability of the existing terms for referencing the Aboriginal and Torres Strait Islander art practices are evidenced in a discussion between curator and critic on the confusion surrounding the labels given to Aboriginal art. After rejecting the convenience of locational terms like 'traditional' and 'urban', Hetti Perkins and Victoria Lynn consider the heading of 'contemporary'. They remind us that this term refers to an art practice which breaks with the past.[11] This would also suggest disqualification since the imbrication between past and present in aboriginalities leads toward a sensibility which paradoxically combines tradition with contemporaneity. As Aboriginal art consistently cross-cuts between the past and present, it activates the political agenda of memory within cultural survival. The significant feature of this claim to contemporaneity is thus not grounded on a break with the past, but in an ambivalent conceptualisation that *articulates together* both continuity and change. This perspective is not a unique result of the violent dispossession in Australia. Parallels can be found in the work of numerous artists whose contemporary identity is represented as also including the historical scars of colonialism. In a work like *Caliban*, 1992, Jimmie Durham chases the fictions and facts of identity in a territory drenched in shame and violence. Colonisation is part of the pulse of this work. It is not referenced as a past event, but as an on-going process. Jimmie Durham's installations are both bittersweet comments on dispossessed survival, and an 'ethnography' of the extinction of at least one sort of Empire.

For about a decade the museums tried to brush these questions aside by pushing them into the 'educational' category of the social history of art. This containment strategy failed to protect the claim that art was by definition timeless and above the history of the social, that is, transcendent. The historicity of artistic production can no longer be justifiably ignored, but as Janet Woolf has argued we must not assume that this can explain the totality of its aesthetic value.[12] The admission of Aboriginal art into the museum would inevitably challenge the colonial presupposition of collecting art 'treasure' and thereby invite a rethinking of the validity of the institution's organisational categories. The definition and location of projects and appointments concerning Aboriginal art invariably cut across the neat distinctions that constituted the habitual frameworks of the institution. Being in-between in the bureaucratic order is equated with mess and confusion. However, as Hetti Perkins observed it was this ambiguity which also emancipatory, for it suggested a possibility in breaking with fixed patterns and roles.[13] The crucial task now is to devise modes of representation that are locally based and which address the specific history of the sense of place from which the art emerges and to which the artist is related.

Is it possible that the complexities of non-Western art practices can be inserted under the broader heading of the modernist tensions? At the centre of the modernist dilemma is the status of individualism. This particular conception of individualism does not embrace all forms of experience, for as noted by Eric Michaels:

> everyone in traditional society is effectively entitled to paint certain designs, not from particular notions of skill or talent (i.e. personal predispositions) but as a result of certain negotiated positions within systems of inherited rights and obligations .... By necessity, the authority of this system would be compromised by an ideology of invention which signalled out individual producers.[14]

For many Aboriginal artists the issue of their status as either individual creator or as representative of a social body is an unsettling problem. This questioning could suggest new levels of interaction between the artist and their context rather than inevitably signal corruption and decline. The radical task is to name this signalling without presuming an automatic transference of the terms of identity to the dominant ideology. Fred Myers is right to stress that the disjunction that circulates within interpretative activities is more complex than commodification and appropriation. He illustrates the enigmas of this transitional state through the words of Myer Rubinstein:

> But for now, as our two worlds meet upon the site of these paintings, we and the Aborigines are in similar positions: neither knowing quite what to think. For both societies the appearance of these paintings is relatively recent and their nature and role is still being discovered. They are in limbo between two homes, sharing their functions and sense of belonging with both, but not fully explicable in either's language. They are like those ancestral beings whose journeys they depict, traversing a featureless region and giving it form. In the words of an Aboriginal man trying to explain Dreamings to an anthropologist, 'You listen! Something is there: we do not know what: something.[15]

This translational task is not fulfilled by the excavation of parallel conventions and standards between the two cultures.[16] The interfaces between such different cultures beg for new metaphors. Merv Bishop's delicate self-portrait, *Is There an Aboriginal Photography?*, 1989, shows himself holding a miniature camera in front of his right eye. It questions the authority of both subjects; who are 'we' who are identified under this name 'Aboriginal'? Can 'photography' hold up the fantasy of the objective and neutral representation? Visual reflexivity over the gaps in identity and ironic displays of muteness are ways in which the language of colonialism still resonates, against itself.[17]

REFERENCE NOTES

Throughout this essay the notion of Aboriginality is used to address the diverse indigenous communities in Australia. The very concept of Aborigine is a Western construct and is part of the contested terrain in the politics of representation. Aboriginality is conventionally defined in opposition to the dominant concepts of Western, Modern, European. Aboriginality not only invokes an artificial homogeneity, but also conforms to a racialised binarism.Use of the term 'Aboriginality' overlooks significant differences between regions. More recently self-defined names for such groups, like Koori and Murri, has entered the popular discourse. I use the term Aboriginality only as a contradictory marker in the politics for collective struggle and specific recognition within both a local and global framework.

1. T. McEvilley, *Art & Discontent: Theory at the Millennium*, McPherson & Company, New York, 1991.
2. *ARATJARA*, curated by Bernhard Luthi, Hayward Gallery, London, October 1993; *ARATJARA: Art of the First Australians*, ed. Bernhard Luthi, Kunstammlung, Nordhein-Westfalen, Dusseldorf, 1993. For further discussion on the strategy to debunk the myth of timelessness in Aboriginal art and the problematics of spatially linking and overcoming the distinction between 'traditional rural' work with 'modern urban' work see my review of *ARATJARA*, 'Framing the Message', *Third Text*, No.24, Autumn 1993. For a discussion of the *Dreamings* exhibition in New York see Fred Myers, 'Representing Culture: The Production of Discourse(s) for Aboriginal Acrylic Paintings', *Cultural Anthropology*, Vol.6, No.1, 1991; Jon Stratton, 'Landscapes: Central and Western Desert Paintings and the Discourses of Art', *Theory, Culture & Society*, Vol.11, No.1, 1994.
3. Quoted in the catalogue, *ARATJARA* op.cit., p.114.
4. George Petelin, 'Richard Bell', *Perspecta*, Art Gallery of New South Wales, 1993, p.8.
5. Ann Stephen, Hetti Perkins and Avenel Mitchell, 'Repatriation, Race, Representation', *Photofile*, No.40, November 1993, pp.12–18. In Nikos Papastergiadis, *The Complicities of Culture*, Cornerhouse, Manchester, 1994, I develop a similar argument to outline the emergence of black arts in Britain.
6. Bob Lingard and Fazal Rizvi, '(Re)membering, (Dis)membering

"Aboriginality" and the Art of Gordon Bennett', *Third Text*, No.26, Spring 94. This essay contains a powerful critique of the argument that the success of Aboriginal art will be monopolised by white art administrators and dealers while Aboriginal culture continues to suffer ethnocide.

7. See the artist's statement in the catalogue *True Colours: Aboriginal and Torres Strait Islander Artists Raise the Flag*, Bluecoat Gallery, Liverpool, 1994.

8. Rea, text from the exhibition 'Ripped into Pieces', *Abstracts*, f.stop media station, Bath, 1996.

9. *Disrupted Borders: An Intervention in the Definitions of Boundaries*, ed. Sunil Gupta, Rivers Oram Press, London, 1993. 'Disrupted Borders', curated by Sunil Gupta, Arnolfini Gallery, Bristol, 1993. See also my review article, 'Disputes at the boundaries of "New Internationalism"', *Third Text*, No.25, Winter 1994.

10. Scott McQuire, 'Signs of Ambivalence', *Photofile*, No.43, p.12, 1995.

11. Hetti Perkins & Victoria Lynn, 'Black Artists, Cultural Activists', *Perspecta*, Art Gallery of New South Wales, 1993, p.xi.

12. Janet Woolf, *The Sociology of Art*, Macmillan, London, 1993.

13. Hetti Perkins et.al., op.cit., p.17.

14. Eric Michaels, 'Bad Aboriginal Art', *Art & Text*, No.28, March-May 1988, p.61.

15. F. Myers, op.cit., p.30.

16. On the uses of televisual technologies by indigenous peoples and the transnational connections that they have developed in global mediascapes see, Faye Ginsburg, 'Indigenous Media: Faustian Contract or Global Village?', *Cultural Anthropology*, Vol.6, No.1, 1991 ; 'Aboriginal Media and the Australian Imaginary', *Public Culture*, No.5, 1993.

17. My thanks to Scott McQuire for pointing out the work of Merv Bishop. See *In Dreams: Thirty Years of Photography 1960-1990*, ed. T. Moffatt, Australian Centre of Photography, Sydney 1991 and Jimmie Durham, *The East London Coelacanth*, ICA/Bookworks, London, 1993.

7.
THE LIMITS OF THE DIASPORA
A CONVERSATION WITH ASHIS NANDY

Ashis Nandy lives in New Delhi where he is research fellow at the Centre for the Study of Developing Societies. He was trained in psychology and, from the outset, his writing explored the relationship between science and culture, creativity and resistance. His most influential work has focused on the forms of rationality which sustained colonialism and the cultural practices which ultimately undermined this regime. The legacies of colonialism were also the subject of his most recent studies on the cultural politics of cricket and Indian film.

Nandy's groundbreaking book, *The Intimate Enemy*, offered a fresh perspective on the cultural frameworks and psycho-social dynamics that were mobilised under colonialism and which he argues are the most brutal expressions of the central tendencies in modernity. Following on from Franz Fanon, Nandy has shown that the ruthlessness of colonialism is not confined to physical oppression by military supremacy, but also found in the systematic dismantling of traditional social structures and the banishment of indigenous cultural systems to the historical dustbin. Colonialism was not just a coercive external force, but also the application of values and priorities which altered the internal practices. It reshaped the imaginings and split the developmental mechanisms of the colonised peoples. Like Edward Said, Nandy looks at the victories of colonialism not only in its overt display of might but also in the way the victors articulated their right to conquer.

It is the modern rationality which privileged new forms of administration and science, and subordinated the emotional and spiritual worlds under a new order of reason and duty that Nandy identifies as the main driving force of colonialism. These radical transformations were the embodiment of the West's theory of progress and superiority. These theories were invariably defined in opposition to the supposedly static, closed and primitive cultures of the non-West. Nandy most powerfully explodes these neat oppositions between self/other, advanced/backward, masculine/ feminine as he demonstrates the complicitous logic by which one knowledge system is pitted against another. In this exchange between what he calls 'players and counter-players' both oppressive and emancipatory practices are born. Thus, for Nandy, there is no essential division between the coloniser and the colonised, he presents us with a more complex and interconnected understanding of how identities are formed in the modern world.

At the time when most Western intellectuals were gripped with outrage over the fatwa that was issued by Khomeini against Salman Rushdie, it seemed appropriate to discuss the status of sacred beliefs in modernity and the relationship between a diasporic community and its country of origin. Rushdie, and his supporters, always maintained that he had the right to interpret the Koran as if it were a text, but his opponents insisted that this form of interpretation is in itself an illegitimate act, for to interpret the Koran as just another text is to relegate it from its sacred context as *the text*. The two positions were seemingly incommensurable — one side claiming defence on the 'free' plateaux of expression, and the other seeking to reinstate the boundaries of cultural difference. Ultimately, the untenability of both positions were exposed by the 'Rushdie Affair'. The grip on modern technology and the mobilisation of the global media system by a so-called fundamentalist spiritual leader, which pointed to a remapping of the boundaries of the Muslim world, was as surprising to some as the notion that cultural hybridity, even in its most aestheticised postmodern forms, carried with it responsibilities as well as pleasures. The convenient oppositions between medieval despots and cosmopolitan authors were found to be entangled within the common space of the modern media system. Nandy's attention to the complicities within colonialism might therefore furnish a useful starting-point for explaining the forces that were at play in these postcolonial transgressions one against Eastern religious dogma and the other against the mobility of Western cultural aesthetics.

Nikos Papastergiadis Ashis, I want to talk to you about the Rushdie affair. However, it is not my concern to discuss Salman Rushdie's predicament, nor respond to *The Satanic Verses*, but rather to consider this affair in terms of its broader consequences, that is, to reflect on the contemporary position of the artist in politics; the relationship between the secular and the sacred in modernity; the distinction between high art and popular culture; the representation of the non-Western cultures as the bearers of fundamentalism and the fetishisation of freedom and tolerance in the West's self-representation. From these perspectives, I want to discuss the 'Rushdie Affair'. Let me begin with a quote from your book *The Intimate Enemy*: 'The West is now everywhere, within the West and outside it; in structures and in minds'. From this perspective whose problem is the Rushdie Affair?

Ashis Nandy Frankly, I do not want to discuss the Rushdie affair. It has already been overemphasised by the global knowledge system, to establish the *a priori* retrogressive nature of all cultures or sub-cultures which do not conform to a given set of categories.

NP What and whose are these categories?

AN They are the categories available within the dominant global culture, which also happens to be the cultural consciousness of the modern West. The Rushdie affair has once again revealed the utter bankruptcy of the global knowledge system, when faced with problems of freedom and dissent. The mainstream scholars have simply failed to make head or tail out of the reaction to Rushdie's book. In their terms, Khomeini's *fatwa* was not only immoral, it was senseless and self-defeating politically.

The frenzied discussion of the *fatwa* in the West can be read as an attempt to make it understandable — by turning it into a marker of a known form of insanity. Few in the modern world were willing to admit that the *fatwa* was an unknown form of communication. After all, if killing Rushdie was the main intent of the Ayatollah, that could have been organised much better if the fatwa was not advertised in the international press and if Scotland Yard had not been alerted beforehand through the *fatwa*.

The moderns totally ignored this issue. They were all too willing to give a clinical diagnosis, without a corresponding critical
social analysis of the political and cultural context within which
such a fatwa could be judged. I disagree with Khomeini's edict,
but I cannot forget the frustration, humiliation, shame, sense of
defeat and incomprehension which triggered the anger of many
ordinary Muslims against Rushdie. In fact, Rushdie himself
understood this anger better than many of his supporters.

No amount of sloganeering on freedom of speech can convince me that this sense of outrage is, as the metropolitan centres
of knowledge would like us to believe, merely a symptom of the
retrogressive and insane responses of a community mired in
primitivism and medievalism. That is why, on our side, sanity
lies in not allowing this issue to be overemphasised.

NP How does this affair reveal the bankruptcy of what you have
called the 'available categories'?

AN Paradoxically, it is revealed through the process of translation
that is brought into play by those using these categories. Once
an event occurs which is outside the conventional frame of reference, it reveals the limits of the frame. We feel we have
understood an event when we establish a correspondence
between the event and our pre-existing general categories. But
in this affair, there are no categories with the help of which the
cosmopolitan world can establish such correspondence. The
only set of molar concepts which the dominant culture has
brought into play is one designed to give the impression that the
affair can be understood as a form of collective insanity. For
example, very few people have talked about the peculiar situation in which Muslims are caught — that they are a defeated
civilisation, trying to reaffirm their sense of human dignity. Even
fewer have mentioned that Muslims have not been unequivocal
about either Rushdie or the Ayatollah. There is also the fact that
the hostility against Rushdie has been deepest in societies in
which Muslims are in a minority. The Muslims who opposed the
fatwa were not all decultured or lapsed Muslims; their opposition to Khomeini was not a step towards their induction into the
modern Western world. On the other hand, those who sup-
ported the Ayatollah were not the ones most deeply rooted in
Islam. The Arab West Asia, for instance, did not spend sleepless
nights over *The Satanic Verses*; none of the more respected

Islamic seats of learning considered the *fatwa* a great innovation in the concept of Islamic justice. Some of them rejected it outright as un-Islamic.

NP Which 'molar concepts' do you have in mind?

AN Concepts such as the Muslims are intrinsically violent. That they were unified in their support for Khomeini. That Islam doesn't care about freedom of speech.

NP Can you say something about the traditions of dissent within Islam?

AN I know very little about the traditions of dissent in Islam. In any case, there are many others much more competent than me to talk about them. But I know that the only person who has been assassinated in connection with the 'Rushdie affair' is not Rushdie but a devout Muslim opposed to the fatwa. He also died for an Islamic cause. He died for his understanding of his faith.

Speaking more generally, I do not believe that any major religion can survive without a tradition of tolerance and pluralism. Totalitarian or fully closed systems do not have good track records: Nazism promised a thousand-year Reich but lasted only twelve years. The Russian revolution survived less than a century; its East European versions less than five decades. Religions are more serious affairs. Any faith or system of ideas which has the ambition of crossing the boundaries of time and space must give scope for dissent and plurality. It is essential for the survival of the system.

NP In order to focus on the creative role of dissent in the survival and resilience of traditions, as opposed to the self-destructiveness of systems that seek to negate oppositions, let me quote again from *The Intimate Enemy*:

This century has shown that in every situation of organised oppression, the true antonyms are always the exclusive part versus the inclusive whole — not masculinity versus femininity but either of them versus androgyny, not the past versus the present but either of them versus the timelessness in which the past is the present and the present is the past, not the oppressor versus the oppressed but both of them versus the rationality which turns them into co-victims.

AN Cross-cutting oppositions are like a multi-dimensional space.

They open up the possibility of a play in which one player must include the others. That is why what is basically called fundamentalism is so anti-traditional and anti-cultural. There is nothing fundamental about fundamentalism. When fundamentalists look towards science, technology or the state they do not turn to traditional texts for inspiration. They look towards and use modern categories. Fundamentalists often are products of a sub-culture of partial modernity which carried the 'stigmata' of defeat. They are the sector that has internalised a sense of defeat and seeks its remedy in the methods and categories of the victor.

In South Asia, for example, all forms of fundamentalism reject indigenous traditions of technology and statecraft. What they want is a modern Western-style nation-state armed with Western weapons pursuing the causes of Islam, Hinduism or Buddhism. In this sense, the fundamentalists are the illegitimate children of the colonial West. This is how they have coped with their perceived civilisational defeat — by becoming comic versions of the West, a West that does not even exist in the West. My argument here is the obverse of Aimé Cezaire's proposition that Nazism was the logical culmination of the modern West, in that the West turned upon itself through that new barbarism. It did unto itself what for centuries it had done to others. I am talking about a psychological process which allows you to do to yourself or to your kind or to your enemies what has been done to you by others, even if it means disowning the most important part of your own moral and cultural self.

NP This paradoxical process whereby the victim internalises the victor's rationality in order to find compensation for his or her threatened self-image, is one of the central axioms to *The Intimate Enemy*. But as you also claim 'India is not the non-West; it is India'. This implies that there are other choices that go beyond the self-negating and complicitous tango of the West's players and counter-players. This also has implications for minority cultures in the West where identity is doubly inscribed by the dominant culture's articulation of its other.

AN We shouldn't be reduced to being passive participants in the West's dialogue with itself and with its chosen others. For, in this dialogue, minority cultures are read as Western replicas of what you perceive in the non-West. In other words, it is not our responsibility to contribute to, criticise, reform or defend that non-West which is a projection of parts of the West's self-hood and carries the load of the West's hostility, guilt, anxiety and fear.

NP Can you elaborate on this concept of the imperfect replica of the non-West within the West?

AN Let me give a rather trivial example. In some early colonial writings, British women were warned against getting involved with Indian men. Apart from the usual inconsistent stereotypes of the Indian men as violent and amoral on the one hand, and effeminate and overly philosophical on the other, in one writing, I am told, the Indian men were described as attractive to British women in the way the Italians sometimes could be. This analogy to the foreigners within Europe is an attempt to understand the other as a version of something that is familiar to the self. Even when we describe the totally unknown, we can do so only in terms of the partially unknown or the known. Instead of admitting the failure of our categories, we love to clobber our empirical experiences until they fit these categories.

The problems of such translations are not unique to the West. There is an Indian folktale about some people who saw a pig for the first time. At first they were bewildered, then one of them confidently claimed that it was a rat that had eaten too much. Another disagreed, and as confidently said that it was an elephant, shrunken due to starvation. Neither was willing to give up his or her categories and admit that this was a new experience.

Diasporic South Asian communities are a new experience. The communities do not know that. Even when they know that, they do not like to admit it. They look to the mother country to redeem their self-respect whenever their dignity is threatened in their adopted country. And the more their dignity is threatened, the more tightly they cling to the mother country and the more angry they become if she does not live up to their expectations. But people like us, who live in the backwaters of Asia, we cannot allow the expatriates to set the tone of public life of our societies, however deep might be our sympathy for their predicament. We also have to be aware that the expatriates often constitute the most chauvinistic and homogenising pressure groups because of their feelings of inferiority *vis à vis* the majority community in the countries they stay in. Some of the most blood-thirsty, ultra-nationalist South-Asians I have encountered stay in the West.

NP Minority cultures are cut off from the generative nucleus of the mother-country, but assuming that the mother-country does not have a monopoly over cultural change, can you give an example of how a culture can develop in the diaspora?

AN There are two alternatives: either to integrate fully, or to define oneself as a different kind of Indian — one with less links to the mother-country. Like the way Australians feel towards the British. Australian authenticity is not dependent on British performance. But the authenticity of the Indians in West Europe or North America, many Indians feel, depend on how India performs.

NP But the 'healthy antagonism' that defines Anglo-Australian relationships is also restricted to those who see themselves as belonging to Australia in a relatively unproblematical manner, that is, to those who would make an unequivocal claim to the dominant culture within Australia. However, those who belong to minority cultures within Australia have a different sense of history. While they too can feel rather dispassionate about British performance, they nevertheless do tend to hold on very passionately to an image of their own other country. This process of retaining the frame of another time and place is important for their own identity.

AN Yes, it is, and we must grant them the right to that memory. But we are not talking here of small marginalised cultures but of a cultural region in which every sixth human being in the world lives. We are also talking of a minority which, though it may be discriminated against in their adopted country, enjoy levels of income, education, and access to media which the average citizen in the mother-country can only dream of. The analogy cannot be with the minority cultures of Africa but with the black minority in the US. The American blacks have every right to talk of their African heritage. But they cannot hope to influence the public life and governmental policies of their countries of origin in Africa.

The exploration of new and creative possibilities requires that the minority cultures in the diaspora develop a dialogue among themselves, and this in turn requires a certain disruption in the community with their mother-countries and some erosion of the ambition to play a special role in the affairs of the latter. I have found that many first-generation South Asians in the diaspora use and internalise a blinkered and uninformed concept of 'proper' nationalism. They cling to the memories of a South Asia which no longer exists and to a myth of return to the homeland which is no longer shared by their children or grandchildren. In the process, these South Asians neglect to reconcile themselves to their immediate empirical context and fail to make a political issue out of their position in the West. Only now do we see evidence of South Asians involving themselves in British or North American politics.

NP Forgive me Ashis for this metaphor, but you sound like the father who has come from the mother-country to tell the children that the way to maturity is to let go of the idealised mother and to learn to play with other siblings, or rather to foster new relationships. And when discussing the failure of migrants in politics, we must also consider the failure of politics for the migrants. Would you put the onus of participation purely on the shoulders of the individual, or on the structural parameters of the polity?

AN I am merely suggesting that certain possibilities that existed have not been explored by the South Asian expatriates in the West. For instance, in the early part of the century, even when India was a colony and the number of Indians in Britain small, there were important Indian Members of Parliament in Britain. They won elections to the House of Commons from Britain. Then there was a long break, and only now do I see some Indians taking an active part in politics again. It is not clear why there was such a break.

I suspect that the diaspora has created identities which do not open up the older Indian identities but narrow them. Hinduism in the diaspora, for example, is much more exclusive and homogenic. Out of feelings of inferiority, many Hindus have tried to redefine Hinduism according to the dominant Western concept of religion. The result has been a more globalised, more Brahmanic — and even a more semiticised — version of Hinduism which endorses some of the most atavistic elements in Indian politics.

NP Are you suggesting that the cultural codes have not survived the various negotiating stages of migration? Rather than cross-cultural borrowing proceeding according to the multiple categories of all the various minority codes, these codes have been redefined so that there is a basic congruence with the dominant culture.

AN Yes, I am suggesting that. Borrowing is vital to all cultures. There must be a constant dialogue between cultures, without one culture giving up its frame for the sake of the frame of another. As it happens, at this point in time, all the cultures except one are facing extinction. Cultural pluralism as well as plural cultures have become endangered species. Already many cultures have been reduced to museum pieces, stage performances, and life in reservations, conveniently displayed for slothful tourists.

Living cultures have other dynamics. Culture as a way of life is a form of resistance. We resist through culture the homogenising categories of our ideological forms, once they get powerful and institutionalised. I have this basic belief that human beings are capable of transforming any emancipatory idea into a new means of oppression, given a sufficient stretch of time. Culture is one means through which we can ensure that there is resistance to categories which have ceased to be emancipatory, and to find ways of generating or keeping alive alternative ideas of emancipation.

NP When describing the formation of the Indian polity in *At the Edge of Psychology*, you credited the modernist intellectuals and the revivalists as the key players and counter-players for the construction of this new form of political community. This synthetic process, whereby one vector legitimised the extraneous and the other sought self-affirmation by reviving the indigenous, maintained a dialogue between the old and the new. Can you see this operating in the diaspora?

AN I do not really know. The Indian diaspora seems embarrassed about traditional culture as a life style. In matters of culture, the diaspora tends to emphasise only the classical components, and expects the nation-state that represents their mother-country to act as a repository of this high culture. Add to this the absurd and paradoxical demand that the mother-country must also transcend its non-classical cultures and, through this process of uniformisation, become equal to the nation-states in the West.

Thus, the Indian diaspora is not only caught in but also being destroyed by such paradoxical demands on the mother-country. The main responsibility of the 800 million Indians who live in the land mass called India is not to be re-engineered by a multi-national corporate alliance between non-resident Indians, as the Indian officialese calls the species, and the resident non-Indians, as sociologist D.L. Sheth calls the Westernised section of India's ruling classes. The ordinary, everyday Indians who live, toil and die in India have other responsibilities to themselves and to their country.

Even for the diaspora to be itself, the expatriate Indians must acknowledge that one cannot have it both ways. One cannot be an expatriate and, at the same time, demand the right to set priorities in the mother-country. Psychologically, this means that one must not just develop cultural links, but also severances.

NP These expressions of dependency between the diaspora and the mother-country are very complex and are symptomatic of both the contradictory wishes of the migrants as well as the contradictions in migration.

AN I grant the complexity of the situation. But I do believe that the Indians in the diaspora have already achieved a certain degree of economic prosperity and professional security; now they must also develop a distinctive politics, culture and tradition. They must see this as an opportunity to create a new life, just like other settlers did in Australia, North and South America. Their demands on India should be cut. They should not expect India to redeem their self-esteem. Nor should they seek a proxy presence in the public realm of South Asian societies. The diaspora must work towards dismantling links with the mother-country and entering the political realm of their new country.

NP Perhaps the diaspora's links with the mother-country are not just a matter of dependency but a constant attempt to validate the necessity for their severance from the mother-country. For example, the enquiries that you must have received about conditions in India may not be a simple expression of genuine interest in life over 'there', but also a search for evidence that endorses their decision to remain 'here'. The justification for resettling requires multiple forms of confirmation, for it means no less than redefining the centre of the world. I certainly felt that the urgency with which some of my more distant relatives would like to see me 'back' in Australia, has as much to do with a need to confirm their presence in Australia as with an expression of lament over my absence.

AN Yes, this is an important point. Whenever I have been asked about my decision to live in India by Indians in North America or Britain, I have always tried to give a balanced answer, outlining the pros and cons of resettling in India. But you are right about this need to find confirmation, because these people always seemed dissatisfied with my 'balanced' answers. They were probably seeking justifications for being in the West.

NP Do you think that Rushdie represents the diaspora's contradictions in *The Satanic Verses*?

AN Rushdie is a gifted writer, but Rushdie is only one voice in the diaspora; he speaks only for a few. He represents a self-confident breed of Indians in the diaspora. His novels have made no compromises in terms of language, images and phrases which are not parts of mainstream Western literature, and his use of such Indianisms is neither esoteric nor apologetic. It is integral to the content of his work.

NP Then why does it only speak for the minority within the diaspora?

AN While Rushdie's use of language is intrinsic to his subject, it is also related to the formal demands of expanding the parameters of the English novel. It follows the tradition of cultural outsiders such as Joyce, Conrad and Nabokov. By introducing a new idiom, using names with foreign connotations, mixing the comic and the serious in a new way, Rushdie has expanded the range of the English novel. His contribution is based on a profound understanding of that part of Indian consciousness which is hitched to global cosmopolitanism. Very few people have described so sensitively and successfully the aspirations and anxieties of the Indian middle class. He has expressed what they would think is wrong with religion, and he has shown that the Indian middle class is not as uprooted as we sometimes think it is. To have offended people so successfully, Rushdie must have had access to the mind of the believer.

NP Is Rushdie's contribution to modernism in the West a reciprocal contribution to modernism in India?

AN Probably not. An Indian writer living in India probably would have understood the limits of his craft better. He would have shown more self-restraint. After all, he would have had to show his face to his next-door neighbours, to his milkman, perhaps even to his aged grandfather. Even as a critic of modernity, I have to admit that Indian modernism has always maintained a minimum responsibility to society. Authors have not been, usually, so dismissive towards traditions as Rushdie has been. Indian modernism is not entirely a cog in the wheel of global modernity. What has been forged in India over the last one hundred and fifty years does not share all the presuppositions of Western modernism. In practice, Indian modernism is neither fully the inheritor of the Enlightenment vision, nor coeval with a form of modernity that conforms to textbook definitions. In that sense, it has its built-in contradictions which give one a lot of play. Though these contradictions are now diminishing, and so is the scope for play.

In theory, things are, however, very different. Indian intellectuals have often over-corrected for what they see as flawed practice. And the Indian middle class has a pathetic faith in the nation-state as an instrument of cultural and social engineering and a matching faith in scientific rationality as a cure-all. Such uncritical faith is not shared by the Western world, and it is a consequence of importing a model of the state and a sociology of knowledge which exist only in theory for the West, not in practice. The contradictions and qualifications introduced by life itself, and the normative and empirical criticisms in the West of the Western state and science, were omitted from the Indian adaptations of the models.

NP Your recent work has moved towards an investigation into the role of the state and an analysis of popular culture. Can you outline your interests in popular culture?

AN I have become interested in various forms of popular culture for mainly one reason. Such forms have captured something of the unrecognised anguish of the South Asians, which has not been audible either to the high culture or to the emergent mass culture in the region. Folk culture is relatively innocent of these new forms of anguish. Popular cultural forms such as the Bombay films, have *by default* a built-in critique of modernity from outside modernity, usually, and perhaps unwittingly, from the point of view of cultural traditions. Whereas the art films in the region have either criticised cultural traditions from the perspective of modernity or criticised modernity from within modernity. Popular culture, in trying to be popular, implicitly recognises and criticises the main props of modernity by tracing the point of view of a culture as it is experienced and lived out.

Aesthetics is a separate question. Popular films, for instance, might be doing things crudely. But then, they are doing things that nobody else is doing. In the West, popular culture is mass culture. Indian popular culture is not mass culture. It is only one of the four strands of cultural production: high, folk, mass and popular. In India, folk culture is still the culture of the majority, whereas in the West it is the most marginalised form. My attraction to popular culture comes from an awareness of the scope it gives to rethink and redraw the base lines of social criticism. At a time when many of the theories of liberation and social progress have been exhausted or have turned out to be oppressive, popular culture has a different meaning and importance. Especially when it had already anticipated some of these developments in its critique of modernity.

NP How will your analysis differ from, say, the Frankfurt School's assessment of mass culture?

AN I essentially agree with the Frankfurt School's assessment of mass culture. However, the School, being uncompromisingly Eurocentric, cannot differentiate between mass and popular culture. Popular culture, I insist, is not unequivocally retrogressive in the Southern world. Popular culture has provided an arena in which to express the shortcomings of modernity and that of the rationality of science and technology. It can help us identify the pain and the concerns of the victims of our times. It has often done so through melodrama and stereotyping, but nevertheless it has kept open a space for social criticism of the new forms of oppression which are unleashed not in the name of religion or culture, but in the name of scientific progress, revolution or development.

To the modernists, it may seem that popular culture in India is simply pandering to superstitions. Maybe it is, but it has also taken on a responsibility that the modernists in India have shirked. Satyajit Ray thinks that his last movie, *An Enemy of the People*, which is based on one of Ibsen's stories, is a very contemporary film. But, despite being an admirer of Ray, I think that, politically, the film has come at least thirty years too late. In its analysis of political pathologies of Indian public life, it is certainly far behind some of the aesthetically third-rate popular films. Ray's new film is an unqualified criticism of tradition from the point of modernity. This in a decade when most of the violence, superstitions and prejudices are associated with modern categories, not traditional ones.

NP The tensions between the secular and the sacred in the nation-state has been a persistent theme in your work.

AN For it is in the name of secularism that the Indian state has tried to marginalise all forms of ethnicity and culture. It thought them to be liabilities.

NP Could we in this context return to Rushdie for a moment? What are your thoughts on Rushdie's representation of the sacred?

AN Rushdie has no theory of sacredness. He views the sacred as only a special — essentially pathological — case of the theory of the secular. In this respect he is a lost child of the 1930s. A true theory of sacredness assumes a certain empathy with the believer and grants the believer a democratic right to believe. And because most South Asians are believers, I would like to see the debates on the Rushdie affair cast in a language which would make sense to them. But Rushdie has responded to the sacred only in secular terms; his language is the language of modern art and aesthetics. He must have been totally confused and hurt by the outcry over *The Satanic Verses*. His worldview and that of his non-modern critics are incommensurable.

NP In an attempt to break with tradition, the rationality of Western science and modernity has equated empathy with subjectivity, and insisted that objectivity presupposes critical distance. When referring to Rushdie's contribution to the English novel, you compared him to Joyce, Conrad and Nabokov. It is interesting, and probably not coincidental, to note that none of these authors were English. Those modernist authors who have been canonised by literary discourse also seem to embody the very condition which modernity has brought to the centre of social experience: displacement. And for the modernist, liminality is the space from which objectivity speaks.

AN The question of objectivity and its links with liminality requires a studied response. I can here make only an off-the-cuff remark. Some traditions of knowledge claim that if you identify with an object deeply or passionately enough you understand it more than if you study it objectively or dispassionately. The truth probably is that any civilisation, to qualify as normal, must give scope for a dialogue between these two modes of under-standing. As it happens, modernity has no place for a theory of empathy and has banished it as a remnant of pre-modern pan-theism. As a result, the dialogue has broken down. The theory of critical distance has been a theory of objectification not objec-tivity. Much of the new violence and hatred in the world flows from this development.

Hence, the need for a play between the secular and the non-secular, to keep alive and reaffirm the existence of a moral universe within which a dialogue is possible between what have become incommensurable values-compassion and objectivity, empathy and criticism. I say this as a non-believer. Because I want social criticism today to include what the early psychoan-alysts contemptuously rejected as an index of primitive, infantile pantheism — projective identification.

This is the awareness Rushdie lacked. *The Satanic Verses* directed its criticism towards the defeated, not towards the imperial structure of thought that rules the world. The book did not criticise too much or too radically; it criticised too little and did so while playing footsie with the rich and the powerful.

WORKS CITED
ASHIS NANDY

At the Edge of Psychology, Oxford University Press, New Delhi, 1978.
Alternative Science, Oxford University Press, New Delhi, 1980.
The Intimate Enemy, Oxford University Press, New Delhi, 1984.
Traditions, Tyranny and Utopia, Oxford University Press, New Delhi, 1987.
The Tao of Cricket, Penguin, Harmondsworth, 1990.

Salman Rushdie, *The Satanic Verses*, Viking, London, 1988.

8.
MINORITY DISCOURSE
AND GLOBAL CULTURE

OLD AND NEW INTERNATIONALISM

Throughout this century part of the definition of modern art is the aspiration towards internationalism. Ever since Apollinaire declared,

> I am everywhere or rather I start to be everywhere.
> It is I who am starting this thing of centuries to come.

Borders were there to be broken. For the avant garde the local was the place you left. The 'national schools' of art which dominated Europe in the late nineteenth and early twentieth century were seen as expressing discrete cultural values and reflecting the interests of the old aristocratic and landowning classes. The cultural field of modernism, and the avant-garde in particular, sought to challenge this connection between art and the dominant order. Formal experiments with new technologies and the affiliation to rhetoric of the social revolution were the two key planks for breaking away from the past. The power of modernism was therefore invariably linked both to a reaction against the particularistic culture of the *ancien régime* and a projection towards a new internationalist culture.[1]

In the post-war period the radical spirit of modernism was truncated as it was increasingly incorporated within the mainstream institutions of art. This institutionalisation within an aggressively nationalist framework, pitting West against East, was not only antithetical to its founding principles but also conducted in a selective fashion. At a time when there was an increased traffic between people from different parts of the globe, and a greater exchange in cultural symbols. The contribution and participation of artists in the peripheries or from former colonies were excluded from the official discourses. Western modernist artists could lay claim to universal values and find global appeal. The populist image of Picasso, as the Western artist who could incorporate non-Western artforms, is the clearest example of the Eurocentric bias in the modernist sensibility. While the Western artist could freely move across borders, the passage of non-Western artists was more problematical. Non-Western artists who embraced the modernist movement were routinely dismissed as 'mimic men'. Non-Western artists could, at best, aspire to reproducing static and closed traditions. Their representation of the local was only that. The suggestion that an intimate representation of the local may also be an allegory for the global was never extended beyond the boundaries of Western modernism. The Eurocentric construction of universalism and internationalism of modern art has so far escaped rigorous critique precisely because it felt empowered to distance itself from those characterisations of nationalism which stressed a backward and introverted mindset. At this end of the century, as the concept of the nation state undergoes another crisis, it is the banner of internationalism which is once again raised as a possible site for cultural renewal.

The notion of internationalism has never been an open and all embracing concept. Colonialism was by definition an internationalist project. How could we overlook the devastation and suffering that was ruthlessly executed in the name of a uniform and global modernisation. Colonial rule may now be formally dismantled, but as Ngugi Wa' Thiong'o reminds us, decolonising the mind is far from complete. The notable lack of conviction given by successive British governments to the institutions formed under the umbrella of the Commonwealth is testament to their inability to explore a multiracial vision of internationalism. While the indigenous elites of Africa and India may have expressed suspicion and distrust towards the Commonwealth in the immediate postcolonial period, this opportunity has been most crucially undermined by the shift from sentimental appreciation to outright disdain by the British Foreign and Commonwealth Office. As Robin Cohen has argued,

Britain turned its back on the Commonwealth but, in so doing, it hardly embraced a new European internationalism. In this new, uncomfortable union with Europe, Britain still insists, for instance, that it retains independent immigration policy on the grounds that 'it is an island'.[2] The current committee which discusses issues of migration for the European Union is the same group set up to advise on the threat of terrorism and drug-smuggling. By keeping the issue of migration in the same frame as these other forms of violent transgression, the EU maintains a continuum with the so-called 'histrionic tendencies of social life'. The stigmata of migration are deeply engrained in the political imaginary. The ongoing complicity between globalisation and Eurocentrism only adds new levels of insecurity to the current modes for interaction and integration in the world economic and communications system. Such challenges are inevitably at the forefront of the way we understand artistic production.

It would be naive to celebrate the fluidity of cultural exchange that follows from transnational capital, rapid telecommunication, and mass tourism which in fact operates against a background of deepening economic divisions between the North and the South, and the ever stricter policing of refugees and migrants along political borders. For while the idea of an authentic nationalism is the antinomy of modernism, the liberating projects of new internationalism also threatened to homogenise cultural differences. The choices today should not be reduced either to local nationalism or to global modernity. What we need to consider is how can we rethink the relationship between the axes of cultural contact and political equality without reinscribing the exploitative models of centre and periphery.

GLOBAL VISIONS

In the past decade a growing field of cultural criticism seeks to challenge many of the fundamental misconceptions in modernism and to offer counter-histories of cultural exchange. The publication of *Global Visions*[3] which brings together the papers delivered at the conference entitled 'A New Internationalism' — the first conference of the Institute of International Visual Arts held at the Tate Gallery in London in 1994 — is an index of this problem of examining the framework of contemporary art from a global perspective.

The contributors to this collection vary from critics like Hal Foster who commented on the utility of quasi-anthropological paradigms in the visual practice of representing other cultures, to the curator and writer Gerardo Mosquera who cautiously mentioned that the precedents for 'new internationalism' lay between a form of complicitous multicultural relativism and the axes of globalisation which divide and alter the zones of silence to satisfy the dominance of the West as a cultural centre. This scepticism is also to be found at the centre of Jimmie Durham's essay, as he asks the deceptively simple question, 'how might we imagine internationalism without it being among nations?'.[4] A distrust of nationalism may be healthy, but is the disavowal expressed by more complacent members of the art world both premature and counter-productive? By pointing to dramatic shifts in the practices of geo-political administration, much of the discussion on globalisation presupposes the obsolescence of the nation state. Therefore it may be more appropriate to think of the reconfiguring rather than the withering of the nation. Rasheed Araeen's comments on the shallowness and hypocrisy of earlier experiments with internationalism within the parameters of an ideologically divided British state and Durham's reflections on the delusions of transcendence are careful reminders of the gaps between the promise and the performance of a concept.

Global Visions provides a necessary reference point for the rethinking of the legacy of modernism as well as offering an indication of the issues that have come to preoccupy the mainstream art institutions. This collection illuminates a number of new political and cultural trajectories. There has been a contestation over the term 'ethnicity' as it has been moved out of the political domain of anti-racism and into the cultural field of identity. With the influence of psychoanalytic literature on the necessary and not just negative relationship between the self and the other, and an increasing awareness of what Kobena Mercer calls the 'diasporic aesthetic', the status of difference in identity has also been re-evaluated. These new shifts have provoked many new questions. How will the traditional be cross-cut with the modern? What is the geopolitical framework which will contain the transnational pattern of cultural exchange? How valid is the national as a category for identifying a contemporary sensibility and identity? What capacity do the mainstream institutions have for understanding and responding to the histories of exclusion and marginalisation?

The institutional responses to such radical questions are at best uneven and at worst defensive. The forces pushing for change are conjunctural, a combination of activism and legitimation implosion. However, this conjunctural energy is often diverted and the sources blurred. A common trope for this form of misrecognition and diversion is found in the representation of the other in the guise of the virgin origin. For instance, while speaking on the panel for the opening of the mega-exhibition *Magiciens de la Terre*, Paris, 1989, Gayatri Spivak pondered on the distance between this title and the expression *artistes du monde*.[5] The separation was not innocent, and she suggested that this was consistent with a certain hesitancy in the way the institution of art can cede some of its ground. By turning to face the problematics of the margin in the name of *terre* it seeks to erase the preceding space of the *monde*. She reminded us that the reception of other practices are often preceded both by the inscription of their world as a 'virgin' territory, and the by hope of constructing an elevated plane for new forms of cultural interaction. In another instance, the 1992 Sydney Biennale, the promise of transgression made explicit in its title — *The Boundary Rider* — rebounded into symbols of reinforcement and containment: the principle for presenting the non-Western artists tended to reinforce the archetype of the other as outrider or as the defender of territory that was already staked and mapped.

The way the dominant institutions respond to the issues of cultural difference is also bound by their very conceptualisation of crisis. It has varied from the recognition of the necessary renegotiation of existing resources to a rethinking of the very paradigms within which cultural practice is conducted. The first level is often conceived as the *crisis of culture*. The factors behind this claim can be clearly listed. Mass migration, decolonisation, emancipatory social movements, feminism are routinely cited as the forces that have generated new levels of expectancy, stimulated further demands, heightened consciousness of the gaps between formal and substantive rights, redefined the horizons of the permissible and the desirable — in short, challenged the certitudes and order of the dominant culture.

In a world of transition and rupture it is not just hierarchies that are contested, the rules of the game also come under scrutiny. For example, Terry Eagleton claims that the current crisis is so deep that the very concept of culture cannot be introduced to reconcile or redeem material struggle, for culture itself is perceived as complicit with the construction of the struggle *in* the social. Culture and other transcendental values are no longer neutral concepts. 'Culture is now part of the problem rather than the solution.'[6] As we witness the breakdown of the conventional models for integrating and organising the question of difference — when both universalism and particularism are seen as inadequate, or when neither evolutionism nor relativism seem satisfactory — then we can we twist the level of understanding crisis: modernity is the *culture of crisis*.

This crisis is most palpable in the difference between the rhetoric of inclusion and the practice of participation. The crisis is thus not confined to the process of assimilating a foreign entrant but involves both restructuring and reorientation. Pragmatic switches and genuine reforms, while dominating the sensibility of the guardians of institutions, offers paltry compensation for the complex demands being imposed by a world of heterogeneity and the cultural dynamisms of difference. At the broad level of how an oppositional strategy is construed, Meaghan Morris has observed a shift in the left-leaning assumptions of solidarity and common struggle. The projected unity and essentialist identities that sustained the earlier ideological critique of crisis in culture is being fragmented. She notes that:

> Real dilemmas are emerging, some of which will make it more difficult in the future for the old 'left-liberal' and leftist cultures to maintain their political imaginary by identifying with a spectrum of causes once smoothly construed as coherent — feminism; anti-racism; gay activism; land rights; environmentalism; opposition to uranium mining.[7]

NEW ETHNICITIES

In his influential 1988 essay 'New Ethnicities', Stuart Hall argued that black cultural politics in Britain was undergoing a significant transition. Hall distinguished two 'moments' in black cultural politics. The first was 'the moment when the term "black" was coined as a way of referencing the common experience of racism and marginalisation in Britain'.[8] Notions such as the 'black experience' provided a unifying framework for building up a common identity across a variety of ethnic and cultural groups, and was instrumental in providing a coherent challenge to dominant conceptions of British national identity. This unified and unifying notion of black identity also informed the development of what Hall calls a cultural politics 'designed to challenge, resist and, where possible, to transform the dominant regimes of representation'. Critical in this struggle over the 'relations of representation' were questions of fetishisation, objectification and negative figuration, manifested in a concern 'not simply with the absence or marginality of black experience but with its simplification and stereotypical character'. The key demands of this form of struggle were for *access* (representation by black artists) and for *contestation* (the provision of positive images to counterpoint existing negative stereotypes).

The second 'moment' of black cultural politics that Hall identifies arises in the context of a struggle over the 'relations of representation' to a struggle over the 'politics of representation' itself. By this, Hall points first to the increasing acceptance that representation does not merely reflect culture but is *constitutive* of that culture; and second, to the increasing awareness of the limits of the 'essential' or unified black subject.

> What is at issue here is the recognition of the extraordinary diversity of subjective positions, social experiences and cultural identities which compose the category 'black'; that is, the recognition that 'black' is essentially a politically and culturally *constructed* category, which cannot be grounded in a fixed transcultural or transcendental racial category and which therefore has no guarantees in Nature. What this history brings into play is the recognition of the immense diversity and differentiation of the historical and cultural experience of black subjects.[9]

At the forefront of this diversity is the recognition that the black subject cannot be represented without reference to the dimensions of class, gender, sexuality and ethnicity. Moreover, awareness of the complexity of affiliations which traverse subjectivity necessitates the recognition of the contradictory processes and investments which constitute identity. As Hall notes, racism is powered not only by the negative positioning of blacks but also by an 'inexpressible envy and desire'. 'Just as masculinity always constructs femininity as double — simultaneously Madonna and whore — so racism constructs the black subject: noble savage and violent avenger.'[10] It is in this sense that Hall posits the emergence of a new ethnicity. Instead of operating as a form of closure in the name of purity of nation and race, Hall points to:

> ... what I think is the beginning of a positive conception of ethnicity of the margins, of the periphery. That is to say, a recognition that we all speak from a particular place, out of a particular experience, a particular culture, without being contained by that position as 'ethnic artists' or film-makers.[11]

THE GHETTO OF ETHNIC ARTS

The history of the shifts in cultural policy is rarely in step with the changes in British society and this complex relationship is in need of further research. Parenthetically, it may be noted that while most of the research on cultural practice stresses the prevalence of an internationalist perspective the research on cultural policy is nevertheless conducted on an almost exclusively national basis. Despite the increasing international circulation of institutional models and the identification of parallels in the construction of the social world in various nation states, there has been very little research conducted on a comparative basis. It would be valuable to consider the relationship between the formation of arts policies and the broader processes of social negotiation and political contestation. Further research is needed to trace the peculiar ways ideas migrate across national boundaries, and how they are consequently institutionalised *within* specific state structures.

The concept of a new internationalism in the visual arts emerged primarily from the ideas and struggles of black arts in Britain. Throughout the 1970s and 1980s black artists and critics in Britain critiqued the prevailing models and categories for representing cultural identity. They attempted to shift the debate on 'blackness' beyond either exotica or stigma, and to expand the political horizons that were set in the anti-racism discourse. This new cultural movement challenged the funding practices of the major government institutions and was a crucial part of the groundswell that led to the formation of the Institute of

International Visual Arts.

One of the earliest documents to specify the limitations in British cultural policies was written in 1976 by Naseem Khan. Khan was commissioned to write the first-ever report on the diverse nature of contemporary British culture and to evaluate the access that 'ethnic minorities' had to state funding. She identified some of the glaring contradictions and failures in the financing of the minority arts. Her report was titled *The Arts Britain Ignores*. This report was subject to immediate criticism.[12] Black artists and critics were quick to contest the very frame of reference and the validation that it lent to the term 'Ethnic Minority Arts'. Such commentators felt that the state's ethnocentric cultural policies would not be revealed merely by identifying the gaps and flaws in the allocation of funds. They argued that black artistic production should not be defined by such patronising terms, which only further polarised the cultural positions and reinforced an oppressive social hierarchy. The question that was repeatedly asked was, how will a dominant culture recognise the achievements and significance of individuals from other cultures, when their cultural traditions are being constructed as not just the origin, but also the limit, to their creative potential? By working on the assumption that multiculturalism was an ideology which legitimised the status of all forms of cultural production, Khan failed to look into the power differentials that ghettoised specific practices as it relegated them to the margins of the national culture. Thus from the beginning we see a clear critique of a form of multicultural policy which confines black artistic practice to narrow notions of community, or as an exemplification of static forms of tradition. Embedded within such a conceptual framework the dominant discourse would inevitably ignore the linkages between black art and other forms of contemporary artistic practice.

Following this report very few significant steps were taken to alter the frame of reference. The commissioning of the Roundhouse Project which promised to serve as a 'superstructure' that would accommodate and enhance a wide range of black cultural practices was a spectacular failure. Throughout the eighties, the Arts Council of Great Britain commissioned various reports which tested the relationship between the rhetoric of cultural diversity and the implementation of funds. The emphasis was on the evaluation of the commitment to funding, the monitoring of attendance to events, the consolidation of specific bases and the possible out-reach to new constituencies or sponsors. Most of these reports concluded by noting the double disadvantage that confronted the black arts organisations, and they all called for long-term strate-gies which would tackle structural problems associated with the racism that blocked the integration of hitherto neglected con-stituencies within a broad pluralist framework.

STAGING NEW INTERNATIONALISM

The publication of the report on *The Institute of New International Visual Arts (INIVA)*[13] in December 1991 was her-alded by Sandy Nairne, the then Director of Visual Arts, as 'a new stage in the development of the Art's Council's thinking about the visual arts and its support to cultural diversity'.

What is unique about INIVA is that it aims to develop a new kind of institute which not only builds on the history of black arts but will also play an active role in shaping a plural cultural aes-thetic. The intention is to challenge the prevailing Euro-American axioms in the discourse on contemporary culture by giving partic-ular recognition to the vitality of non-Western practices. They propose to tackle the limitations of the dominant views in two ways: first, by confronting the exclusion of the majority of the world's cultures and second, by addressing the marginalisation of minority cultures within Western states. Thus the concept of 'new internationalism' calls for both a wider understanding of global culture and the history of art. It also presumes that in this partic-ular moment of ideological transition and the rupture of social and cultural certitudes the issues of difference and hybridity have to be given greater cultural value.

The cultural and intellectual promise of INIVA thus rests on establishing a critical negotiation of the cultural formations that are emerging as a consequence from the twin pressures of cultural diasporas and socio-economic globalisation. INIVA not only offers the opportunity to excavate and 're-present' the works of signifi-cant artists who were repressed by the mainstream, but it can also act as a spur for rethinking the criteria for institutional inclusion and mount a critique against the ethnic patterning of cultural hege-mony. Cultural difference is no longer posited as an optional

addition but as a constitutive force in the dynamism of plural societies. From this perspective the frame of 'new internationalism'
cannot be defined by merely attacking the chauvinistic aggressivity that marks the re-emergence of nationalism(s). 'New
internationalism' cannot be simply implied as the congregation of
those previously excluded from the institution of modernism. The
concept needs to be defined in terms of its points of departure, the
horizons it sets out for, and the associations it seeks to encourage.
The concept should be a frame for enabling connections in all the
processes of engagement rather than just in the positive network-
ing and unintended consequences that result for those who
participate within its own structures. The concept needs to suggest
a method which others can either adopt or reject.

While the agenda for work to be done is rich and demanding,
the broader cultural predicament in which the concept of 'new
internationalism' is located is not so optimistic. Sandy Nairne has
noted the poverty of cultural policy within the European Union.[14]
The Treaty of Rome was only concerned with maintaining the heritage of national culture within its respective borders and
reinforced the priority of market principles so that contemporary
art can be traded freely. The Maastricht Treaty was no significant
advance. There was a generalised acknowledgment of the responsibility for developing a common culture while respecting the
specificities of the existing cultures. However, as Nairne observed,
this policy is limited by two flaws: first, the absence of any detailed
clarification and second, the failure to acknowledge the role of
minorities within the respective national cultures. The combined
effect is to undermine the potential for establishing the diversity of
reference points and the pattern of interchange in a broader cultural formation.

The flaws that Nairne identified at the transnational level cannot be overcome simply by imposing models and practices within
specific nation states. For instance, who could dispute Secretary
General of the Arts Council of Great Britain, Anthony Everitt's
claim that we need both a 'value free space', and a broader framework than that which Eurocentric modernism established?[15] Yet,
when it comes to defining the basis, the criteria and the boundaries
of 'new internationalism', the main initiatives and responsibility
are invariably passed back to the cultural producers. Gavin Jantjes,
who is one of the key advocates of 'new internationalism' and the

main consultant of the INIVA policy, has linked the shift in the Arts Council of Great Britain, cultural policy to two phenomena: first, a step away from the paternalistic absolutism that was constitutive of the earlier 'Ethnic Arts Policies', and a move towards a form of democratic accountability that is responsive to the specific needs of racial minorities; second, Jantjes suggests that just as the figure of the other has taken new significance in the philosophical and cultural discourse of postmodernity, then cultural policy should also be consonant with these broader shifts.[16]

This redemptive narrative is particularly transparent in his essay, 'The Emperor's Spectacles', Anthony Everitt begins by graciously reversing the Thatcherite mania against the threat of 'swamping'. Instead he characterises the arrival of migrant labour from colonies other than Ireland as the injection of vitality that rescued a body from atrophy: 'The country was set to dwindle into a marine Ruritania. But then an extraordinary thing happened. A gift from the Third World to an undeserving member of the First.'[17]

One of the unintended consequences of the reverse migration flows of decolonisation was the emergence of a cultural surplus in the 'mother country'. The resulting challenge, Everitt implies, is what to do with the 'gift' of this surplus. Down-playing and often conflating the significant differences between assimilation and integration, he thereby considers the validity of multiculturalism as cultural policy. Everitt reasserts two fundamental critiques which have been directed against multiculturalism. First, that there was an inadequate application of the principles of equity. Second, that the principles of tolerance were misconceived. Everitt admits that even on a crude economic scale the existing structures did not deliver their services nor respond to the needs of their constituents. This marginalisation was also reflected in the values upon which notions of acceptance were defined. "Multiculturalism is like an invitation a host issues to his or her guests: everyone is welcome to stay provided they obey the convention of the house."[18]

How does Everitt see INIVA going beyond the limitations of multiculturalism when there was never a genuine form of multiculturalism in the first place? With a slight conceptual transposition of Everitt's mapping of the migrant's 'homeland', we discover that the 'surplus' is no longer in 'Gujurat, St. Lucia or Uganda', but in 'Brixton, Leicester and Liverpool'. The margin appears to be relocated but the asymmetries of 'gift exchange' that sustain paternalism are far from shattered. In contrast, INIVA should be seen as a way-station rather than as a terminus. INIVA should embrace the future-oriented principles of initiating research in new methods for representing cultural expressivity that *articulates* the condition of itinerancy and transition, *heightens* the modes of syncretism and translation, *negotiates* the spaces between binarisms and *explores* new media, the potential and the security of INIVA also rest on a broader historical consciousness. We need to complement the principled promises of policy-makers with the counter-histories of INIVA. Faith that the turn towards Europe will facilitate an intercultural and relativist sensibility is not necessarily well founded when the British state has consistently disowned the informal and formal experiments in internationalism that emerged after the implosion of Empire. In recent years we have witnessed not only the dismantling of institutions which were born out of the integrative aspirations of the Commonwealth, but also the utilisation of multiculturalism at all levels of education and social welfare has been targeted out as the soft option. The political context for a 'new internationalism' is still bound by xenophobic border control and a parochial surveillance of cultural utility.

THE PROCESSUAL FRAME OF GLOBALISATION

For some time the term globalisation has been used as a starting-point for conceptualising the patterns of integration and destabilisation that have occurred in many aspects of every day life. In more recent debates this term has been shorn of its critical edge and simply used as a description of the way the world is: globalisation has moved from being a concept for defining the context and the pattern of forces that construct a socio-economic field to an everyday term for rationalising the patterns of domination. In order to avoid the pitfalls of 'anything goes' that are so often pinned to nebulous terms like the 'global postmodern' I return to the question: how has the globalisation of cultural production affected the relationship between dominant and marginal cultures? When considering the shift in the discourse on art history from formalism and 'primitivism' to hybridity and 'new internationalism', it is tempting to construct this transition as a progressive movement from the cultural blindness of appropriation and displacement to the political insight of negotiation and compensation. However, faith in such progress is qualified whenever a closer examination is made between the stated intentions and structural practices of the art institutions. As regards the levels of change that have been initiated we must always consider who initiated change, and what are the axioms which mark change? This level of questioning now demands a further examination of the broader frameworks in which such debates are situated.

Thinking global is not the same as thinking of universals. Despite the ever-increasing evidence of global effects and processes, a critical analysis of globalisation still remains difficult. With the collapse of the totalising schemas for explaining social change and cultural formation, there has been an increasing interest in the sphere of the social world which was previously considered to be the underside of modernity. It is at this theoretical juncture that the symbolic status of the migrant and the subaltern are also being re-evaluated. Such belated attention can encourage various forms of exaggerated claims. We can begin to note a certain perversity in the celebration of the migrant as exemplifying modernity's potential either to liberate or exploit through detachment. Three types of migrant dreamings seem to stake out the modernist quest. Can the migrant *stand in* for the history of the place of origin, to *stand up* as an intimation for the future of the place of arrival, or act as a *shuttle* between these temporal and spatial axioms?

Writing against the grain of the recent debates in cultural studies which have elevated the status of the migrant, Gayatri Spivak has issued a firm warning against the strategies of false continuities. "The trajectories of the Eurocentric migrant poor and the postcolonial rural poor are not only discontinuous but may be, through the chain-linkage that we are encouraged to ignore, opposed."[19] With righteous disdain Spivak has poured scorn on the mobilisation of a homogenising heading like 'the other' to contain everything from the ethnicity of the migrant, the history of anti-slavery and the politics of decolonisation. The tactical strategies of oppositional politics, she judiciously reminds us, are not automatically transposable for the benefits of consolidating the parameters of minority discourse within academic and cultural institutions.

Spivak goes on to suggest a number of problematics in the representation of the transnational dynamics of culture. The transnational cannot be identified simply by extending the logic of comparative work, that is, by adding together or substituting categories of the national.[20] The identity of the transnational is always catachrestic, in the sense that the original meanings can only be secured by reference to another place which is beyond its own borders. This tension between naming and ontology makes "postcoloniality a deconstructive case" and heightens the utility of deconstruction in countering the reification of ethnicity in postcolonialism.[21] This implies that the multiracial inflections in the dominant culture of plural societies like the US and Britain cannot be raised as evidence of globality. Globality has no paradigmatic form, it is only found in the incessant process of 'negotiation between the national, the global and the historical as well as the contemporary diasporic'.[22] Thus if globality is not just an extension of earlier forms of multiculturalism, and transnationalism is not only an extrapolation of internationalism, then the difficult task is to grasp these new phenomena in their precise measure and to define a conceptual language that can address these cultural shifts.

IN CONCLUSION: LEARNING TO THINK GLOBAL

In the 1990s, critical theory and cultural politics stressed the importance of addressing the specificity of the local while maintaining a vigilant eye on the global frame. This suggestion, which had a polemical urgency underpinning it, now seems under threat from a different angle. Homi Bhabha has noted that one of the consequences of the liberal discourses on multiculturalism is a shifting in the burden of who defines culture. Attacking Charles Taylor's dismissal of hybrid cultures and his inability to address the issue of belatedness within the terms of the 'politics of recognition', Bhabha alerts us to the pernicious logic of conversion or deferral in liberal discourse when it is confronted by the partiality of minority culture.[23] One of the tactics within liberalism for defusing the crisis of the difference in culture is the stress given to the putative tolerance and equality of diverse cultures. Yet, if globalisation involves the increasing interconnection of social processes across time and space, then how will the discreteness of the local be sustained? Bhabha points to this difficulty when he reminds us of the necessary perils in what he calls 'simultaneous translations', whereby the compulsion to speak to others is caught on the dilemma, either of elevating communication to a false universalism, or of being caught in a mute particularism. With some frustration he notes: 'The common coin of cultural exchange in modern societies, at the international level, is still the national community and the national culture, even though their representations may be more complex.'[24]

Even when the national is marked as hybrid, the representation of culture still proceeds as if all its mixtures still add up to a discrete and unique geo-political unit. In the liberal schema of negotiated congruence and continuity the difference of cultural difference must always be presented in discrete and concrete terms. Like Spivak, Bhabha is more concerned with the processual in cultural difference, rather than the products of cultural diversity. Their attention to the question of cultural difference is connected to a critique both of the legitimacy of the prevailing hierarchies in which identities are inserted and of the construction of frameworks for evaluating respective positions. Part of the problem is that the symbolic and political institutions which have a formative role in our preconceptions of history and which forge both concrete and abstract relationships to place, have yet to construct frameworks either for evaluating the 'new' cultural identities based on hybridity or for imagining the tensions of globality.

REFERENCE NOTES

Once again I am grateful for the advice and direction of this essay from my friend Scott McQuire.

1. Peter Wollen, *Raiding the Icebox: Reflections on Twentieth-Century Culture*, Verso, London, 1993.
2. Robin Cohen, *Frontiers of Identity: The British and the Others*, Longman, London, 1994, p.30.
3. *Global Visions: Towards a New Internationalism in the Visual Arts*, ed., Jean Fisher, Kala Press in association with the Institute of International Visual Arts, London, 1994.
4. Ibid., p.113.
5. Gayatri Chakravorty Spivak, *Outside in the Teaching Machine*, Routledge, London, 1993, p.210.
6. Eagleton's astute observation concerning the pitfalls of transcendentalism and

relativism in contemporary culture is marred by his consistent conflation between deconstruction and an apolitical form of pragmatic relativism which is inevitably an alibi for free market capitalism. See T. Eagleton, 'The Crisis of Contemporary Culture', in *Random Access*, ed., Pavel Büchler and Nikos Papastergiadis, Rivers Oram Press, London, 1995.

7. Meaghan Morris, 'Future Fear', *Mapping the Futures: Local Cultures, Global Change*, ed., Bird et al., Routledge, London, 1993, p.37.

8. Stuart Hall, 'New Ethnicites', in Mercer, K., ed., *Black Film, British Cinema*, ICA Documents No.7, 1988, p.27.

9. Ibid., p.28

10. Ibid.

11. Ibid., p.29.

12. See Rasheed Araeen, *Black Phoenix*, No.2, 1978.

13. Gavin Jantjes and Sarah Wason, *Final Report: The Institute of New International Visual Arts (INIVA), 1991*, London Arts Board and Arts Council of Great Britain, December 1991.

14. Sandy Nairne, 'European Fusion', *Frieze: International Art Magazine*, No.11, Summer 1993, p.18.

15. *Cultural Diversity in the Arts: Art, Policies and the Facelift of Europe*, ed. Ria Lavrijsen, Royal Tropical Institute, The Netherlands, 1993, p.57.

16. Ibid., pp.59-66.

17. Ibid., p.53.

18. Ibid., p.56.

19. Gayatri Chakravorty Spivak, 'Scattered *Speculations on the Question of Culture Studies, Outside in the Teaching Machine*, Routledge, London, 1993, p.257.

20. Ibid., p.262.

21. Ibid., p.281.

22. Ibid., p.278.

23. Homi Bhabha, 'Culture's In Between', *Artforum*, September 1993, p.167.

24. Homi Bhabha, 'Simultaneous Translations: Modernity and the Inter-National', *On Taking a Normal Situation*, Museum van Hededaags Kunst, Antwerp, 1993, p.163.

9.
GLOBAL PROPOSALS
A CONVERSATION WITH
GILANE TAWADROS

As the balance of geopolitical power swings and twists in new directions, and forms of art activity that were previously ignored have come to prominence, the bankruptcy of a Eurocentric framework has grown increasingly palpable. If we see the selections and concerns of the major biennales and large-scale museum exhibitions as an index of the dominant values, then it is clear that the themes of migration, postcolonialism, hybridity and the role of the non-Euro-American artist are now considered to be a vital force within the institution of contemporary art.

How do we measure this change of attitude? While nobody could really call this admission of the 'other' a revolution, many have already characterised it as selective incorporation — an appropriation that ultimately consolidates the institution. Perhaps both approaches miss the subtleties of difference. I would call this change a swerve in the established practices. When the impact of the 'other' became unavoidable, a swerve was necessary in order both to switch orientation and widen the base of recognition. It remains to be seen whether this swerve is sufficient to take us towards the promised land of 'New Internationalism'.

It is worth remembering that political economists have always been conscious that the flow of capital has little respect for national borders. They called this transmission 'internationalism', and it was only when non-Western hands began to guide the flow that they renamed this transmission 'globalisation'. Within the art world, concepts of globalisation have been at best nebulous and at worst oversimplified. Two general strategies are evident in the plethora of group and thematic shows that have toured in recent years. First, an undoing of imperialist oppositions where the intention is to reverse or complicate the pattern of influence. Second, a focusing on the differences within the boundaries of a national culture, thereby acknowledging the activity of artists previously ignored. We thus see a re-evaluation of the status of both the global and the regional.

It is into this lively arena that the Institute for New International Visual Arts (INIVA) was launched. INIVA can be seen as a direct result of various critiques of the mainstream British art institutions by black artists and critics in the eighties. After a long period of inertia and sporadic consultations, the Arts Council of Great Britain and the London Arts Board finally responded. Earlier experiments such as the Roundhouse project were closely scrutinised and a cautious but optimistic report that laid the foundation for the Institute was drafted.

INIVA aims to explore a broader vision of contemporary art. The central concept, 'new internationalism', contends that the prior frameworks for understanding contemporary art, were confined by Eurocentric boundaries and standards. INIVA seeks to develop 'new ways of looking at contemporary visual arts ... by giving priority to artists who have been marginalised on the basis of race, gender and cultural differences.'

There is still much to negotiate in terms of criteria of influence and the rules of evaluation. It is toward this end that we could see a radical cultural project for the future — one which could seriously question the category of the nation as a valid concept for understanding the enigmatic affinities between a sense of belonging and the creative act. Is it not time to think of possible connections between different places rather than the perpetual excavation of the histories of displacement? How would we define the cultural formations that do not rest on a national territory? It was with such questions that I approached the director of INIVA, Gilane Tawadros.

Nikos Papastergiadis Why do you think INIVA came into being?

Gilane Tawadros The Institute grew out of the work of the artists, writers and curators in this country. People like Rasheed Araeen, David A. Bailey, Guy Brett, Eddie Chambers, Lubaina Himid, Maud Sulter, Sunil Gupta, Keith Piper and Gavin Jantjes. It grew out of a specifically British context. Some of those artists were also working as publishers or curators because they perceived gaps in what was being written and exhibited. There was an absence of non-European artists within exhibition spaces and in the teaching of art history. But also an absence of alternative cultural perspectives on contemporary visual art and scholarship.

NP Do you think that this engagement, as artist/curator, or critic/artist, will be an important feature of the Institute?

GT Yes, it is concerned equally with visual art practice and with ideas about contemporary art. Artists had to work at both levels because they didn't feel one was sufficient. There is the sense that they were not allowed to act simply as artists in any kind of a neutral way, separated off from the curatorial and critical world.

NP What was the relevance of the Roundhouse Project?

GT The Roundhouse was a failed attempt to reconcile a number of initiatives by black artists, performers, theatre writers, directors and so on in one building. After that fell through, the Arts Council's Visual Arts department was left with the problem of how to reallocate funds that had been designated for that project. They were committed to funding exclusively for the visual arts and so held a number of consultative meetings to see how the money should be spent. The resounding response was 'whatever you do, don't build a black art gallery'. There was a time when it was important to make black arts visible in the same way that women artists were making themselves visible, but that time had passed. You cannot differentiate black art history and practice from white. These things come together and both their currencies are intimately intertwined.

NP How would you define INIVA's role?

GT The legitimate subject area for this organisation is both the recent history and contemporary practice of black artists in the UK and the re-evaluation of Western art. The organisation will look again at what modernism meant and redefine it. Its structure is unique, since it wasn't set up to be either purely exhibition-making or purely education-led. There is the opportunity of cutting across those two spaces, to bring ideas and practice much more closely together. The best analogy is like a sort of production company that will work with institutions or individuals to produce exhibitions, publications, seminars, research projects and build up a library and archive. There is no other arts organisation with that degree of breadth and flexibility.

NP But these issues and problems are not unique to Britain. They have been articulated in various forms throughout the world, and I wonder why this Institute didn't happen before and elsewhere?

GT I think it has to do with the history of migrant cultures within this country. The nature of the relationships between Britain and other countries, and of its colonial history is specific. The French colonial experience aimed to extend 'Frenchness' around the world, whereas the British experience was not one which made the people of those different nationalities British, but brought them together under the umbrella of a British Empire.

NP Let's shift the comparison away from France to another colonising country — the US. Why isn't there a comparable institution there?

GT It's a very different history. That the designation 'African-American' is used alongside 'Irish-American' and 'Italian-American' shows how different this hyphenated identity is. What struck me very much from discussions with African-American artists was the nostalgia for an Africa as a mother country, as an original homeland. It is something that was expressed by black political movements in America early in the twentieth century. In Britain, the nature of this relationship with a mother country is expressed in much more ambivalent terms. It's much less a question of nostalgia than of negotiating two cultures without being romantic about either of them. Whereas in America you get the sense that there is a desire for an Africa which can somehow bond together the fragmented experience of the African-American experience and make sense of it. There is a tension between a kind of national identity that erases and supersedes any specific identity, and the specificity of experience that needs expression. The challenge that faces both the Institute, and more generally faces us all as we go into the next century, is how we can maintain the specificity of our particular identity and experience, located in the here and now, and yet also speak beyond that specific experience to other people and to other experiences. This involves a mode of inclusivity that is not simply premised on the universals of modernism.

NP One of INIVA's central goals is to broaden the cultural aesthetic and get beyond the modernist claims of universalism. But the problem with broadening is that it might move away from rigidity into a sort of open-ended space which is just as destructive, because it moves into flaccidity.

GT I would question whether broadening necessarily leads to that kind of open-ended, 'anything goes' space, or to use Nelly Richard's phrase to an 'economy of sameness', where things become so equalised that they become undifferentiated. I'm more interested in creating a space for the particular and the specific but not so that they are completely self-referential. I'm more interested in how a specific experience and a particular expression can be mediated in such a way that it finds points of reference with other, very different experiences.

NP How do you see this mediation occurring?

GT There are a number of possible hooks for engaging with something that is unfamiliar. In the realm of visual works of art, those can be colour, form, or in some cases, words. Any kind of trigger contained in the work itself. I think memory is, for me, a much more powerful metaphor for explaining how that space is negotiated.

NP But how would I relate to a work which is based on memories that I do not share?

GT You don't share the specific memory, but there are things which act as triggers to memory. There is a difference between the memory which is particular and specific, and the trigger, which needn't be specific or shared.

NP How is this triggering device different from the universalism that underpinned modernism? For instance, the famous appeals by Greenberg and Reinhardt to the purity of colour and form.

GT I'm talking about a space beyond the name of the artist and actually engage with the work itself. I would argue that we have forgotten how to engage with the work, without the artist's name becoming a trigger for a whole set of references, negative or positive, about the making of, say, abstract painting. We should not look at work removed from social, political or historical context. But why is it that the unfamiliar is so scary and why do we have to wade through a wall of information — anthropological, sociological, literary and often literal — to find a point of relationship with a work of art?

NP I agree, that the choice isn't between the extremes of either the pure context-free reading of the work and saturated academicism. There is something in-between, perhaps. But some degree of knowledge will always precede our perception of an art object. Is the Institute also trying to deal with how we construct knowledge about an art and culture?

GT The phrase 'in-between space' is a really crucial one because it suggests a lack of fixity, a kind of partial state. The intellectual framework in which the Institute operates is not about a form of total knowledge, entailing a sense of linear progress, nor presuming a bird's eye view of the world.

NP One of the other central concepts promoted by INIVA and related to the notion of the 'in-between' is the notion of hybridity. What is the significance of hybridity for contemporary culture?

GT 'Hybridity' will always carry with it a kind of dystopian vision of plurality which is chaotic and incoherent. There have been attempts to reappropriate that term and to suggest that plurality and fragmentation are what real experience is all about. While we all pine for coherence, we also accept that this desire doesn't relate to our actual experience of the world. I think a lot of this has to do with a profound sense of loss — the sense that we have not only lost those frameworks which made sense of the world for us, but also the belief that such frameworks could exist. And that's where the experience of migrants and exiles has been such an important contribution to visual-arts practice and intellectual life in recent years. If you have lived in two or three different places, then the possibility of there being one way of seeing the world is not something which you desire or feel that you have lost, you can't feel loss about a sense of unity you never had. The possibility of seeing the world, not in a singular way, but in a multi-accented way opens up such enormous possibilities. This is the contribution of those artists and intellectuals, and is also the intellectual framework for the Institute.

NP What do you do with this desire for coherence?

GT We have to engage with the possibility that there is no answer. That is a very, very difficult thing to do and that desire is not going to go away.

NP Is the difficulty of living with this impossible desire the 'new' part of 'the new internationalism'?

GT I have problems with the term 'new internationalism'. It is not an appropriate label to define the artistic or intellectual propositions of this organisation. It triggers memories of nationalism and internationalism that presume another sort of utopian structure for wholeness and coherence.

NP Is the tone of INIVA anti-Utopian?

GT It is about posing questions. For instance, the INIVA conference ended with a series of questions, but no answers. I think that was right, artists pose questions, they don't provide answers.

NP Does it have the appropriate structure for that sort of questioning?

GT It has the ability to bring together ideas and practice. It has the freedom to operate as a kind of producer of things outside a fixed space while working in collaboration and partnership with other institutions and individuals. Where an organisation is led by its exhibition programme, it is this which leads the way for its publications, seminar programme and research. For such an organisation the exhibition is both the end product and the defining framework. As Jimmie Durham said at the conference, given that we are all obsessed with originality and anxious about repetition, perhaps the only thing left to do is to make art that is necessary.

NP Such needs initially emerged from the initiatives of individuals who were marginalised by the dominant culture. But in the future, what sort of mechanisms would you put into place to ensure that INIVA responds to the needs expressed by those who are being marginalised in their own time?

GT The challenge is to maintain that dynamic, which comes from responding to needs as they are defined by practitioners.

NP Are there organisations abroad that you would collaborate with?

GT There are connections with organisations like the Arab Institute in Paris or the Du Bois Centre in Harvard. There are also smaller groups around the world that do not have such a profile but which are working outside of the recognised art establishments.

NP How would you identify them?

GT We are beginning to follow up potential collaborators so that we know what's happening and where we can intervene strategically so as not to duplicate initiatives that already exist. Also the Institute's library and archive will exploit new technology to hold and retrieve information on artists and writers from different parts of the world, and to share that information with others. I think that new technology holds a lot of potential for what this organisation seeks to do.

NP Don't you think that this very technology will be least accessible to those people that you are most desperately trying to get in contact with?

GT In some cases we will not be able to rely on technology alone. On the other hand, there is the case of some rural aboriginal communities in Australia who are now tapping into satellite technology. Nevertheless, I don't think we should take it for granted that everyone has access to technology. I think that this question of access is another key issue for the next century.

NP You often talk about the next century in a very optimistic way — are you hopeful about what will unfold?

GT I am hopeful.

NP So you believe in progress?

GT Progress on the level of dialogue and exchange, yes I do. I believe in it very deeply.

NP And are you confident that you'll survive, financially?

GT Like any other new organisation, we'll be given a fair crack of the whip. It will take four or five years to establish a body of good practice and then I think we should be judged on that practice, on the criteria that we and those funding us have defined. As long as all the players and everyone is clear about what our brief is, and what we are setting out to do, then I feel confident about being judged according to those criteria.

NP Do you fear that people are already shifting the goal posts?

GT I think that's a genuine fear. In some cases the goal posts haven't been clearly defined and that is something that I need to address.

NP What new directions would you, and your board like to see in the future?

GT At our first meeting, the board was insistent that the Institute should build on our strengths, that is offer a dynamic link between artists, writers and curators. That we shouldn't pre-empt that by looking to build a gallery or seeking any other conventional building solution at this stage. The priority is to work with this unique structure and remit. They've also made it clear that we shouldn't act as a funding agency, but that we should work collaboratively and in partnership with other organisations and individuals. We should be aware of our particular context and stress that the Institute is here in Britain: that it has come out of initiatives and perspectives developed in this country and by the work of artists and writers here. The balance of our activities should reflect this and not to be constantly looking outside. And finally, and most importantly to maintain the equal weighting between our four areas of activity: research, exhibitions, education and training.

NP Finally, do you think its possible to maintain a radical cultural agenda without radical politics?

GT I think its impossible to have a radial political agenda without a radical cultural agenda. At the end of the day we are not a political organisation. Of course politics comes into it, politics always comes into art, we are political beings and I wouldn't ague with that. But I'd hate to think that the organisation became pigeonholed as a sort of narrowly defined political organisation which it's not. Whatever politics exists is in the work; it can only come from the work produced by the artists themselves.

10.
WARRING ETHNICITIES AND
GENDERED VIOLATIONS
RAPE IN BOSNIA

MAPS AS SCARS

At Christmas in 1994, the artist Dennis Del Favero, who had been working in the Former Yugoslavia, showed me a map of Bosnia with 27 black points, each one signifying the location of an alleged rape camp. One of the perplexing experiences of simply looking at this map was the sense of recognition. A few years earlier this map would have signified unfamiliar territory, now the name of every town brought with it a chill of horror: we recognise the names Banja Luka, Bihac, Mostar, Prijdor, Gorazde. Together these points seem to form a circle around the dreaded memory of Sarajevo, a history lesson almost forgotten. At the end of the twentieth century, Sarajevo is the symbol of another failure.

The maps of Bosnia have been drawn and redrawn by generals, politicians and peacebrokers. Maps never show the asymmetries of movement: a red line may indicate the path of fleeing refugees; it may also identify the crushing route for the advancing tanks. During the nightly news bulletins, the lines of Bosnia were cut deeper into our consciousness. Borders were pushed and pulled like elastic barriers both to shield one community from another and to signal the end of a history of co-existence. This war raised fundamental questions about the status of cultural difference within nationalist discourse as well as broader issues of transnational responsibilities. Who belongs to and who is excluded from

Europe? What are the boundaries between Europe and the non-European? A definitive answer to these questions is well beyond the reach of this essay. Similarly remote is an outline of the causes and solutions to the Bosnian crisis. My focus is more specific here. It analyses the representations and testimonies of atrocities committed in the infamous rape camps in order to understand the way representations of gender and ethnicity were mobilised to sanction the fury of war.

BACKGROUND TO THE CONFLICT

Located on the cusp of the ancient schism between Eastern and Western powers, the identity of Bosnia has been criss-crossed by different influences. The modern demands that a nation must belong to a singular notion or people who share a memory of common past and who have developed a comprehensive system for communication that supports a unified culture and common language,[1] cuts against the grain of Bosnia's diverse cultural history. Before the outbreak of the conflict in Bosnia, the identity of the people was defined by reference to at least three 'other' nationalities: 43.7 per cent Muslim;[2] 31.3 per cent Serbian; 17.3 per cent Croat; with the remainder 7.7 per cent referred to as Yugoslav or others.

With the breakup of Yugoslavia, Bosnia's future was poised between two divergent trajectories: either a unified state with a multinational polity, or partition according to ethno-specific borders. It was increasingly obvious that the Serbian political elite was not prepared to negotiate over the destiny of the State within a multiracial and democratic framework. For, when the Muslim-led government called for a referendum over the question of independence, Karadzic withdrew his party's participation. Nevertheless, 63.4 per cent of the electorate participated in the referendum of February/March 1992 and 99.4 per cent voted in favour of independence.

With this clear mandate, Izetbegovic called for the international community to recognise Bosnia as an independent state. On 7 April both the US and the EU recognised Bosnia, and on the same day Karadzic declared the existence of the Serbian Republic of Bosnia-Herzegovina. This declaration was backed by the support of the

Serbian-dominated Yugoslav National Army which led all the military advances of the Bosnian Serbs and did not formally withdraw from Bosnia until 4 May 1992, and even then left behind considerable arms and troops. Tensions and occasional fighting between the Muslim and Croat community revealed the fragility of their alliance, and, on 28 August 1993, Mate Boban proclaimed the Croatian Republic of Herzeg-Bosnia.[3] The consequences of this war have been astounding, according to a US Senate report, at least 35,000 killed in the first year, with 2 million refugees in the first six months, and something between 20,000 and 60,000 rapes.

THE STATUS OF STRANGERS

The slogans promoted by ethno-nationalists leave no option for the co-existence of different people, and this proclamation is always premised on an aggressive rewriting of history. To declare 'wherever a Serb, Serbia' or to demand 'Croatia for the Croats' is symptomatic of a belligerent polarisation that removes the space that might include the presence of others. The sudden cult of auto-identification proceeds more out of a system of rejection and hatred, than a slow historical process and intimate scrutiny of self-knowledge.[4] The symbolic debasement of the enemy follows from the transformation of the distinction between 'us' and 'them' into an opposition of absolute difference. On one side there is virtue, justice and humanity and on the other vice, crime and barbarism. In this context it is habitual to think of the enemy as a monster.

> Modern-day nationalists are interested only in the destructive forces that ethnic differences can unleash. When they talk about the right to self-determination, they mean their right to determine who will be allowed to survive on their territory, and who will not.[5]

This conflict between a singular and plural identity raises fundamental questions about the constitution of society and civil space. What is the status of the stranger in a state where no single collectivity has an absolute majority? How does a modern society which is so radically composed of difference negotiate its way out of the demands for purity? This paradox, which is a constitutive feature of modern society, is precisely what the Bosnian war exposed.

With the official withdrawal of the JNA and the attenuation of the links between Serbia and the Bosnian Serbs, it became difficult to conceptualise the advancing forces as alien invaders. The international community has difficulty in enforcing international standards of human rights without evidence of a violation of national boundaries. Yet, to insist that the conflict in Bosnia is an outburst of mere particularistic ethnic violence is another means of avoiding the construction of a transnational framework of social and cultural responsibility. This strategy of avoidance and rationalisation has been well mapped by Branka Magac.[6] Her typology of the West's inconsistency is framed, on the one side, by the reckless disregard of the contradiction between the enthusiasm to dismantle a socio-economic system and the nostalgia for the political unity in the former state and, on the other, a generalised disavowal and repugnance at any expression of nationalism. Somehow the West would like to see itself above and beyond the petty rivalism and particularism of nationalism. The media representation of the war was rampant with denunciations of 'primitive savagery',[7] and sweeping statements like the 'Slavs are genetically programmed for violence'. As one commentator noted:

> What we have encountered among some policy-makers is a sense of scorn and contempt toward the victims of this war. 'The Balkan people are predisposed to violence. This is just a centuries-old tribal war for which there is no cure. It's part of their mentality.'[8]

The repeated accentuation of 'their' difference from 'us' in the media gives ground to those who wish to proclaim a policy of distanciation and containment. Success in policy terms is thereby measured by the prevention of a 'spill over' of the conflict. Analogies drawn between Bosnia and Vietnam, Cyprus or Latin-America say more about the difficulty of naming the causes of the conflict than they reveal common symptoms.[9] Western commentators have, in turn, described the uncertain correspondences between political pledges and military practices as 'Balkan roulette'. By stressing the conceptual and historical otherness of this region such representations attempted to create a secure distance which would buffer the West from a sense of moral implication in the knowledge of and proximity to the conflict. Bosnia became an 'other' place whose conceptual distanciation allowed the West to think of 'ethnic conflict' as 'their problem and not ours'.

THE PRICE OF PLURALISM

In opposition to the accounts which represent the 'inherited antagonisms', and 'primordial characteristics' of ethnicity as the cause of the conflict, Michael Barratt Brown focused on the economic pressure that was mounted primarily by the International Monetary Fund and the unequal distribution of wealth and economic structures in the Former Yugoslavia.

The collapse of economic relations, the resulting administrative chaos combined with the devaluation of the dinar in 1989 and spiralling rates of inflation, reaching at one point 1300 per cent, sharpened the divide between those regions which not only had economic autonomy but also access to foreign currency. Bosnia, the state most dependent on the internal economic structures and one of the poorer, was in that sense a double victim to this process of decentralisation. Michael Barratt Brown argued that the collapse of the regime left the poorer regions more exposed to suffering and susceptible to conflict.[10] The historian Susan Woodward proposed a similar argument as she stressed that the concept of primordial ethnic differences were rationalisations for the struggle over material rewards and political power by new elites. Historical hatreds and cultural resentments, which often contradicted recent experiences of social integration, were successfully staged and manipulated by all sides once the economic crisis had spilled into open conflict.[11]

The crisis in Bosnia is implicitly connected to a contemporary phobia in modern society: ethnic difference. The failure of the West to defend a multi-ethnic society is rooted in a deeper failure to acknowledge that this is also the constitutive feature of its own social order. Society is composed of strangers. However, the unresolved racism that lurks in the nineteenth-century romanticism that underlines all nationalist discourse prevents the West from fully acknowledging, let along defending, the significance of difference. For the West to continue to seek solutions which are devised in terms of separation via cantonisation, is both a denial of its own constitutive process, and a way of indirectly rewarding the aggressor. If the principles of tolerance are precluded from the negotiating process, then there is the presumption that the lines between the different collectivities are non-negotiable and immutable, or that the specific practices of co-existence are alien to this region. From this position, the negotiators are held hostage to the belligerent paradigm whereby the identities of 'others' are not deemed as strangers that can be integrated into a new form of the social, rather they are enemies who have to be destroyed. Zygmunt Bauman reminds us of the hubris of modern totalising systems.

> From our grandfather's dream of a pure and translucent world of rationally managed certainty, our fathers woke up inside, or in the close neighbourhood of, totalitarian prisons. The dream of purity made humans into polluting agents, while reason decrees them redundant, promptly designing the rational technology of waste-disposal. Both the Nazi and the communist experiments had their intellectual enthusiasts. They promised, after all, to do what other addicts or victims of modernity wished, but did not dare: to cleanse the human world of all contingency and messiness; to do away with everything useless and inimical to ultimate harmony and self-confidence of the human species; to put within reach the most daring ambitions or remaking the world. It so happened, though, that what those experiments are likely to be remembered for, more than anything else, are Auschwitz and Kolyma.[12]

THE VIOLENCE OF RAPE

According to reports issued by the United Nations and Amnesty International rape and sexual abuse were widespread in the Bosnian war and all sides committed atrocities. However, Muslim women were the chief victims, and the main perpetrators were members of the Serbian armed forces and Serbian paramilitaries. Within the first year of the war, the European Community reports concluded that at least 20,000 women had been raped. One woman said she had been raped about 150 times during her two-month ordeal. While many of the survivors were reluctant to give testimony — too traumatised to repeat the details, too fearful of further retribution, or too ashamed of the stigma — nevertheless some have broken the silence that generally surrounds this crime. As Nina Kadic has stated: 'For the first time in history we are breaking the silence about mass rapes in the middle of war'.[13]

The scale of rape executed in Bosnia can be compared with the horrors of other wars. Throughout history there are reports of invading armies raping women. This would suggest that rape is a constant in war, a universal feature of aggression. Rape in Bosnia is like rape in Berlin or like rape in Troy. However, the way rape has been used as a *policy* of war and as a means for ethnic cleansing suggests that this is a unique case. It is the combination of five factors; the scale of rape; the targeting of victims; the form of violation; the construction of the rape camps; and the ideology of insemination, which suggests that what was manifested in Bosnia was a new extreme of brutality. There is little to be gained by searching for the right historical precedent, these rapes are both like and unlike other historical examples and, most importantly, it is an event which goes beyond our limited capacities for understanding evil. In this case, appreciating all the facts does not facilitate a clear and absolute judgment.

This does not, by any means, imply that military and political leaders should be absolved from responsibility. The military leaders of the occupying forces not only failed to establish effective preventative orders, but ignored their responsibility to investigate the allegations into abuses of power. In places where they did not encourage rape, local authorities often condoned it. Accounts of the rapes in Bosnia point not only to the random and individual abuse of women but to a pattern that conforms to a general policy of genocide. Apart from the more conventional raping of women and children in their own homes, there were accounts of prominent women being publicly gang raped, girls whose vocal chords have been torn because they have been repeatedly raped in the mouth, pregnant women whose stomachs have been ripped open, the foetus removed, and pig's flesh stuffed into the stomach.[14] Violations such as these were conducted by, or with, the aid of the military, police or para-military forces.

Rape and sexual abuse in Bosnia had been conducted in three types of situation. First, there was the regular abuse of power by the military forces or local authorities, whereby women were abducted temporarily or raped on the spot. Second, women were often raped while being held in places of detention. Third, there were other detention centres to which women were transferred solely or mainly for the purpose of rape and sexual abuse.[15] These infamous 'rape camps' were sometimes to be found in remote hotels, mining camps, or sawmills and on other occasions located in local schools, halls and civic buildings.[16] Few women returned to their families; one, who survived a three-month detention in a 'worker's hut', told her story to Amnesty International. They reported her account of the conditions in the following terms:

> Twenty-four women were held in her hut, although she believes
> she saw about 100 women in total as they were unloaded. She and
> others were beaten upon arrival and on later occasions. Twelve
> women, including the informant, who were held in her room were
> raped in the room in front of the other women on multiple
> occasions, sometimes by more than one man at a time. Other
> women who tried to defend her on one occasion were beaten and
> one of the perpetrators told her, 'You will bear a Serbian child'.[17]

THE CONTEXT OF RAPE

Accounts of rape are present in almost every record of war. For
every Troy there is a Helen. Every call to war is spliced with the
imperative to defend the honour and chastity of mother, wife,
sister, daughter. The enemy, by definition, stands accused of being
a rapist. Since the French Revolution, the identification of the
nation as either the combative *mère-patrie*, or the defenceless
woman raped, has become part of the routine repertoire of
propagandists. The gendered image of the nation has been linked
to the prior association between the fecundity of the mother and
the fertility of the soil. In Bosnia we are witness to a unique twist
in this horrific but universal feature of war. The myths and hysteria
of rape that accompany the battle-cry have been pushed to the
limit, both by the scales of actual horror that even defies the reach
of the propagandist's rhetoric, and through the *explicit* incorporation of rape in the practices of war.

At this point the conceptual links between war and rape become
obvious. Rape is the meta-metaphor of war, it is the metaphor of
war that is implicit in all the other metaphors of violation in war.
Consider the parallel between the strategies of aggression through
appropriation, submission and penetration and the syntax of rape.
The very language for occupying other spaces is linked to the language for violating other bodies. The order for rape does not just
come from above, it comes from within the culture of war. It also
comes from a fear of non-identity, whereby a sense of who I am is
constructed not out of reflection and exchange but from a system
of rejection and hate. The militant Serb is defined in opposition
and through the negation of the Non-Serb.

THE USES OF RAPE

In the Bosnian war the rationale for rape was articulated through the discourse of patriotism. Rape was almost always ethnicised: the perpetrator and the victims rarely shared the same nationality. Even in the cases where Croat soldiers were accused of raping Croat women, they claimed that rape was a punishment against those 'treacherous' women who aided their Muslim neighbours.

Cris Corrin has argued that the raping was done 'in the name of one nation against another'.[18] Rape was inflicted in order both physically to violate the body and to assault the mental and social stability of the victim. The psychological injury and social upheaval was part of the perpetrators' aim. For rape was not only a means of gaining revenge and intimidation over women, but also a weapon for destroying the social fabric by violating sacred codes, attacking the concept of family honour, coercing confessions, extracting information and punishing women for the activities of fathers, husbands and brothers.

The incorporation of women's sexuality into a culture of militarism was extended beyond the occupation of other women; it also, and primarily, involves a scrutiny of one's own women. Some women's groups in Bosnia have claimed that the practice of raping the enemy's women was conceived as a form of desecration against the symbols of that nation. This link is made explicit in the discourse of nationalism which is articulated through the metaphor of the idealised mother. Going against the substantial historical grain of mixed marriages, love for land and language is thus inflected through an idealised image of a pure maternal figure. The mother binds together the family of the nation and an exclusive allegiance to her cedes the basis of belonging. As the idealised image of mother shapes the discourse of the nation, the politics of the nation reinforce the expectation of women to be judged according to the idealised standards of these symbols. Corrin has observed that the Bosnian Serbs resurrected medieval symbols of motherhood, such as: 'Yugovich, the long suffering, brave, stoic mother of nine offering her children up to death'.[19] A woman's contribution to the nation was thereby defined through a militarised cult of blood and soil.

The status of women is thereby defined not by her subjectivity but by her maternal function. By offering children to her husband

and the nation she donates her body to the perpetuation of a name and the protection of the 'fatherland'. It is this donation of the body for the service of the 'patria/patriarch' that becomes a target for appropriation and usurpation by the enemy. To break this cycle, the rapist aims not just for violation, but also impregnation. The woman's body is reduced to a 'cocoon' that can be captured and manipulated to ends that suit the other side. Amira S., a survivor from a rape camp, recalls the words of one of her rapists.

> It is our responsibility to bear a child who is the carrier of specially required genes. We Serbs have a particular code in our genes that has already been transmitted for centuries through our descendants. You are only carriers of our future offspring.[20]

This reference to 'particular codes in our genes' recalls the collective hysteria over the rape of French women by German soldiers in the First World War. At that time, the scientific thesis of the telegonist imprint, or the contaminating seed, had gained plausibility. It was presumed that the qualities and traits of a primary male were passed on to succeeding offspring via the mother despite impregnation by a second father.[21] The Serbian ideology on rape has a similarly bizarre presumption, and it is this transmission of the 'superior gene' that defines the duty to rape. Once the Muslim women were impregnated their own bodies were reduced to the role of an incubator for the Serbian sperm. There is an obvious biological flaw in this argument but, in military terms, the logic is appallingly simple: the supply-link for future Muslims has now been converted into a carrier for the Serbian race.

Rape exposes both the male anxieties over possession and the ambivalent role of women in the discourse of the nation. The link between rape and dispossession in war is a deliberate inversion of the domestic bonds that constitute patriarchal marriage where possession is consummated by the woman bearing a man's child. The woman is meant to deliver a child that will carry his name and defend his nation. The aim of impregnation in rape runs along the same lines of logic, but in reverse: the invader steals the woman from the patrial space, sexual appropriation signifies the break from this community and threatens the continuity of its bonds, and the ultimate impregnation initiates the deliverance of his child. If a woman is, on the one hand, a mere 'cocoon', and on the other a privileged symbol of social order, then she will always be the site of rivalry among men — tied to their demands for (un)broken bloodlines. Impregnation not only drills at the male fear of impotence to defend his home, but also threatens to disrupt any future reintegration of the family. In Bosnia, rape was also a form of banishment: it was done so the victims could never return to their community. Shame and stigma would sever relationships to the past, kin and family. In the words of one victim: 'We all feel that we have lost everything. We have been abandoned.'[22]

The objectives of war in Bosnia were not confined to capturing territory and subjugating the occupants. The policy of ethnic cleansing demanded the erasure of others. It was not about controlling others but about displacing them. Wiping them clean off the surface and eliminating their historical presence from the territory. Every trace of the historical legacy of Muslims had to be expunged. Overcoming the military 'muscle' of the opponent by crushing their army was accompanied by the elimination of their cultural memory: twelfth-century libraries burnt, mosques dynamited, doctors, lawyers, judges, professors targeted and then 'disappeared'. This war attacked the body at all levels. The symbol of the other and the process of elimination proceeded on three fronts, from muscle and brain to reproductive organs. To eliminate any trace of the other in the psycho-geography of a community was an exercise in the genocidal fantasy: the extermination of the other for the security of the self.[23]

NARRATING RAPE

The consequences of rape in Bosnia are difficult to predict. The status of the few survivors and that of the 'rape babies' is uncertain. Little research has been conducted on the fate of such women and it is impossible to comment on the barriers and stigmas they may face, or even on the intensification of the very bonds that the rapists tried to destroy.[24] Responses are thereby caught in a complex bind whereby the urgency to speak out and intervene is held back either by the fear of deeper shame or by the futility of inspiring counter-productive revenge attacks. Women are therefore hesitant in speaking out because it is uncertain who will assume the responsibility of justice.

The difficulty with narrating rape is paralleled with the difficulty

painters have in showing rape. Mieke Bal's illuminating commentary on Rembrandt's two paintings of the rape of Lucretia picks
up on his tendency to represent the events leading to or following
from the actual rape. Looking at the paintings we can reflect on
the act only from the distance of time, or the perspective of another
who was not involved. The act itself is depicted, at best, metaphorically. Bal argues that Rembrandt failed to show the rape not
because of the restraints of public taste but because the act of rape
makes the victim invisible. The classical images of rape tend to
abstract the pain and displace the site of violation so that the spectator may identify with the victim.[25]

Will the call for acknowledgment only lead to greater personal
and social injury? If the onus of proof is put on the woman to
prove that she either did not 'provoke' or failed to display sufficient resistance, if the community stigmatises the innocent victim,
and if the father, husband or brother feels compelled either to pun-
ish the woman or put himself into a state of suicidal vengeance,
then this will only compound the woman's personal trauma. Jenny
Sharpe has argued that the reporting of raped English women during the Indian wars of independence was used to sanction the use
of colonial force. Violence, it appears, is never so extreme as when
it is executed under the banner of morality, for the mere uttering
of violation to women and children, 'exempts the male from sanity'.[26] Similarly in Bosnia, the metaphors of rape which focus on
the suffering of women concentrate on the sense of guilt and shame
and imply that a third party — a custodian — has responsibility
to seek retribution if not exact revenge. This appeal entwines the
brother, husband, father — as legal defenders — with the rapist —
as illegal assailant — in a battle of outrage and a contest over honour. Her own violation is thereby addressed, but only indirectly,
that is, through the male's desire to seek revenge for the transgression against his chattel. It was a crime in so far as his authority
was challenged. It was a violation as his bloodline was stained. It
was an appropriation as his household was damaged. If this is the
only justice that the victim can find, is it any wonder that they may
chose silence.

Kate Millett argues that memories of rape are often mediated by
an inherited guilt that trails from the assumption that 'sex is
female, a female responsibility'.[27] Amira's rapist, Milan, re-enacts
this fantasy when he declares that he is not just punishing her, but

also unleashing the secret that lies in her unspeakable desire. He projects himself as the one who responds to her treacherous femininity, in his eyes she *is* sex, the embodiment of bestial rhythms. Amira describes the way her body is fragmented by the gaze and clutches of the rapist.

> Who cares about legs here? The breasts are needed here. The
> breasts that can be bitten or cut off or grabbed so violently that a
> woman could die from pain. But the rest, the spot that is
> considered by each male to be the centre of the world, is saved
> until last and then used in any way imaginable.

The violence of rape is thereby framed in a matrix of incarceration, appropriation and violation. As the body is taken by another, physical pain and symbolic wretchedness spiral into an infernal votex. Amira describes how even when the pain ebbs the fear raises again from the uncertainty of when she will be attacked again, and the constant search for an answer to the question: 'when will this ordeal have an end?'. Humiliation is manipulated as all parts of the body are made open, available, public. The shattering of the traditional codes of dignity, privacy, intimacy, surrounding the genitalia is the first objective. Without bodily intimacy social boundaries start to collapse. Then time begins to warp, not just by the enclosures of space, but by the arbitrariness of containment and the impossibility of rescue. The boundaries between pain and relief blur and a rush of panic sets in.

Amira fears that she will always stand accused, as if her very nature had provoked aggressivity. This interpretation does not come from an understanding of her 'nature' but follows from the ideology which has constructed feminine sexuality as the arousal of bestial desires. The effect of patriarchal ideology is thus projected as the cause of rape. Self-recrimination is accounted for in these terms: she provokes sexual aggressivity because the husky desire of being taken is already within her, and he both obliges by giving 'it' to her and then punishes her for taking 'it' from him. A cycle of vengeance and attribution. She wanted 'it' and therefore deserved being violated. After the rape there is the further 'self' punishment that comes from a sense of worthlessness, a feeling which follows the experience of appropriation, which is how the rape began. The raping continues as it rebounds inside the memory of the act and against the consequences of the act itself. A murderous cycle of victimage and self-destruction begins with the expression, 'I must have deserved it'. It is echoed in the resentful eyes and averted gaze of neighbours who could offer no defence, and then staged most gruesomely in the public procedure of the trial. The victim is often mentally raped again by others.[28] To avoid such further pain many women wrap the agony of rape in silence.

THE BANALITY OF EVIL

The motivation for rape in this war cannot be explained purely in terms of the sexual gratification of savage *chetniks*. A more complex answer is necessary, one which takes into consideration the specific combination of political ideologies, historical traumas as well as psychic drives. In her profound interpretation of the technologies for internalising Fascism, Rey Chow points out that the underlying sentiment is not of hatefulness and destruction but one of loyalty to a higher body, 'Fascism is about love and idealism'.[29] The drive to eliminate the other is the same drive as the purification of the self. By incorporating rape into the strategy of ethnic cleansing it has been perversely linked both to national duty and the banal exercise of power over the enemy. Although populist rhetoric invariably caricatures the enemy as a 'crazed savage', the real identity is not that alien or distant. The men who rape are often neighbours getting 'revenge'. Soldiers doing their 'duty'. One soldier admitted to his victim that he was ashamed of being a Serb, 'We have orders to rape the girls'.[30] They are ordinary men seduced by their inflated powers and excited by the powerlessness of their victims.[31]

Whether the torturers be vengeful opportunists, hardened bullies or petty officials, all simply following the brutal flows of nationalist policies, the crux of their complicity lies not in their personal motivations but in the construction of political frameworks that validate and encourage such atrocities. Responsibility has to be directed both at the individuals who executed the suffering and at the leaders who created the framework in which a torturer is permitted to exist. A situation had been created where minor injuries could be projected on to abstract political claims or personal grievances conflated with vague historical traumas.

> After the actual fighting ended, most of the killing was personal.
> It was settling accounts with someone who stole your girlfriend or
> who didn't lend you a cigarette.[32]

It is surprising to note that the task of the torturer is framed by such banality and that it invariably includes elements of pleasure and sociability. The now familiar rationalisation expressed by Nazi torturers, 'I was just doing my job' draws a continuum between the obedience of the torturer who was 'just following orders' and the dispassionate administrator who stated that 'neither do I have any personal hostility against Jews, nor am I a sadist'. The proximity of administrator to the torturer turns open the question as to whether we all have the capacity to be a torturer. Who has the moral strength to question and refuse the standards that he or she has been told to fulfil? It is the force of circumstance — the promise of rewards, the satisfaction of pleasing authorities, the desire to participate in a new social order — rather than pathological inner drives which dominate the worldview of the torturer. The torturer does not act alone; no matter what ingenuity or vigour he displays in the execution, he does not invent the framework of torture and, crucially, to underline the social aspect of torture, it is always conducted by a group. Gang rape not only bonds the members but also compounds the victims' sense of worthlessness. With public rape, the humiliation is magnified by the very knowledge of its perpetuation. It is not just that one man has overpowered the victim, but that everybody on his side is symbolically entitled to violate her. Amira states in her diary: 'There was no man within hundreds of kilometres who was not entitled to come up to us and ask to be served in any imaginable way'. Utter worthlessness is engrained deeper as the very status of the torturer is made indiscriminate.

FRAMING EVIL

The prevailing explanations of rape in war proceed from two diametrically opposed assumptions. Rape is either a result of the essentially destructive instincts in human nature, or it is part of the techniques of institutionalised terror. Yet both explanations fail to grasp the totality of the horror. The first view gives far too much weight to the internal and supposedly unfathomable features within the psychology of the perpetrator. According to this view men do not *become* rapists. For this would imply at some earlier point in their lives they were not rapists. Rather, it stresses that the potential of rape is always present and within. Whereas the second approach emphasises the way terror is orchestrated, it addresses evil as if it had a function and intention. From these perspectives the horror of rape makes sense only if we accept that the individual and the system already had the potential for evil and that, given the right circumstances, it would be unleashed and explode into this infernal destiny. However, the closer we get to evil — the more we see it in both its random outbursts and its chilling rationale — the less convincing these explanations seem.

In Primo Levi's powerful account of survival in a concentration camp we are constantly confronted by the question in his title, *If This is a Man*. This question rebounds in every description of suffering, hunger, cunning and endurance. We see it being answered in the documentation of what is done to this man, and what this man must do to preserve his dignity and survival. The closer we read the more we learn about *how*, but the further we get from understanding *why* the Germans killed the Jews. Near the end of this book he admits, 'No one can boast of knowing the Germans'.[33]

We still have little understanding of why evil takes root. Evil does not listen to logic. It opens its own ground and feeds from within its own drives. It can be a reckless fury with centrifugal energy driving itself towards an enemy, but from all directions at once. It does not follow the straight lines of malice. The madness of evil is not an individual folly, and it is a delusion to presume that evil can be bridled within the professionalisation of the military machine. Evil is intrinsic to the culture that makes war. No legal scale which holds the norms of human dignity and social order on one side can hold evil on the other. The two cannot be compared in any sense of positive or negative, they refuse to be translated into each other's language. Evil is not commensurable with habitual thinking and, in one sense, there is no space for evil in modern law.

While the wars in former Yugoslavia have been described as the 'most listened to, photographed, monitored, overheard and intercepted entity in the history of mankind', the dissemination of information by the primary gatherer, the CIA, has hardly been motivated by moral concern for human justice.[34] This agency had compiled comprehensive lists of existing concentration camps, identified sites where massacres had been conducted, determined which leaders had sanctioned war crimes, but it refuses to pass on such information for fear of also divulging its 'methods and sources'. Requests for evidence from the United Nations, The International Tribunals and Red Cross were met with stonewalling and footdragging. The idea that protecting 'sources and methods' should take precedence over the prevention of genocide says a great deal about the hope for justice in the 'New World Order'.

The international response to the Bosnian crisis has failed to conceive a framework that can establish peace within multi-ethnic parameters, or genuinely to understand the suffering of rape victims. From the outset, the prevailing strategies for peace have only considered different ways of mapping segregation. This in turn has fuelled nationalist sentiments and ethnicised both the causes and the responses to the war. The political shortcomings have been compounded by a complex set of legal barriers that have not only limited the possibility of apprehending known war criminals but also constrained the very definition of war crimes. For instance, rape is not in and of itself a crime against a specific gender, it can only be legally addressed as a crime against humanity. Yet the primary 'evidence' that rape was conducted in such a way that meets these criteria is often lacking. The rape camps, for example, are often difficult to locate. They were located in temporary centres, and their identity was easily camouflaged and routinely denied. The difficulty of identifying perpetrators and then documenting their whereabouts is heightened by the problem of establishing a neutral authority that will have the capacity to conduct investigations and execute arrests. International agencies can offer little assistance, the UN does not have the power to make arrests, the International Tribunal on War Crimes in Former Yugoslavia cannot try people in absentia, and the International Red Cross is forced not to disclose information that might compromise its neutrality.[35] The contradictions between high-sounding principles and shabby political practices, which numerous critics have exposed,[36] also point to the hesitancy in constructing what Edward Said calls a 'new universality'.[37] The failure of the West to defend a multi-ethnic society is rooted in a deeper failure to acknowledge that this is also the constitutive feature of its own social order.

The International Criminal Tribunal for the Former Yugoslavia does not have jurisdiction to try the crime of rape as a crime in and of itself. As the crime of rape has to amount to a crime against humanity,[38] the incidents of rape conducted by soldiers who seized the opportunity to abuse women cannot be considered by the Tribunal unless it can be established that this specific abuse of power has been committed as part of a policy of war.[39] Thus the Tribunal draws a clear distinction between the individual acts of rape and the organised or systematic practice of rape. Only cases where there is a certain mass or concentration of victims can be considered as a gross violation of the human rights of non-combatants. Françoise Hamsen has also pointed out the precise criteria against which rape can qualify as war crime. Only those cases of rape which can be clearly linked to the policy of ethnic cleansing could be investigated by the Tribunal. To demonstrate this link the victims must not only prove that they were raped but that these rapes were conducted in any of four circumstances. First, that rape was used to terrorise the civilian population or forcing people to flee from their homes. Second, in circumstances where the raping of women was conducted while being detained. Third, when women were being held for the explicit purpose of being raped. Fourth, if there was the added intention to impregnate the women in such a place, then this, she suggests, does raise questions about genocide.[40] Thus the crucial part of a victim's testimony is the need not only to establish that she was actually raped in the course of the war, but that the course of the war included rape.

Even if such cases were successfully brought to trial further questions remain. Would the judgments appear legitimate to both sides? Would the structures of justice seem adequate in the face of the inflicted pain? Visna Kesic, from the Centre for Women War Victims in Zagreb, doubts whether the legitimacy of a trial would be respected as long as one ethnic group sees itself as being persecuted by everyone else. To be judged by one side is often the cause for vindication by the other. Your pariah is my martyr. She argues that, without the groundswell of internal initiatives and commitments for justice, the neutrality of the procedure and the justifications for punishment will not be accepted, they will appear as another imposition by a foreign and illegitimate will and only block any steps towards reconciliation and catharsis. Kesic also argues that the provisions within International Law that have been set up for the protection of human rights are far too abstract and generalised to safeguard women from violation. The inadequacy of prosecuting rape as a war crime is revealed in the definition of the consequences of rape. Kesic states that the 1949 Geneva convention 'describes rape as a crime against integrity, dignity, chastity etc., it is never defined as a crime against a gender, that is, a gender crime'.[41]

Even if all the rapists were identified, and brought to trial, how do we treat the convicted? Revenge is the act of inflicting as much damage as you can to the object which caused you harm. Retribution and reprisal demand reciprocal but proportional punishment. Who would rape the rapist? What value is there in further indulging in these abhorrent acts? To reintroduce the vengeful tactics and callous mentality of the perpetrator would not display any further reverence for the qualities of human life. The question is not whether the convicted deserves the same that he gave, it is not a matter of seeking justice in terms of such diabolical balance, but rather an opportunity for looking for an exit from the tragedy. With the impossible burden of corroborating the testimony of rape victims, the legal system makes itself more receptive to the man's fury than it does to a woman's voice. If the law were more responsive to the women's testimony rather than being shaped by male anxieties over national possession, family honour and racial continuity, then what would it say now? People always have to live with other people:

> As for those who have been struck by one of those blows which leave a being struggling on the ground like a half crushed worm, they have no words to express what is happening to them. Among the people they meet, those who have never had contact with affliction in its true sense can have no idea what it is, even though they may have suffered a great deal. Affliction is something specific and impossible to describe in any other terms, like the sounds of which nothing can convey the slightest idea to anyone who is deaf and dumb. And as for those who have themselves been mutilated by affliction, they are in no state to help any one at all, and they are almost incapable of even wishing to do so. Thus compassion for the afflicted is an impossibility. When it is really found we have a more astounding miracle than walking on water, healing the sick, or even raising the dead.[42]

REFERENCE NOTES

1. For an outline of the characteristics of nation building see, Miroslav Hroch, 'From National Movement to the Fully Formed Nation', *New Left Review*, 198, March-April, 1993, p.5.
2. The Muslims got the right to declare themselves as a nation in 1971 when instructions for national determination were adopted.
3. Philip J. Cohen, 'Ending the War and Securing Peace in Former Yugoslavia', in Stjepan G.Mestrovic, ed., *Genocide After Emotion*, Routledge, London, 1996, pp.44-5. The term 'ethnic cleansing' was first introduced by Serb intellectuals who promoted plans for the territorial expansion of Greater Serbia via the displacement and elimination of all non-Serbs. Its most explicit articulation was found in the 1986 'Memorandum' of the Serbian Academy of Arts and Sciences.
4. The phenomenon of obfuscating facts through the manipulation of latent emotions and buried historical traumas has reached complexity and variety in the Former Yugoslavia, that this has prompted a sociologist to devise the term post-emotionalism and edited a collection of essays on this subject. See Mestrovic, op.cit.
5. H. M. Enzensberger, *Civil War*, Granta, London, 1988, p.22.
6. Branka Magac, 'The Destruction of Bosnia-Herzegovina', *New Left Review*, 196, November-December 1992.
7. J. Keegan, 'A Primitive Tribal Conflict only Anthropologists Can Understand', *Daily Telegraph*, 15 April 1993.
8. I. Nizich, 'Crime and Punishment', *War Report*, No.33, May 1995, p.29.
9. See for instance the representations in AIM (Alternativa Informativna Mreza) a network of independent from all the republics of former Yugoslavia.
10. Barratt Brown, op.cit., p.267.
11. Susan Woodward, *Balkan Tragedy*, Brookings, London, 1995.
12. Zygmunt Bauman, 'Age of Extremes', *New Statesman and Society*, 3 February 1995, p.19.
13. Nina Kadic quoted in *A Weapon of War,* produced by T. Morten, ABC Radio National, 10 April 1994.
14. A. Ahmad, 'New Metaphor in the New World Order', Impact International, March-April 1993.
15. The Final Report of the Commission of Experts (established Pursuant to Security Council Resolution 780) 1992 documented the existence of rape camps and the use of rape as a policy of war.
16. Amnesty International, *Bosnia-Herzegovina: Rape and Sexual Abuse by Armed Forces*, AI Index: EUR 63/01/93, January 1993.
17. Ibid.
18. Cris Corrin, 'Issues of Violence Against Women in Eastern and South-Eastern Europe', unpublished paper, June 1994.
19. Ibid.
20. Of the numerous testimonies from the victims of the rape camps that I have read, I have chosen to quote from only one. All unreferenced quotations are from the diary of Amira S. from Foca, whose testimony has been submitted to the United Nations International War Crimes Tribunal for the Former Yugoslavia.
21. Ruth Harris, '"The Child of the Barbarian": Rape, Race and Nationalism in

France during the First World War', *Past and Present*, No.141, Nov. 1993, p.196.

22. Roy Gutman, *A Witness to Genocide, Element*, Shaftesbury, 1993, p.72, Roy Gutman was the first Western journalist to document the existence of Serb run concentration camps in Northern Bosnia.

23. I. Nizich, 'Crime and Punishment', *War Report*, No.33, May 1995, p.27.

24. The policy of women's centres in Zagreb was to allow the women to have an open choice from keeping the child, putting it in an orphanage or having an abortion. Most of the women in the rape camps died and very little is written on them. Personal correspondence with Helen Durham, member of the Australian Committee of Investigation of War Crimes in Former Yugoslavia.

25. Mieke Bal, *Reading 'Rembrandt'*, Cambridge University Press, Cambridge, 1991, p.61. See also a report by a psychologist working with victims of rape who has described their symptoms as 'mostly intensive fear, dream disorders, obsessive pictures and memories, and very often depressive and delayed depressive reactions. Almost every day the women have a new reaction, because of facing intensive trauma, and also because of lack of nutrition. They also have feelings of guilt, feelings of diffused anger, distrust of others and loss of self-esteem. We work in group therapy on transactional analysis crisis and circles.' Marjana Sanjek, 'Regional Reports: Bosnia Herzegovina', *Helsinki Citizen's Assembly: Violence Against Women in Eastern and Central Europe*, Publication 8, p.31.

26. E. M. Forster quoted in Jenny Sharpe, 'The Unspeakable Limits of Rape: Colonial Violence and Counter-Insurgency', *Colonial Discourse and Postcolonial Theory*, eds Williams and Chrisman, Harvester, London, 1993, p.235.

27. Kate Millett, *The Politics of Cruelty*, Viking, London, 1994, p.174.

28. An index to the depth of silence in which rape is held can be found in the recent exposure of the mass rapes of German women by Allied forces. For a commentary on Helke Sander's film Befreir and Befreite which depicts the confusion and resentment of rape victims in this war, see Irit Rogoff, 'From Ruins to Debris: The Feminization of Fascism in German History Museums', *Museum Culture*, eds, D. Sherman and I. Rogoff, University of Minnesota Press, Minneapolis, 1994.

29. Rey Chow, 'The Fascist Longings in Our Midst', *Ariel*, Vol.26, No.1, January 1995.

30. Gutman, op.cit., p.68.

31. See also P. Lancaster, 'The Gender Weapon', *The Middle East*, No.210, April 1992, p.8.

32. R. Block and P. Ellingsen, 'The Inhuman Moment', *Spectrum*, 3 June 1995, p.4.

33. Primo Levi, *If This is a Man*, translated by Stuart Woolf, Abacus, London, 1987, p.145.

34. Charles Lane and Thom Shanker, 'Bosnia: What the CIA Didn't Tell Us', the *New York Review of Books*, May 9, 1996, p.10.

35. R. Marthner and R. Van De Krol, 'UN Seeks to End Convoy Attacks', *Financial Times*, 18 November 1993.

36. See Branka Magac, 'The Destruction of Bosnia-Herzegovina', *New Left Review*, 196, November-December 1992; Barratt Brown, op.cit.

37. Edward Said, 'Nationalism, Human Rights and Interpretation', *Freedom and Interpretation*, ed. B. Johnson, Basic Books, New York, 1993, p.196.

38. See Article 5, Statute of the International Tribunal.

39. Graeme Blewitt, deputy prosecutor for the Tribunal, *A Weapon of War*, op.cit.
40. Françoise Hamsem, *A Weapon of War*, op.cit.
41. Ibid.
42. S. Weil, *Waiting on God*, Routledge & Kegan Paul, London, 1951, p.65.

11.
ZONA DI TRANSITO
WITH IMA KORJENIC

The following collage of voices is taken from a radiophonic documentary feature called *Diaspora* produced by Tony MacGregor and Virginia Madsen for The Listening Room, ABC. My text was first written to accompany *Pietà*, an installation designed by Scenario Urbano which was commissioned by the Art Gallery of South Australia. Scenario Urbano is a collaboration of artists and designers — Dennis Del Favero, Tony MacGregor, Derek Nicholson and Eamon D'Arcy who are engaged in the production of multimedia projects for museums, radio and urban sites. The group was initiated by the Italo-Australian artist Dennis Del Favero. Zona Di Transito was a project which examined the experience of the refugee — the experience of dispossession, of being 'in transit' between a place called home and somewhere else, a twilight beyond relationship.

Nikos Papastergiadis What did you see on the other side? Who received you? What will you do?

Ima Korjenic My name is Ima Korjenic. I came to Australia five months ago. I live in Sydney, in Liverpool, with my father Ismet Korjenic and my mother Sadia Korjenic. We came to Australia as refugees. Actually we were driven out from our town, the town of Mostar in Bosnia-Herzegovina.

A DREAM WHICH IS NOT IT

The cherry trees in my town bloom in April. Every April in Mostar is florid with purple petals.

The gardens of Mostar in its spring sun, in the twilight are full of marvellous poesy and majestic music.

Everything creates a perfect harmony — the fiery colour of the setting sun; the emerald green Neretva river, the glittering of the roofs in the moonlight; the neon lights of the city.

But the spring of 1992 was a dreadful contrariety. The colossal black smokes from the burning buildings and the dense red blood of the wounded and killed in the streets.

Horrible cannonades and tank attacks.

War, fearful war. Screams horribly resound in the night.

No this is not a dream.

This is not me any more. I look at the bullets in the wall of my room, the broken pictures on the piano. The pain and anger in my father's eyes. Pippy my dear parrot does not talk any more. The days are passing by in the fear. I am leaving. Fear. Faithlessness. Doubtfulness.

I have counted the days in a refugee camp with a couple of books in the corner of the little room, and with photographs from my childhood. Very often, before bedtime I wet them with my tears. The avaricious news on the radio does not say anything good.

My Mostar still flames and slowly disappears.

So my hope is that I will walk again with my friends in its flowery alleys.

I came back to finish my schooling because the news said the war was finally coming to an end. Unfortunately that was only a false hope. On Sunday at 5 am we were taken to the concentration camp. Strange and savage soldiers have robbed, threatened and beaten us up.

Thanks to my father we managed to escape. After a couple of days hiding in a cellar, we reached the free territory.

And here I am now in Australia.

My suitcase is my life. There are only my books, awards, diplomas, souvenirs, and memories from Venice, Sarajevo, Paris. I have also taken my études from Bach, Chopin, Grieg, and two old framed edelweiss from a little Swiss hotel. I could not take my Pippy with me so I left him with my best friend.

But I will live. I will fight. I must do it for my dear Mostar, for new Australia, and friend Moya who has gifted me her piano.

Perhaps the sun is sad and bloody, but it grows and rises and I want to shine stronger and stronger everyday.

After 18 springs spent in Mostar, filled with odorous blossoms of the cherries, I hear the new sounds, I hear the sound of the Western spirit and impulse.

> When we imagine our lives, certain images and stories come to mind, arrivals and departures; places, faces, journeys.
> Sometimes we can reconstruct these events and passages.
> Sometimes we can invent such moments through stories.
> For most of the time the ability to remember and to visualise is governed by someone who I will call the internal narrator.
> When I curse myself, it is this person who I despise; when I feel glad, it is he or she who fans my heart.
> This voice is a capricious guide.
> Sometimes I wonder what it would be like to leave home not only alone but without the voice at the centre of my movements.
> Would this be the way to madness, or the beginning of facing the unknown? Perhaps when all things come apart, and some of us become refugees, it is this faint voice which we seek to hold with tremulous gestures.

This is how it actually happened. It was 7 May 1993. We were in our flat, everything was quite peaceful, it was Saturday night. We could feel something, the situation was tense.

> What is exile other than the last chance before death?
> Please remember two facts. Exile begins with the impossibility of staying at home and in the necessity of starting again somewhere else.
> Between near and far, hope and fear, there is a chance, and it is for this that everything is risked.
> I try to think of the multi-directional risk of exile. And I suspect that what fuels the gamble is the vortex of the present suspended by the conflicting energy of the past and of the future.

My Dad said, 'The Croatians started to burn the Muslims' houses and their shops and their properties ... And the Croatian army was there all the time ... and we saw them coming closer to our house, early on a Sunday morning. We saw lines of people going from their house, from buildings, ... thousands of them ... But we didn't know what was going on ... we didn't know where they were taking them ... We knew something was wrong, and everyone went out of their houses ... First they said Croatians are looking for military persons, soldiers ... but of course, that wasn't true, because all of us were civilians ... They bashed the door with their guns and things ... And they came in and said: 'We're going to kill all the Muslims here. Get out as soon as possible.' And we couldn't take anything from our house. We went out in our pyjamas and slippers ... We didn't know what was going on ... and suddenly I realised we were surrounded by all those Croatians with guns and ... waiting to die or something ... and then we saw them coming in, just ruining everybody's flats ... And they took everything, everything from us.

> Think of those moments when you were caught
> between two poles,
> suspended in panic, and forced to wait,
> wrapped in darkness,
> your torso frozen by its own sweat,
> and the blood burning your feet into the ground.
> An unbearable stasis that brakes the urge to start and to get on.
> But no, you must not, and cannot move,
> trapped inside the walled tense of nowness,
> you scream, but like a mute.
> Second by second
> Bang following thud. Time against time.

My mum said she didn't tell our neighbours or friends that she was leaving. She says, 'Because I was too scared and I couldn't trust anyone .... By that time our town was full of enemies already and they ruled the city. We had to be really silent ... we couldn't make a move ... and we were very suspicious, everyone was suspicious who was in the street, that was why I didn't say that I'm leaving, and I didn't say where I'm going or anything ... that's why ... two bags would be enough ... you know ... to get killed ...

> Better the Devil you don't know.
> Is this the peculiar motto for survival in exile or the modern
> dilemma of differential damnation?
> Given the choices a refugee is thrust into, the parameters of the
> question dissolve into the horizon of luxurious arrivals.
> Then again, which of us can claim the privilege
> or even desire the position of arrival or fixity?

There is a race for difference, a new symbolic hierarchy.
Look at a migrant and a refugee.
Hold on to their commonalities as you witness the measure of
compulsion in departures.
Yet it is the very measure which has been blurred by the 'new
world order': how do we now distinguish between the dream of
opportunity and the search for security?
Who is to judge between an economic advance and a political
retreat?
The difference between the two is as marked as it ever was.
The difference is blood.

Our baggage still has the shape of that old bridge that was torn
down ... of course there is no old bridge now, but still we think it's
going to go through some kind of transformation or metamorphosis to exist again ... and sometime perhaps our luggage may be
the luggage of return.

My father told me of a dream he had long ago, and now I want to
hear it again, he refuses to tell it.
There is not even an explanation, just a swift 'nope', and a
shifting of the eyes.
Picking up the dice he continues with our game of backgammon,
ignoring my repeated requests.
There was something familiar about the landscape of his dream,
it had an intimate texture, even the faces of the strangers
seemed familiar to me.
I wanted to enter this space again and to witness his encounter
with those three men dressed in long dark robes.
I wanted to hear his bemusement over their Latin reply to his
Greek greetings, and their ensuing dialogue in English.
These three men were wandering along the frontier of his village,
they were not lost for once they had lived there, and were now
passing by without coming into the centre of the village ...
He knew they were his ancestors, and so he rolled his double sixes
again.

What did you take with you when your village was burning?
What could I take, it was not the first time, my feet took me.
Where did you go?
Away. At first we didn't know where to go. There was just the
need to escape. You must understand how your sense of direction
changes when you are desperate. The difference

between here and there becomes everything. All you see before you is a horizon which you call 'there', and this horizon is all that seems solid. Nothing in your life prepares you for this.

Nomads are always on the move, but they know where they are going — they are on supply routes. Migrants follow the routes of their vague hopes and try to reroot their ambitions.

We were just fleeing without direction, knowing that what was behind us was our own destruction, and if we stood still it would swallow us. To stand without falling, this was the pressure of fear.

What did you see on the other side?
I saw the lights and I saw that not one had been lit for us.
Who received you?
Only the poor let us stay near by, but this was not always easy, we could not see each other's limits so we still have to defend ourselves. As for the rich, their pity is confined to two things, first their need, then their guilt. If they need hands to dig their dams then they will take us, and if our faces do not reflect back the sins of their fathers we are invisible.

What will you do?
We will stay until we can return, but we already know that our homes are gone for ever.

12.

THE ENDS OF MIGRATION

The starting-point for critical elaboration is the consciousness of what one really is, and in 'knowing thyself' as a product of the historical process to date, which has deposited in you an infinity of traces, without leaving an inventory. Therefore it is imperative at the outset to compile such an inventory. Antonio Gramsci

All that we know we know by direct action — such as a bee sting — or by metaphor. Jimmie Durham

Stories and images of the self, on what ground do they rest when the 'I' has been dislocated from home? Who is represented under the sign of 'I' when the boundaries of the self seem unstable and the history of identity uncertain? The radical transformations of modernity have fundamentally altered the form and representation of identity. The social and the personal are always intertwined. Migration often accentuates the complexity of this relationship. Physical bonds might be severed but symbolic links and cultural values persist within the memories and adaptive practices of migrants.

This essay examines the relationship between the experience of migration and the forms of representation that are utilised to make sense of the self in a foreign place. I will focus on three artists who live in Australia and present a reading of their work which includes a dialogue with the postcolonial and deconstructivist theories of identity. This dialogue, between critical theory and cultural practice, is motivated by a deeply held belief that these contrary forms of inquiry and representation are also parallel attempts to address the open questions of identity in modernity.

The 'migrant experience' is often cited as a symbol for the dynamic of rupture and integration that cuts across the whole epoch of modernity. The nature of this symbol is itself deeply problematic and contradictory. Does it construct another set of universals that deflect attention away from the specificity of historical experience? Is the very figure of the migrant adequate given the vast differences in the form of displacement? It seems that we must now reflect upon the conceptual language that is available for representing the 'migrant experience'. For instance, Australia has been described as a nation of immigrants and indigenous peoples. While the extreme cases of marginalisation: genocide and ethnocide have only been inflicted upon the indigenous peoples, the violence of appropriation has not been confined to such a neat dichotomy. The institutional claims of belonging and the powers of displacement have always been inflected through complex racial and cultural axioms. 'In Australia,' Juan Davila observes, 'the only options for identity are alienated ones.' But what is the language for representing this interminable alienation?

The central concepts of minority discourse — displacement and alienation — have been recurring themes in the humanities and the social sciences. This shift has brought new levels of attention to the concepts of border and cultural identity. Hence a few qualifications need to be stressed from the outset. First, borders do not presuppose isolation. Or, conterminously, we cannot make the automatic assumption that the increased mobility of people and the intensification of information exchanges will dissolve borders. Borders persist despite flow and continue to exist through the social processes which regulate exclusion and incorporation. Therefore, the function of the border is not only to keep particular individuals out but to maintain the discreteness of cultural categories. Second, the distinctiveness of self-identity is not based on the exclusion of the other, nor does cross-cultural interaction lead unequivocally towards acculturation but, rather, relatively stable identities are formed across boundaries and within dichotomised cultural zones. This is not a process of being singularly bound by the gaze and practices of dominant institutions, however, when these institutions do turn their eyes to the margins, they should at least consult the histories that have been excluded by its own practices.

The tensions between the centre and periphery in Australian art discourse is stressed by George Michelakakis's recent survey — a study which highlights the differentiation that occurs even in the margin.[1] There is, he argues a part of the margin which the centre deems to be too marginal to be even acknowledged as the margin. The oppositional model of centre and periphery needs to be reconsidered, for in a culturally heterogeneous society the dynamism between centre and margin which was operative for the avant-garde may prove to be too limited.

Thus it should be clear that, in this context, to address the other is not to summon a figure that is always outside mainstream discourse. The migrant drama of suffering, nostalgia and reconciliation has become a story with which we are more or less familiar. If different migrants have different stories to tell, then we are left with two tasks: specifying the particularity of these stories, which would test the range and depth of permissibility and responsiveness in storytelling and storylistening; and second, to investigate the lines of institutional selection, which would reveal the way the storytellers are divided.

Let me now face my own title: 'The Ends of Migration'. It implies, paradoxically, that migration seldom finds an end for, at the point of arrival, the journey forks delta-like. In his novel, Wilson Harris suggested that the voyage begins with the fear of death and that arrival is greeted with 'Mixed metaphoric senses in voiceness, voicelessness, speech prior to speech, dumbness prior to eloquence'.[2] The protagonist who is named Hope, finds himself alive but caught in a triangle of questions.

> When one descends into breakdown — part physical, part mental
> — and is drawn up into space, what equation exists between the
> multidimensionality of the mind and the multidimensionality of
> the ship of the globe written into one's sense? How shall I begin to
> put it? How shall I translate untranslatable truth?[3]

The transition from silence to language may seem lonely but it is never a solo journey. 'Untranslatable truth' is always regarded from myriad positions, and, in these times, the language which oscillates between the axioms which Wilson Harris eloquently invokes, is the language of minority discourse.

The work of Elizabeth Gertsakis is but one of the many possible starting-points from which we can witness the persistent dialogue between recuperation and projection in the interpretation of absence. Her photo-essay 'Innocent Reading for Origin', 1987, uses the images from her parents' past to address the silences and gaps in her own history. Her own narrative is, in part, built up from the old photographs that showed her parents in Greece, their place of origin. These are images which immediately speak of the distance travelled from Europe to Australia, and within the two tenses of past and present. They confront a seemingly insurmountable gulf between a traditional community of peasants and the modern city, nevertheless these images are gathered as fragments of the self.

Looking at her relatives dressed in their 'good suits', posing before they go to an annual carnival, one begins to reflect how the muddy soil under their shiny shoes is always home and work. Viewed from another country and a different generation, this place assumes a dream-like quality: deeply personal but also unfamiliar. Gertsakis's selection of images and the readings that she makes of them demonstrates a fascination with hierarchies, gestures, appearances and objects which are only partly familiar to her. It is in the shadow of this fascination that bodily poses and objects inspire an investigation into an order and cultural interaction that cannot be explained by the language of the present. By a strategic use of symbolism, these images reveal the 'poverty' of sources with which she can invent her past. After all, the 'archive' from which she draws is but the small collection of black-and-white photographs that her parents had stored in an old Italian shoebox. Gertsakis knows that the whole story never was, and probably never will be fully articulated. What is significant is not just an acknowledgment of the details of the other life but the residue which calls for admission into this life. They attempt to read the story of origin not within a linear narrative but from a position of incommensurability. The only symmetry between past and present is the oscillating value of lack and plenitude, within these images of hardship and deprivation there are also stances of strength and courage. The banality of their everyday can today appear heroic.

But what makes these images innocent? Is it in the hope for salvation through the logic of Christian inversion? It is not the act of reading that can summon the nostalgic allusion that 'things were better then'. Nor is there a promise of inheritance. The timing of innocence is neither in the future nor in the past but in the present. These images of origin can only be read innocently in the absence of a history that would otherwise frame them. The borders of these images are the questions she asks in the adjacent texts. The aesthetic response is, to a large extent determined by a specific context. If these signs have a claim to priority, that is that they speak of a lack in cultural signification before this lack had already found a place in the narratives of migrant discourse, then this marker of emergence must also be a factor in its reading. What could once be read with innocence, through retrospection and in the clamouring din of multicultural competitiveness, could today be misread as naïve. There is no protection for the past.

THE TROPICS OF IDENTITY

Minority discourse is coeval with all the migrations, displacements and ruptures of modernity. The grand and petty journeys of conquest, the expulsion or marginalisation of strangers, the dismantling and undermining of the traditional: these quests did not lead to the great house of transcendence. All these dreams and energy did not construct a world free from darkness. Rather, the counterpointing legacy of the West's enlightenment is indelibly stamped in the rapid torsion and teeming hybridity of the post-colonial city. If we take the nation state as the political, cultural and administrative unit which exemplifies the trajectories of modernity, then we can see the deep contradictions between difference and similitude that lies in the belly of the beast: the unisonant calls for the birth or the resurrection of 'a people' has always had to contend with the dissonant languages of 'the people'. The constant challenge for the nation has been the negotiation of the limits of difference in a context that seeks to strive towards unity.

Given that there is an increasing rhetorical acknowledgment of demographic diversity in the modern urban landscape which has, in turn, created new forms of identifying and labelling others, and if the new form of 'tagging' identity is expressive of another level of repressive tolerance, then the theoretical framework for investigating the questions of subjectivity will also require rethinking. The tropics of identity, the way we see and the means through which identity is articulated, are also shifting. We can no longer presume that engagement with minority discourse elevates us to the moral

highground outside the mainstream. The radical is not just oppositional any more. This does not mean that the centre has collapsed,
fragmented or deconstructed itself, but it does mean that the mar-
ginals are now in a radically different position. When we refer to the
shifting of borders of exclusion and contestation there is also a need
to draw attention to this dual process of containment and transgression. How then can we broach the new politics of inclusion?

There are, as Stuart Hall outlines, at least two ways of understanding the signifying practice of cultural identity. On the one
hand we can think of cultural identity as a symbol: on the other,
we can think of cultural identity as a metaphor.[4]

As a symbol, cultural identity is often transformed into a fixed
and rigid construct. Its potency rests on its putative timelessness;
its ability to radiate, to signify incessantly throughout history. It
becomes the token which is at once the source of a people's unique-
ness and the basis of its unity. It is by forging a relationship to this
symbol that the person is distinguished from 'Them' and becomes
one of 'Us'. While seeming immeasurable and eternal, the status of
the symbol can however, vary according to the cultural and political power of 'the people'. In times of oppression and struggle, the
symbol can serve as the catalyst for the redemption of self-esteem
and the demand for self-respect. In this sense, the symbol can be
seen as the last vestige of value and also the call to recapture the
values it once embodied. It suggests a sense of plenitude and unity
that existed in the past, and by virtue of this existence it condemns
the condition of lack and fragmentation in the present. As Benedict
Anderson has demonstrated in *Imagined Communities*, the formation of such imaginary constructs was crucial for the emergence
of nations.[5]

To think of cultural identity as a symbol which needs either to
be resuscitated or brandished is to presuppose a belligerent condition. The symbol is well suited to warfare. It enables the
production of an identity that can oppose the identity of the other:
often, the oppressed have begun their resistance to the oppressor
with re-searches into the self. In this sense, cultural identity as symbol becomes a resource in the opposition to or the unyoking of the
identity conferred by the dominant regime. The problem with cultural identity as symbol is that it draws its energy from the
binarism of purity and corruption. The potency of the symbol rests
on its intactness, its uncompromising and intransigent survival

throughout millennia. The symbol thus also inspires the language of exclusion and defensiveness.

There is another more open-ended but not necessarily less vigilant way of thinking about cultural identity. To see cultural identity as a metaphor is to think of the difference in similitude, and vice versa. With cultural identity as metaphor, the significance of identity is not fixed on to a singular track that maps origin and destiny according to primordial and immutable laws. Metaphor stresses the inventiveness in the inventing of one's past. For, after all, to intervene into the present and to suggest possibilities for the future requires creativity. And metaphor, which is nothing but the seeing of thisness in thatness, is therefore also a recognition of the other in the self, and again, vice versa. In metaphor, the emphasis in cultural identity shifts from being to becoming. Metaphor acknowledges that cultural identity comes from the past but it also gives voice to the transformation that occurs in the history of the sign, that is, in its coming to the present. The past no longer stands as the imperious judge of authenticity. For cultural identity is not just the recovery of the essence which was lost, but is also the discovery of the plurality in history. Cultural identity is thus not achieved by 'fencing off' of a particular cultural territory but is found in the way we are represented and how we represent ourselves in relation to a particular construction of the past.

With symbol and metaphor, we have two radically different ways of understanding and utilising cultural identity. Symbol suggests a rather defensive and backward-looking conception of identity and defines itself through the aggressive binarism of essence and purity. Metaphor is a more consensual mode. It illuminates the possibility of continuity within a configuration of difference and similitude, it demonstrates the productive, rather than the destructive side of mixture and hybridity.

These distinctions could be worked through with reference to many of Juan Davila's paintings. The titles alone resonate with the theoretical debates in cultural identity; Hybrid, 1989, and Portrait of Bungaree, 1991, Self-Portrait, 1984, This is not Juan Davila, 1983, Self-Portrait, 1984, Politically Incorrect Self-Portrait, 1988, Fragile Self-Portrait, 1992, Pre-Modern Self-Portrait, 1988. These paintings do try to portray a self, but in no way are they self-portraits. Even when the artist's subjectivity figures in them there is no attempt at solitary introspection, there is no search for the true self.

Nor is there any attempt to reproduce outward appearances. In the metaphorical sense of cultural identity, these works are autobiographical. They could not be autobiographical in the conventional sense of the genre, for where in this intense traffic of signs is there an origin? The relationship to the self is one of conscious and imaginary distortion. Self and other is split, only to be grafted back together in a perpetual doubling act. The sources are not in a personal past, nor in the interiority of a particular stream of consciousness. Rather, the identity that emerges is one which simultaneously deconstructs the stereotypical cultural identity as it implodes the various intersections and missed opportunities in the discourses of art history. These self-portraits are not testaments of character or explorations of inner worlds, they are revelations of possible configurations between one body and another, whereby the body becomes a screen upon which languages commute. This is what Juan Davila represents, the autobiography of missed opportunities in dominant art history.

After rejecting an academic or literal reading of the history of each sign, how do you interpret a Juan Davila portrait? Understanding these paintings is not as simple as decoding the history of the respective signs that are portrayed within them, for the meaning is not just in the culmination but also in the juxtaposition of the difference between signs. It is by their being put together and by the rupture of referential codes, that is, by virtue of the method rather than a narrativisation of the content, that an allegory for the contemporaneity of these images can be found. In these portraits one can see three histories: Australia, The Americas and Western Europe, and more importantly, an 'hysterical' shuttling amongst all three.

When confronted by an artist who so self-consciously shuffles between various self-images, why should we continue to use artistic practice as proof of some form of identity or another? Juan Davila, despite his protestations, has been described as 'Australia's foremost sodomitical artist',[6] presented as an iconic 'queer artist',[7] a 'satirist'[8] who exposes hypocrisy in the institution of art and debunks high culture. A recent debate over the homoerotic staging in both the death struggle of the nineteenth-century explorers Burke and Wills, and the now cracked relationship between Hawke and Keating, was trapped in the stereotypes of whether or not the representation of anal sexuality is a symptom of a deeper aggressivity.[9] The figures that are cast in his paintings may have anomalous associations for some. They are often interpreted as coming from his own subjectivity and as messengers for new social norms.[10] 'I am not a man,' he has said. 'I impersonate one.'[11] I would not see him as the artist as transvestite, but I would say that as an artist he transvests all the components of identity and representation.

Instability in the staging of identity should not be confused with moral vacillation and political procrastination. Nor should the profusion of cultural symbols and the collision between national symbols be taken as a sign of either dazed loss or passive consumption in the traffic jam between either formalism and kitsch, or bucolic idealism and pornographic smut. Davila's attention to both the intersection and the instability between images and things suggest an awareness of the porousness of the boundaries which the dominant culture would prefer to see as impervious. The desire to demonstrate sloppiness, contamination and interpenetration can also lead to a mis-interpretation of the energy within intention. Is this sheer perversity? Perhaps, but then to be a pervert suggests that you are seeking not only to gain pleasure by disturbing somebody else's moral development via playing with their sexual orientation, but also that the playful intervention or just the passive observation is in itself an act of harming. Harm is done because the subject is either weaker or caught in a moment of weakness. The vulnerability of youth or the defencelessness in the moment of intercourse are not situations which Davila manipulates. Quite the contrary, his attention is directed toward the subjects of macho-political strength. He prefers to paint Paul Keating bending over. He represents the legendary machismo of a liberator through the unbuttoned tunic of Simon Bolivar. He 'sodomises' the figures, not the bodies. It is the symbolic space given to 'our leader' that he attacks, not their biography, or rather it is the gap between these two discourses that he seeks to expose. He attacks the historical legacy rather than twisting the potential for a moral judgment. Much of the criticism that has surrounded Davila has focused on the literal side of perversity. What is missed is the complexity within his resistance. Davila is a very dirty artist, because more than anything else he is opposed to purity. According to Mary Douglas's definition, dirt is simply:

> matter out of place ... When there is dirt there is a system. Dirt is the by-product of a systematic ordering and classification of

matter, in so far as ordering involves rejecting inappropriate elements.[12]

Guy Brett also argues that Davila confounds the conventional notions of the body. In his paintings, the body, like the distinction between inside and outside, is always out of place, 'shattering traditional unities and amalgamating things which are not supposed to touch. It is plain to see that 'body' is both carnal and sexual and an argument of visual codes.'[13] Much is said of the figures that Davila desecrates, but there are other figures where the painterly spirit shifts from malevolence to benevolence. For instance, there is both Juanito Laguna and Bungaree. It is no coincidence that, given the multiple layering and processual formation of identity, that Davila concentrates on the ambiguous in-between figures, or rather the go-betweens of colonial encounters. The most difficult element to see within these paintings, but perhaps more generally the crucial one in the images forged by Davila, is this attention to the dynamism of exchange and the politics of submission. The subtle sense which discriminates between giving in and giving up, the fine silky patience implicit in the tactical and tactile appropriation of the forms of the other to secure survival.

The 'go-betweens' like Laguna and Bungaree that Davila identifies with are neither representatives of the subaltern, nor are they visualisations of his own alter ego. They should be seen as imaginary and fictive identities, mythical and metaphorical spaces, which are relatively open-ended. These are identities which exist between pure virtue and absolute vice. Davila sees them as a zone, a surface upon which others have projected and they themselves have introjected fantasy and fear. With these figures we can begin to see the price of the exchange between the coloniser and the colonised. Or, after a closer examination, we can consider the fluidity within maleness and femaleness, then we can ask, 'what am I trying to pass as?'. These questions are powerfully answered in Baldwin's writing.

> Alienation causes the negro to recognise that he is a hybrid .... In White America he finds reflected — repeated, as it were, in a higher key — his tensions, his terrors, his tenderness. Dimly and for the first time, there begins to fall into perspective the nature of the roles they have played in the lives and histories of each other. Now he is bone of their bone, flesh of their flesh .... Therefore he cannot deny them, nor can they ever be divorced.[14]

From this position we can ask who are the figures in Davila's paintings? Why did he pick up Juanito Laguna, an imaginary boy who holds the aura of an angel and promises release? Why the double-dressing Bungaree, who walked naked with the Aboriginal people and wore Western clothes when among the colonial officers? Perhaps his concern is not only with the heroism in these risky characters but the fact that they are metaphors: they connect like with unlike, translate difference, carry meanings across borders, move us from here to there. After all the etymology of metaphor is linked to the function of a porter, and it is to and from this humble service that Davila pays and gains tribute.

With metaphor we can witness the vital dialogue between the two vectors in cultural identity. For, without metaphor, how would we investigate the tropes for the construction of similitude and continuity, or consider the position from which difference and rupture operates? To quote from Stuart Hall's essay on 'Cultural Identity and Diaspora':

> What recent theories of enunciation suggest is that, though we speak, so to say 'in our own name', of ourselves and from our own experience, nevertheless who speaks, and the subject who is spoken of, are never identical, never exactly in the same place. Identity is not as transparent or as unproblematic as we think. Perhaps instead of thinking as an already accomplished fact, which the new cultural practices then represent, we should think, instead, of identity as a 'production', which is never complete, always in process, and always constituted within, not outside representation.[15]

As one is constantly speaking from the 'bodies' of the self and the other one must also ask how it is received?

READING THE OTHER

The antennae of the mainstream are well tuned into the margin when its delegates speak with the voice of sentimental realism. Sentimental realism is achieved by exaggerating the base of experience and sacrificing the complimentary axioms of methodology and perspective in the creative process. That is, the validity of a work is measured by what it purportedly represents, rather than the way a subject is observed and the manner in which it is ordered. This is a fundamental truncation of the working out and working through that occurs in the image/text. And there is a tendency when a new discourse emerges that its critical reception is often limited to an identification of the artist's subject position. The shock of the new is somehow broken if it can be tied back to a particular set of experiences, that is, if it can be observed without the threatening fear of ubiquitous ruptures — of being engulfed by a sense of alienation in the text. For if the alienness of the author's experience can be brought forward to house, or even to ghettoise this sense of difference, then it can be contained, fixed and observed with the comfort of pity. Its realism can then be sentimentalised, and the links between us and them can be safely attenuated — abstracted to the level of paltry platitudes and spurious universals.

The perception of minority discourse as a category which contains a unified body of writing is always in danger of jeopardising the chief characteristic of this field, that is, cultural difference. How do you categorise such diverse writings under one heading? One way of getting around this paradox is by exaggerating the base of experience and by sacrificing the attending axioms of perspective and methodology. I think that such strategies are counter-productive. In order to address the cruciality of the migrant's perspective in critical theory, I would like to reconsider the status of narratives which reconstruct the history of the self. The conventional genre for such narratives is autobiography. However, in the case of minority discourse this genre could not be applied automatically.

All autobiography confronts the task of excavating from the remains of history: a search for the fragments that signify the qualities of lived experience. These are problems that a diasporic writer also confronts in an accentuated form. Since there are few fragments to be found other than those that have been retained by memory. The historical sources that one can turn to are often either inaccessible because of the 'tyranny of distance', or have been annihilated by the ravages of history. However, above and beyond the substantive problematic of rewriting the past, of the arduous pain of finding the 'facts', there is also the issue of how such a story can be written. What language, what genre will accommodate such stories marked by such intense pain and which often involve an experience of epochal shifts: from the traditional to the modern, from Fascism, to Communism and then to capitalism, all in one lifetime.

If autobiography is the genre which conventionally privileges the subjective experience of the author, then the relationship of its three component parts — auto/bio/graphy — is radically deconstructed by the representations of identity in minority discourse. Given such unstable conditions for both the subject matter and the process of writing, the heading 'autobiography' was probably inadequate, also because of the curious relationship between the other and the self in these narratives. The supposed stories of the self were more often than not a discovery of the otherness in the self, the multiple identities that struggled within the personal, and an awareness of the profound difficulty in deciding who is the true 'me'. Since needs and names mutually define themselves, I will give a name to this supplementary genre. I will call it allography: 'other-writing'.

To evaluate the representations of the modern self we need to extend our understanding of autobiography. There is no doubt that all autobiographical accounts of the self reveal the instability of memory, that is, the profound oscillation between history as self-recollection and fiction as self-invention. Steering this dialectic and fuelling these narratives, is the great expectation of discovering the 'real me'. Yet what would autobiography mean if the first principle was not the retrieval of a stable set of past experiences but the need to recoup a possible past in order to invent a stability for the present? To this paradoxical claim — that access to that which we are most intimate with, the self, is uncertain and obscure — there are additional facets that one must also investigate. What happens to our self-image when the symbolic space is not only uncertain but seemingly deformed and truncated? That is, when the images for the construction of the self are also weapons for the destruction of another part of the self? What happens when the subject who writes a history of the self is also the subject of West's ethnography of the other?

These questions are symptomatic of a reflexivity that is characteristic of the body of thought generated by feminist and cultural theorists who are redefining the concepts of identity. My concern with the developments within this minority discourse is in how it impacts on the categories and practices of self-representation. For if the notion of the self is radically deconstructed in minority discourse, then surely the evidence for this will not be merely witnessed in the rhetorical and exclamatory discourse of ethnocrats. The energy and trajectories of these transformations is more clearly evidenced in the works of artists who converted the tools and forms of representation that were used to describe them into instruments of self-projection. When the artists who had been previously relegated to the margin take over the prerogative of representation, then there is not just a sort of 'theft' back of power but also a challenge to the traditional structures of agency. Those histories which were described in static and distant forms are now the sites of vibrant activity and unsettling intimacy.

DECONSTRUCTION AND AUTOBIOGRAPHY

It should be noted that autobiography itself is a far from stable concept. In his seminal essay 'Autobiography as De-Facement', Paul de Man has traced the problematic literary assumptions upon which autobiography rests.[16] He begins by challenging the claim that autobiography is a genre whose literary status ought to be elevated in the canonical hierarchy. He presents his critique from two positions. First, that due to the looseness in the definition of style and periodisation there is no coherent autobiographical mode. Second, while genre conventionally designates a duality and hence a distance between an aesthetic and an historical function, autobiography rests on an unstable convergence between the aesthetic and the historical.

In autobiography the distance between fiction and reality is collapsed: the perspective on life always rests on one subject and the aesthetic of this perspective must also emerge from the identity of the subject, that is, the author. However, in characteristic fashion, Paul de Man, after opening out the anxieties of autobiography's claim to being a genre translates these 'weaknesses' into strength:

> We assume that life *produces* the autobiography as an act produces its consequence, but can we not suggest, with equal justice, that the autobiographical project may itself produce and determine the life and that whatever the writer *does* is in fact governed by the technical demands of self-portraiture and thus determined, in all its aspects, by the resources of his medium?[17]

Thus, for Paul de Man, the significance of autobiography shifts from being one of the lesser genres in the literary canon, to being a figure of reading, a trope for interpreting and understanding that occurs more or less in all texts. The interest that he attaches to autobiography is not in its reliability in revealing self-knowledge, but in its demonstration of the self-inventiveness of self-representation and the openness of the text. For Paul de Man, autobiography is of interest not because it can offer another category within the literary canon, but because it is a perspective which challenges the construction of categories and hierarchies in interpretation and understanding. However, these insights would take on further shades of complexity if they engaged with minority discourse.

The subtle filiations between autobiography and fiction can be cut across by a third term: allography. In the first instance it refers to the process of representing another, but more importantly it gives a name to the genre that emerges from the postcolonial and migrational confrontation of the other within the self. Allography is the text that is produced in the enunciation of cultural and sexual differences. It addresses that writing which commences from either the shattering of the previous self, or the process of writing the self into foreign spaces and in turn reinscribing it as 'familiar'.

Thus my purpose is twofold: to re-evaluate of the status of autobiography and to supplement this genre/figure by sketching a possible outline for allography. These two concepts do not stand together in any oppositional framework, and there are other parallel attempts to define the status of texts which cross the border between the life of the author and the life of the work. Jacques Derrida's essay 'Otobiographies' similarly attempts to restructure rather than dissolve the genre of autobiography.[18] He, too, problematises the oppositions and the categories which lend stability to the identity of a life as opposed to the identity of a text. The 'oto' which he offers as a substitute to the 'auto' — a substitute which ironically is almost inaudible — comes from the ear of the other. It is this ear rather than the self which signs as it multiplies the story of origin in the text. With the example of Nietzsche's *Ecce Homo*, Derrida shifts the locus of meaning away from the author and locates it not just at the point of reception but across the tremulous borderline, or what he calls the *dynamis* between outside/inside, life/death, autobiography/thanatography:

> Whenever the paradoxical problem of the border is posed, then
> the line that could separate an author's life from his work, for
> example, or which, within this life, could separate an essentialness
> or transcendality from an empirical fact, or yet again, within his
> work, an empirical fact from something that is not empirical —
> this fine line itself becomes unclear. Its mark becomes divided: its
> unity, its identity becomes dislocated. When this identity is
> dislocated, then the problem of the autos, of the autobiographical,
> has to be totally redistributed.[19]

Derrida has frequently used the trope of *prosopopeia* to identify
the disfiguration of a face, or a voice as it passes into language. He
has eloquently invoked the future oriented dynamics of memory.
He knows that memory can harbour that which cannot be anticipated in the present as it holds 'the past as experience of the
promise'. But if we cross the hallucinatory trope of *prosopopeia*
with the gifts of memory and run this through the problematics of
cultural difference, would this then take us into allography?

Extrapolating from this question, we can see that the gift of
allography is not merely a familiarisation with the past and a reconciliation with that which has passed. Its pleasures do not derive
from the comfort of plotting journeys taken. Rather, it takes a
more unsettling programme, by defamiliarising the assumptions
that gloss over the fissures in identity, allography begins as it plots
the journey that beckons.

Derrida's critique has radical implications in terms of the interpretative practices. He is drawing our attention to the enigmatic
link between the body and the corpus of the author as he attacks
any reductive equivalence between the I that writes and the I that
is written. He is questioning the status of the so-called empirical
facts which motivate psycho or socio-biographies. But my attention to autobiography is more concerned with the problematics
of writing and representations. I am trying to evaluate the status
of those texts whose notion of identity is radicalised prior to and
at the point of writing. Derrida would challenge this difference
but I will draw attention to the claim that the question of cultural   difference   radically   inflects   the   process   of
self-representation and that this question had not been addressed
in Derrida's *Otobiographies*.

THE POLITICS OF ALLOGRAPHY

For those who come from the margin, the entrance to the space of cultural representation is preceded by a questioning of the jagged line between the formation and deformations of identity. From this point on, the processes of recognition and dialogue are neither symmetrical nor parallel. This is why every intervention from this perspective is a political as well as an aesthetic gesture. One must fight for the claims that are attached to the name of the space into which one's production and identity are being inserted. Allography is about the process of writing oneself into the political arena — it is the political act of making oneself visible within cultural discourse. We could turn the emphasis around and ask, what concepts and frameworks have emerged which can carry the foreign across the border and into the familiar, or even better bring the familiar in proximity to the foreign? How has the non-modern, or the part-modern, been conceptualised in terms which exceed the paradigms of Primitivism and Romanticism? With the acknowledged heterogeneity of metropolitan culture, how has this redefined the structures of language and interpretation? Have the migrants smuggled in foreign concepts; tucked in different ways of seeing with their labour? In the buckling and yoking of foreign words is there a new syntax of cross-lingual conjunctions? Do we have metaphors for the state which is a patchwork of arrival and departure? Or from another angle, is any of this traffic acknowledged in the modernist discourse of incorporation and postmodernism's articulation of incommensurability?

What are the categories, the grammar for the in-between states, the neither-nors and both-ands of the modern world? One solution is to say that everything is modern. Yet the prize of modernity can be a hollow one, especially when it presupposes the disavowal or the obsolescence of cultural otherness. To map the contradictory traces of this age is not a task that calls for preserving the pre-modern past nor an open embrace of techno-Utopias, but a focusing on the present from these pressing and contradictory tenses.

My concern here is not with the rhetoric of victimage which equates authenticity with suffering. I wish to explore the bases of subjectivity, but not through the small doors and narrow corridors of sentimental realism. We must go beyond the armchair assumptions which relegate autobiography to the preservation industry.

There is some perverse comfort in making the margin conform; making its story clear with fixed beginnings and discernible ends. The more predictable the passage, in terms of the structural laws of tragedy and redemption, then paradoxically the more valuable it appears to the mainstream. Autobiography is not just about remembering the place you have left behind but could also be about what emerges from the 'nostalgia' for the place called the future. Autobiography need not always begin with a search and end with the rediscovery of the home in the past, but might commence with the continuous homecomings and incessant beginnings within the present. Allography embraces these qualifications on the historical and aesthetic functions of the autobiographical text and is the torch which illuminates the impact of cultural difference in the construction of identity within dominant discourse. Allography refers to those texts which are written from the borders or the unacknowledged positions within the West. It comes from the problematisation of the first person pronoun 'I'. While autobiography is born with the simultaneous validation of individualism and the crisis of individuality, allography emerges from the crisis in defining a subject position both experientially and philosophically. It is not just the trauma of entering modernity but the problem of defining the relationship between identity and solidarity in modernity.

Returning to the role of metaphor in the representation of identity, and to the re-evaluation of autobiography, consider Gayatri Chakravorty Spivak's essay 'Asked To Talk About Myself ... '[20] From the outset, Spivak presents us with the theatrical metaphor of 'staging' (a metaphor which she will sustain throughout her essay in order to challenge the 'pernicious' linkage between origin and agency), to test the degree to which a language has the capacity to mirror experiences which are incommensurate with its own history. The tension between Western discourse and the everyday experience of people that have been violently catapulted into the West by colonialism is situated on a number of levels, and Spivak consciously shifts the boundary that separates the public from the private to illustrate the metaphorical 'invagination of identity'. The second part of her essay is introduced as a 'palimpsestic rememoration'. She is recounting the memories, that another person, a psychoanalyst, no less, made her remember. But the palimpsest (that surface of secondary inscription which effaces the original) serves as a metaphor for cultural identity as 'becoming'. Consider her opening remarks, the way she sets out her problematic, and juxtapose these statements with Stuart Hall's earlier formulation of 'identity as "production"'. For Spivak, the question of identity is always a staging of identity.

> To feel one is from an origin is not a pathology. It belongs to the group of groundings, mistakes that enable us to make sense of our lives. But the only way to argue for origins is to look for institutions, inscriptions and then to surmise the mechanics by which such institutions and inscriptions can stage such a particular style of performance.[21]

It is not necessary to give an account of her autobiography; the focus is on the necessity of staging an *aporia*. (An aporia is the understanding that emerges when one finds oneself between two undecidables and discover the capacity to remain within this situation. It is a scenario where you are 'damned if you do, and damned if you don't' and you therefore go on.) In Spivak's case, the aporia arises from the fact that there is no mutual correspondence, no form of equivalence or echoing, between the institutions and inscriptions of her formative years in India and those of her current place of residence in the US. This autobiographical dilemma is then ingeniously staged by reworking the ellipses in her dialogue with the psychoanalyst, through the classical myth of Narcissus and Echo. We can then ask: what are the options for a global-feminist-Marxist-deconstructivist like Gayatri Chakravorty Spivak? Is she to stay within the institutions and inscriptions of the Indian self (the androgynous seer Tiresias has already warned that this is the way to madness) or is she to be an Echo — one who always gives back to the First World Narcissus the end bits of 'his' utterances. Is Spivak caught in the undecidability of echo or counter-echo, disavowal or mimicry? In the teeth of the undecidable either/or, Spivak talks about the capacity to internalise conflicting and incompatible models. She, as always, opts for the both/and. The position that she claims for herself is the position of movement. In this configuration, she claims for herself the position of the shuttle: 'In this stumbling double bind, the impossibility even of echoing a rejection, is the postcolonial woman's (formal, not substantive) shuttling predicament'.[22]

Spivak is conscious that this feeling of, or for, origin is double-edged. It can be both a resource for affirmation and a balm that soothes the pain of homelessness. What then are the options for critical engagement with this 'feeling'? Is it to make a political or moral judgment about the particular destiny that this feeling summons? But even before we launch ourselves in this direction, Spivak reminds us that the function of a critique is to note the location and the trajectory of such institutions and inscriptions. Spivak is drawing our attention towards the disjuncture between the feeling for origin and what might be called the original condition, or home, and that this desire for home occurs in a context of homelessness. Hence, it is the distance between these positions which deflects, displaces the calling for origin on to another sphere. From this vantage point, Spivak asks another question: how to articulate these perceived instances of rupture and return which occur at the most intimate levels of everyday experience, or what she calls 'fragments in clinamen'.

In the attempt to define her own subject position as a postcolonial critic she stresses that this role is not just an echo of the already defined position in either the First or the Third World. To illustrate her predicament she proceeds with a close reading of an Ovidian narrative, one which Freud overlooked in his account of narcissism, and as she reveals, this is not a simple mirror relationship. The coupling of Narcissus and Echo is not confined to a narrative of the former articulating and the latter repeating back. The economy of symmetry which purportedly constructs Narcissus as plenitude and Echo as lack is broken when Echo refuses to answer Narcissus's question 'Why don't you fly from me?'. We are left with a similar silence in response to the question, how does a critical discourse like psychoanalysis fail — because in this context it can only fail — as it addresses the particularity of these clinamens at an untenable level of universality? Spivak stresses that the level of recognition that psychoanalysis offers is too abstract to be *meaning-fully* recognised by the subject.

The discourse and institutions of visual art are faced with a similar aporia. Recent Western extravaganzas like the *Magiciens de La Terre* and *Il Sud del Mondo* were faced with the problem of what critical framework can embrace cultural diversity.[23] The claim that the particular objects on display were all part of universal and much more humanist aesthetic kept undoing itself. But we do not have to go very far to be reminded of these contradictions and the pregnant silences in mainstream art discourse. Everywhere today, the stranger is always already here.

THE STRANGER WITHIN

I want now to consider the work of Constanze Zikos. In works from his 1992 exhibition D.I.E (an acronym for *death is everywhere*), such as *I X Maria, A Lifetime Contained in Black, There Were Two Young Icons* and *Death Double* the funereal evocations and hard-edged forms are like flags dressed in the colours of ridiculous kitsch. These images of mourning and adoration are not concerned with the transcendence of the dead, nor with a resolution with loss, but are an evocation of what Abraham and Torok called 'encrypted discourse'.[24] The 'z' in the artist's first name: Constanze, is also a trace of the mistaken transliteration of his original Greek name. This mistake probably dates back to the first contact with the state's immigration officials. Zisis was the name of his father, and in Greek, 'zisis' means 'to live'. The D.I.E series came shortly after the death of his father.

Zikos's painting have straddled the boundaries between modern abstraction and a variety of visual codes associated with Hellenism. Between these forms is the unashamed exploitation of bridges built by the kitsch of the Greek diaspora and Western popular culture. As in his recent *Fake Flag*, 1994, Zikos reveals a constant delight in kitsch's disruptive order. There appears in this tragicomic mess of transplanted practices an alluring geometry. Learning through appropriation and emulation presupposes access to models; but what happens when this relationship is mediated through the other? The classical references have already been subjected to a Victorian whitewash. The secrets of the past have been smuggled into the antinomies of other Empires. Is the reference to Byzantine and Classical iconographies too distant as code to be tenable; too copied to touch the particularity of the everyday out of which these images emerge? Judith Pascal was right to appreciate that:

> the Classicism Zikos was proposing was neither stylism nor
> revival, but an elaboration of Nietzsche's vision of Greek culture
> with tragedy at its centre, and the theories of George Hersey for
> whom the meaning of the forms of classical architecture can be

understood only if they are seen, as it were, sprayed with sacrificial blood.[25]

Zikos is clear that it is impossible to return directly to the source. The message of the past is as much in the process of mediation as it is in the commingling with the present. For in a sense the reference point is not the discursive formation of classicism, but kitsch. The role of kitsch in Periklean Athens is a moot point: I am concerned with is the role of kitsch in Zikos's Melbourne. And as far as I can see, his work, is in part, a response to the mobilisation of symbols from antiquity into the kitschorama of Melbourne's modernity. Kitsch is commonly interpreted as a sign of a failed or partial entry into modern culture. It makes a mockery of any 'serious' or 'elevated' claim to have reached a higher level of cultural development. Kitsch is the embarrassing reminder that one is but an aspirant before the hallowed alter of the established. Zikos was quick to reject the stigma of kitsch and has persistently incorporated it into his aesthetic. In Zikos's hands, kitsch becomes a source in an autobiographical investigation rather than a mechanism for an ironic distancing from the banality of the suburban everyday.

The key to this sort of interpretation, lies not in the correspondence between symbols and a narrative of origin, but in the disjunction between signs and the technics of representation. For Zikos, the painterly surface is domestic laminex. The geometric registrations are pre-cut from stencils, and the paint is from semi-industrial spray cans. The reason this work can be called allographic is to be found in the relationship between the personal titles, and the formal use of surfaces, colours and symbols. We have learnt about our ancestors from romantic stories told by tourists and travellers. Similarly, the sourcing and processing of symbols in Zikos's work are both diffused and transported via techniques criss-crossing the commercial and the antiquarian. This relationship tends not toward the modernist abstraction of the self and the bracketing of subjectivity, but rather, with the radial energy of memory and mourning, to open new geometries of cultural identity.

For over a decade, an optimistic hope has fuelled a new direction in cultural criticism. It was argued that the migrant perspective, because of its profound awareness of rupture and displacement, could heighten a sensitivity towards the productive tension between the fragmentary nature of identity, the aleatory function of language, and the instability between memory and history. This sensitivity which reversed, crossed and displaced the conventional paradigms of lack and plenitude, self and other, was to serve as the premise, not the basis, for a more generalised movement into a new aesthetic — an aesthetic that institutionally acknowledged and discursively worked against the binarisms and hierarchies which dominated the non-industrialised cultures of the globe.

We are now left with the hard questions of evaluation. Has this aesthetic taken off, if so, how far have we gone? In what ways is cultural interaction no longer bound by what Jean Fisher calls the 'vampiric' structures of colonial domination?[26] For a genuine form of cross-cultural interaction to occur, we would need to recognise that a definition of agency and culture, must also include the subjectivity and structures of the other, otherwise the dialectic is frozen in the gaze of self-reflection.

From a cut with the formative dynamism of the past (place of origin), and in the mediated connection to the generative pulse of the present (the place of arrival), it is possible to imagine the allographic function of autobiography: the two as one, but not in order to lock the part into a grander whole. Rather, this would be a form within which it is possible to redeem the silences, ellipses and radical unevenness in the cultural languages of everyday life.

REFERENCE NOTES

1. G. Michelakakis, 'Cultural Destruction in Postcolonial Australia', unpublished paper, 1991.
2. W. Harris, excerpt from a novel to be called 'Resurrection at Sorrow Hill', *Third Text*, No.19, Summer 1992.
3. Ibid., p.25.
4. Stuart Hall, 'Cultural Identity and Diaspora' in J. Rutherford, ed., *Identity*, Lawrence and Wishart, London, 1991.
5. Benedict Anderson, *Imagined Communities*, Verso, London, 1983.
6. R. Moore, 'Finger Painter', *Melbourne Star Observer*, 4 August, 1995.
7. M. O'Donnell, 'Fragments of Juan Davila', *Outrage*, August, 1995, p.59.
8. A. Wright-Smith, 'Art News', *Herald-Sun*, 2 August, 1995.
9. R. Nelson, 'Angry and Confronting', *The Age*, 16 August, 1995.
10. From this perspective, Davila is only making explicit what is consistently implied in say Clarke's interpretation of the tragedy in Burke's and Wills's relationship. 'Mr Burke and Wills adored each other. Mr Burke called every other member of the expedition by his surname; he called Wills affectionately "Wil".

Neither of them was to know when they first met and liked each other and felt that bond between men to which women must be for ever mighty strangers, that Wills's adoration of Mr Burke was to contribute to their undoing.' C.M.H. Clarke, 'Glory, Folly and Chance', *A History of Australia*, Vol.IV, Melbourne University Press, Melbourne, 1978, pp.144-64.

11. Quoted in *Unbound: Possibilities in Painting*, Hayward Gallery, London, 1994.
12. M. Douglas, *Purity and Danger*, Routledge & Kegan Paul, London, 1966, p.35.
13. G. Brett, *Transcontinental*, Verso, London, 1990, p.38.
14. James Baldwin, quoted in Homi Bhabha, 'Black & White and Read All Over', *Artforum*, October 1995, p.114.
15. Hall, op.cit., p.222.
16. de Man, P., 'Autobiography as Defacement' in *The Rhetoric of Romanticism*, Columbia University Press, New York, 1984.
17. Ibid., p.72.
18. Derrida, J., 'Otobiographies', in *The Ear of the Other*, Schocken, New York, 1985.
19. Ibid., p.45.
20. Spivak, G.C., 'Asked to Talk About Myself ... ', *Third Text*, No.19, Summer 1992.
21. Ibid., p.12.
22. Ibid., p.17.
23. See my 'The South in the North', *Third Text*, No.14, Spring 1991.
24. Quoted in Bhabha, H. K.., ed., 'Dissemination', *Nation and Narration*, Routledge, London, p.315.
25. Judith Pascal, 'Constanze Zikos', *Art and Cultural Difference,* ed. Nikos Papastergiadis, *Art & Design*, Vol.10, No.7/8, 1995, p.90.
26. Personal communication with Jean Fisher.

13.

ON BECOMING AUTHENTIC

A CONVERSATION WITH JIMMIE DURHAM AND LAURA TURNEY

Born in 1940, Jimmie Durham is an internationally acclaimed artist, writer and poet of Cherokee descent. Durham spent a number of years in the seventies on the Central Council of the American-Indian Movement (AIM). In 1977, he co-ordinated the first hemispheric delegation of 98 native representatives to the Palace of Nations in Geneva, where presentations were made before a subcommission of the United Nations commission on human rights. Durham left AIM in 1979. In 1983, he published *Columbus Day* a book of poems. Since then he has worked as an artist and writer.

1993 saw the publication of *A Certain Lack of Coherence*, an anthology of his writings that date from 1974 to the early 1990s. As part of their series of contemporary artists, Phaidon Press published a comprehensive survey of Durham's visual works and writing, *Jimmie Durham* in 1995.

Jimmie Durham's work addresses both the political and cultural forces in the construction of identity and the problems with situating oneself in a sympathetic context. It also illustrates how the tensions between indigenous rights and environmental politics are paralleled by the role of cultural difference in contemporary art in the face of modernism's crisis. Durham situates himself uncomfortably between a specific community and an abstract audience. Whether it is in terms of his advocacy of indigenous rights within a Marxist paradigm, or the identification of artistic strategies in relation to the 'new internationalism', Durham is always addressing the legacy of ethnocide as well as considering the widest possible alliances for the oppressed. His mode of thinking is comparative and inclusive, turning things inside out, starting from etymology and working towards a theory, ricocheting from point to point but also always looking for a position from which the observer can become witness. By implicating himself in the politics of art, and vice-versa, his arguments gain an extra twist, one that does not so much remove the barb from his judgment, but shows that it cuts both ways.

Nikos Papastergiadis Can you talk about the difficulties in forging alliances with the green movements that were the result of conflicting interpretations of custodianship of the land and the purity of nature?

Jimmie Durham Let's begin with a specific example, the Tellico Dam. The environmental groups were never on our side yet they expected us to be on their side from the very beginning. Environmentalists weren't generally willing to be seen on the same side with us because it politicised what they thought needed to be not politicised. For them it was strictly an environmental issue and if you brought in indigenous land rights issues it became politicised. That's been their status from the Environmental Defence Fund, Sierra Club, all the big groups down to the little groups. Some of the smaller groups are actively against Indians because we're just other humans polluting what should be pristine land.

I feel that in Mexico I regained some of the wisdom of my childhood. I grew up in the woods and it was dangerous. There were five kinds of poisonous snakes. There were bugs that could kill you; spiders that would kill you; all sorts of things that would bite you or scratch you or trees that would make you sick if you breathed too close, and so on. It made us careful, it made us move carefully. It wasn't as severe in Mexico but it introduced this element back in my life and suddenly I felt I was back in the world for the first time since my childhood. There were certainly environmental workers who were not prepared to live in such close proximity to scorpions or black widow spiders; they didn't want the wilderness quite so wild, or quite so close to them.

NP Was your strategy in representing the American-Indian Movement (AIM) at the UN in Geneva also an attempt to work at an international level in order to be more effective at the national and at the state level as well?

JD We have always worked at an international level. When the League of Nations started, a man named Deskaheh went to Geneva to plead the case for the American-Indian Nations, he was Iroquois. He stayed six or seven more years because he couldn't get the money to get back and he became a clown there. Cherokee chiefs went to London to talk to the Queen to say, 'Could you get your colonies to straighten up please?' When the UN first started, the Siletz sent their chief, the Sioux sent their chiefs. The Siletz sent someone to San Francisco when they were talking about the UN and said, 'Could we be part of this discussion please?' The desire to negotiate within an international arena is a constant to us. We define it as just being part of the world community that we used to be part of. We don't see it as national versus international because we always want to act internationally and our proof is always that we deal with each other. Because the Cherokee Nation can speak to the Iroquois Nation, this is the proof of our internationality to us. We don't see anything silly about this. But the US seems to think that's crazy.

So when I first came to the UN during Wounded Knee, Frank Fools Crow and two other Sioux chiefs, the three top chiefs of the Sioux Nation went to the UN in New York. They went officially from the Sioux Nation, so they were in their official gear, in official clothes and headdresses, and in New York this was another clown show. It wasn't seen as the US are attacking these Indians. The US army has surrounded these Indians, and they have sent their three top chiefs to the UN to protest. It wasn't seen that way at all. They just arrived at the UN, they did not know what else to do. The guards said that they could not come in, who did they want to see? They wanted to talk to whoever was in charge, the UN. They got their picture in the paper as clowns.

Then two years later we set up our office and I had the job of doing this a bit more methodically, that was all. Since it did not work when we sent our chiefs, let's send someone who maybe knows how to do things the way they do and follow their tricks. I went to Salim Salim, who was, at that point, the head of the League of Non-aligned States, he was the ambassador to the UN from Tanzania, and sought his advice, but he was per-

plexed by our case because he couldn't see how we could be classified as independent nations that had been colonised. The US
was not seen as a colonial entity in the UN. Then there began
to be the idea of Fourth World People. I saw it as a one of the
most urgent things to fight. We were not for indigenous rights;
we were not for indigenous peoples; we were not for Fourth
World Peoples — we were only for the rights of say, the
Cherokee Nation or the Iroquois Confederacy as a nation of
people. As soon as we allowed ourselves to be connected to
indigenous peoples worldwide, we would have lost any support
from the African countries that we needed in the UN. They
would say, 'This is part of some primitivism that England has
put all of us in. Part of our decolonisation process is to get away
from that primitivism.' That's what all the African countries
were on about in the sixties and seventies: to get away from trib-
alism and to get away from people defined as part of the land.
I was afraid we would lose that support completely and all we
would gain would be people who wouldn't help us. We would
gain the environmentalists on some level, who would just be
vaguely sympathetic but who wouldn't be actively helping us.
How would they help us? Would they join in our political struggle? They never have, so I did not think that they would. I
thought the PLO, as an organisation, might. It might join with
us in a political struggle. In the UN, in the seventies, this was a
useful alliance.

Laura Turney Did you think that by allying too much with environmentalists this would depoliticise your case?

JD Yes, especially in those days, when we had to convince people
like Salim Salim that we were genuine from a political stand-
point, that we were worth his time. It never quite worked. He
was very helpful but he never quite believed that we were worth
his time. There was no African who ever believed that we had
legitimate rights. The Africans, more than the Arabs, more than
Europeans, Russians or Chinese, saw us in terms of Hollywood.
If I could sit and talk with someone, as I often did, and say,
'Don't you think that that's part of the political process? Don't
you think that you are colonised into thinking that way about
us?' They might laugh and self-consciously say, 'Well yes, you
have a point', but the next day, nothing had changed. It was not
true with Algeria; it was not true with Cuba; it was not true with

the Communist bloc, they were much more sympathetic.

NP To be acknowledged in the International arena as a political force, you had almost to define yourself as a people or state that was colonised and therefore now needed to be liberated, from another state.

JD Yes, exactly that.

NP Then the crucial task was how you define yourself as a people, as a collective.

JD It was very tricky. Everyone got suspicious of me, rightly so I think, because I had a thousand faces. I said this to this group and this to that group, trying to get someone to be on our side. I got known as a kind of Soviet-style Communist for a while, just because I saw that the Soviets were willing to help us in the UN in a certain way. They controlled a lot of little parts of the UN. They really needed to know that what we wanted was socialism in the US and not decolonisation of the Cherokee nation. So, to them I said, 'Yes of course, our problem is class in the US, absolutely, there's no question, we don't want to be a thousand independent little nations, with our own passports and our own post offices'. I wasn't lying, that isn't what we want, 300 independent little groups of people, because the US would just crush us. If we had to have our own post offices and our own borders defended against the US, they would cut off the water supply on their side of the border and that would be it. By saying that to the Russians and the Poles, they became my best buddies. Then the Africans would ask about decolonisation. We would say, 'Yes here's our treaty, we are some sort of independent nation, here the US has colonised us and we want to be independent of the US, we have the right and here is the treaty that proves we are some sort of independent nation just like you!'. Then I would go back to the reservations, this reservation says it wants total independence from the US, the other one says, 'They want some tractors'. I say 'Yes, that's our struggle, our struggle is tractors!'. It's the problem of having to make one definition that will last for ever. All we want is some human rights.

LT How do environmentalists actually define or see Indian peoples in the US; and, in turn, how do Indian people actually define themselves in relation to the people with whom there is the possibility of making some kind of alliance?

JD I think that really is complex since there is not an Indian people. There begins to be one now — every decade I say there
begins to be now. The Cherokee Nation was once more than one
million people. We had four distinct dialects, we were a big
bunch of people, with a great huge landbase that went from
almost Washington DC down to Northern Florida; from
Western Tennessee to the coast. It was bigger than France. We
first met the Spanish and the Spanish set up missions. Then we
had a fight and we killed the Spanish and then the English came
in. From smallpox and everything we started losing population.
We started losing wars basically when we started losing population. We knew Europeans from the sixteenth century. Other
people say that the Sioux Indians were driven on to the Plains,
much, much later and they did not meet any white people until
1820, something like that. For two hundred years we had been
fighting and the Sioux did not know who we might be fighting.
They did not know what was happening, they just knew that the
Chippewa were driving them out and that they were also losing
population from smallpox. Then they got out to the Plains, then
they found some horses and became the Plains Indians, then the
white people came and started shooting them. So, they think
that they are from the Plains now, they do not remember ever
being in the forest. I remember when I first went out to work
on Pine Ridge, the Great Plains were so strange to me because
I am from the forest. It would be just like if I went to Russia, it
was such a culture shock. If I say, yes — that Cherokees and
Sioux are both Indian — it's only silliness. We are together in
the way — not the way Serbs and Croats are together but the
way that the Serbs and the Irish are together — the distance is
the same. The language difference is the same. Certainly the religious differences are much bigger. It's a history of how you are
colonised, so in the State of Oklahoma now, all Indians are stupidly racist against black people, just because it is the State of
Oklahoma. Everybody is stupidly racist towards black people.
You can't live in Oklahoma in some pure state; you can't live in
a black community. The University of Oklahoma football team
is called 'Boomers', the oil boom, but Indians go to the football
game and shout 'Boomer State, Boomer State'. Why are the
Indian people on the side of the idiots who took your land and
killed you? — 'Cos it's our team!'. I used to have a lot of talks

with Paul Smith, a Commanche, about the fact that we really cannot know too much about who we might have been pre-Columbus. We've been through too many wars and we've lost too much population and we didn't write much down. We cannot remember many songs because we've lost 98 per cent of the population. You might think you do, but you've probably lost 98 per cent of your stories.

NP The stereotypes projected by others are often internalised within your own history. Has this affected the way you connect with other artists or activists?

JD Maybe this answer will be a little mystical sounding. I met a Cherokee artist Kay Walkingstick, she came to my house because I wanted her in the show that Jean Fisher and I curated. I had just met her at that time. She doesn't know how seriously our families are on different sides of the political fence. It's like an Irish situation. Her family is really on the enemy side of my family. We liked each other so much it was as though we needed each other, we just felt completely relaxed and completely at home from the very beginning. I was in Pilsen, in Bohemia and I met Arthur Renwick who I'd met once just briefly before in Montreal. All the time we were in Bohemia, we hung out together, we were best buddies just because we could relax with each other, we didn't say that, we just did it, we knew that we were a couple of redskins who could hang out; it was just that. It seems to always happen, we might be politically against someone but when you're out in the world, you would gladly be with that Indian, even if it's a Sioux or Iroquois. We're not Indians, we're not the same, but in fact by now we have a similarity of some sort. We like each other more, in a certain kind of way, we can relax with each other. I don't think this is easily articulated and I haven't seen anyone articulate it before, but I see it among Indians constantly. At the same time we don't support each other very much, we just hang out together as a way of relaxing.

I had a dream once, but it has stayed with me a long, long time. I'm from an area of Arkansas, next to Oklahoma. It's very close to where Bill Clinton is from, but my side of it is desolated, just very bad country. I know an American white guy, Jay Johnson who now lives in California. He lived in Mexico and he would come by my house and we would talk and he would always ask me where I was from, my land and so on. Partly to check out my authenticity, Americans always do that, so I dreamed that I had taken him back home, and suddenly noticed, when I got there, that everyone was dead and all the land was burned and black and there was nothing left alive at all. I went down to the creek and there were three little black birds only about an inch or so, hiding under a log and they said, 'Don't tell him we're here!'. That dream stays with me and Jay Johnson never said, 'I want to go back with you', he just started questioning me about home, and suddenly something in my brain said, 'Don't tell him where'.

NP That reminds me of a John Berger story. It had a memorable line in it which says, 'When the first axes went into the forest, the trees whispered to themselves, "the handle, it's one of us"'. Can you talk a little more about your project *Here at the Centre of the World*? How did the idea come about?

JD It began quite slowly, in Mexico, where I did live close to the centre of the world, which was an actual tree. When you go to that tree, you see that it marks the centre of the world, there's no argument about it. There is also a magnolia tree, close to where I grew up, that also marks the centre of the world and you can't argue with that either. It is very clear that magnolia tree marks the centre of the world. I already had the idea, what a coincidence that I am so often at the centre of the world! There is a Cherokee saying about when one travels that 'I got there and I saw that half the world was before me and half the world was behind me', therefore I was at the centre. Then, coming to Brussels, thinking about having lived in Europe before, when Geneva was more or less the centre of the world. But the hope of the freedom of money is the new centre of the world. So Brussels is the new centre of the world because it is here that we are hoping that we will get enough money to free us up. That we will have peaceful democracy, brought about by capitalism, that is the Brussels hope and the new European hope.

So, once again I am in the centre of the world, I am in Brussels, the new centre of the world. Then, I was immediately asked last year to do this show in Middleburg which is already a funny contradiction because even Holland agrees to call itself The Netherlands. How can you call yourself The Netherlands, how can you be a Nether to yourself? If you are The Netherlands, you have to call the rest of the world The

Netherlands because the rest of the world is nether to you! Then for there to be this city called Middleburg in The Netherlands seems too strange! Then I started thinking that Europe has all these centres at different times and I find myself doing something with them, so I am doing a show next year in Vienna which has always been the centre of the European world and still thinks of itself as the centre that bridges Asia and Europe. It seemed like there was something worth playing with, the idea of political space and what political space has to do with any kind of other space. They do think that there is a Europe and there is an Asia and you might say that the Ural Mountains is the dividing line, but someone else does not agree. I don't think there is, there is just Eurasia.

NP So, this project *Here at the Centre of the World*, is an exploration of the bridges to the different margins of the world.

JD Yes, exactly that. The thing I am doing in Yakutsk in Siberia, with the City Museum of Porri, Finland, is a project which goes around the Arctic Circle, and it relates to a theory of human migration which suggests that people came from Siberia, across the Bering Straits and into the New World. But, they say that there were no humans originally in the New World. Which we used to hear all the time and I thought that we would not have to hear it any more, because the assumption is always that there were original humans only in Europe. We know that is not the case, we know we are all from Africa. The fact that some people stopped in Paris and some people went on to Cleveland does not make much difference since we are all from Nairobi!

NP What do you plan to do in Yakutsk?

JD I am going to take a mirror with me. Like the figure Kristeva discusses always travelling with a German book, which was his mirror. He said, 'This is my mirror. I carry along this book in German that I am reading, wherever I am in the world. I can see myself by reading a book of my own language, my own people.' It's a very sweet idea, a very gentle idea. It has nothing to do with any truth or power, or whether it is right or wrong, it is really an eccentric idea. Kristeva said that this is narcissistic love, he is using his culture, himself, as his mirror when he is with other people. What if you did not do that? What if you did not bring the baggage with you? Because, Yakutsk is no further away from me than Brussels is. Yakutsk is maybe closer to me than Brussels, except I happen to be in Brussels at the moment. I am not sure in what way I am in Brussels.

When I used to be nostalgic and I'd tell stories about my home, and it's about Cherokee apples, which are real apples. They are black on the outside and red on the inside, very sweet, magic apples. No one would believe me because they don't grow outside any area in Arkansas. I think that they are not there any more either, I haven't seen one since I was ten. Everybody thinks that it is one of my silly stories. When we were coming up from a subway station, here in Brussels that is under the Berlamont building, which was intended to be the centre of the European Union. But, it had too much asbestos, so it's just a giant vacant monstrosity. It's a great big building, completely vacant and will probably stay completely vacant because they don't know how to clean it up, it's too big. So, right across the street they built the new headquarters for EU. The subway comes up under it. I came up at the back of it and there were two apple trees, this was in June so the apples were still young. I looked at them and I said, 'Maria Theresa, wait, I think these are my apples'. I went over and got one, it wasn't quite black on the outside because they were still green. I took one and bit into it and sure enough it was an apple and I said, 'See! see! This is my apple! I was so pleased to see them, to see them there at the real, vacant centre of the new world.

At the time I was looking for a present to give a new godchild in Ghent. So, I quickly wrote her a map of where this apple tree was and a description of what kind of apple it was and the whole story. It's in a very fun place. This street is called Street of the Law, and the other street is called Charlemagne Street. Just over here is the Europe Hotel and over here is Old Hack Pub and here is the vacant centre of the world. So I drew that map — this is where your apple tree is and when you get older you have to go. I just wrote her a letter and that was the gift. There was still one apple left and a Filipino film maker asked me to join a project he was doing about Hiroshima and Nagasaki and a Filipino artist who had died of AIDS. So I said, 'Okay, I'll give you the other apple tree and we'll do a text about it. Here's the same map and here's the same text and you get one apple tree and my goddaughter gets the other one.' So I thought, 'I've done something nice here'. I promised my goddaughter that in September I would go back and get some of the apples, get the seeds and give her the seeds of an apple tree to plant in a safer place, that would be her second present. So, sure enough, last weekend I did, and it's completely cemented over. Not even a trace of the two apple trees. Not even a sign that there were ever any apple trees there. You have to go into the world with no baggage, with no mirror, with no way to do anything but ... I don't know what we're supposed to do.

Except there is that story that I wrote about Quetzalcoatl and his brother. It's a very nice story. Quetzalcoatl had a brother whose name translates as 'Smoking Mirror'. For fifty-two years Quetzalcoatl rules the world and he is a very handsome plumed serpent, but he is also a kind of dandy. Every morning he has to put on his make-up, since he is the god of good times, but his brother, Smoking Mirror is the god of art and industry, so he is the black smoke character and he is also the one who brings corn, most of the crops come from the ugly brother. He really is ugly, he is missing his left foot and he is burned practically to cinders, all scarred up, practically a skeleton face and his chest is torn open and his heart is beating ready to be plucked like a grape, he's a super ugly man. Every fifty two years he comes back and visits Quetzalcoatl and says, 'Let's have a party. I'm your brother. I've just come up from underground and have some of this tequila. Let's sing and dance.' Quetzalcoatl gets completely drunk and stupid. The next morning he wakes up, he has a horrible hangover and his brother pulls out his mirror and says, 'Look at yourself! Aren't you ashamed? I'm going to take over, you're not good enough to run this world, I'm going to run the world.' Quetzalcoatl goes underground for fifty-two years and ugly brother rules the world for the next fifty-two years.

The only way I can be Indian now, the only way I can be Cherokee now, is nostalgically. I can tell the stories but anyone can tell any stories now, stories don't have the weight that we need them to have, they're not the proper baggage. When you open your suitcase full of stories it doesn't serve you the way it might once have served us.

NP Your refusal to sign up to the Indian Art and Crafts Act, which purports to protect as it regulates the question of Indian authenticity, is consistent with your deep suspicion of the paternalistic

gestures in American history. And then there is your public statement: 'I am not an American-Indian, nor have I ever seen or
sworn allegiance to India. I am not a Native "American", nor
do I feel that America has any right to either name me or un-
name me. I have previously stated that I should be considered
mixed-blood: that is, I claim to be a male but in fact only one
of my parents was male.' This is in fact a statement against the
way the government would locate your identity and how you
would be expected to behave and therefore commodify your culture for the consumption of the officially sanctioned commercial
trading culture. So the refusal wasn't a distancing from your
community, but was a rejection of the way in which that community was being defined into the discourse of trade. But a lot
of people interpret it the other way, that you are turning your
back on things and that you were trying to proclaim the law of
the universal artist there.

JD I am certainly turning my back on any organised Cherokee
nation because it is not there. To pretend that it is there is to play
the US Government game against yourself, against the Cherokee
Nation. It's the Cherokee Nation that is against the Cherokee
Nation; if they say we do not recognise you because you are not
enroled, I have already said that to them, 'I don't recognise you'.

NP But what does this mean about the notion of community
today?

JD I was hoping earlier that there would be, not a group of like-
minded people, but that there would always be intellectuals with
an intellectual agenda. I don't see that there is any other human
agenda but intellectuality and that is the very thing that we are
most distrustful of these days. We do everything to deny intellectuality as our agenda, but I still want the Enlightenment in
the sense that I want us to say, 'We should be using our brains
to think about things so that we become the humans that our
brains might allow us to become if we think about it a little
more'; that kind of intellectuality. Politically committed intellectuality. You don't see any other intellectuality, you don't see
intellectuality of pure thought or something because we are not
in an angelic situation, we are in an earthly situation. So, not of
like-minded people but just of intellectuality. In the art world it
is practically against the law again to come out for intellectuality, to be on the side of thinking, it's certainly not commercially

viable. Strategically I have to shut up and say, 'I don't know'. Every question has to answered with Andy Warhol and Warholian statements so that you will be recognised as an artist, 'Yes, that's an artist's statement, I saw Andy Warhol do that once!'. There are signs. I put myself in a circle of people who grab my interest and I think that this is my community but it's not those people who are necessarily my community. It is intellectuality itself, not a sentimental idea of intellectuality that has to be my community.

NP I wonder whether your project, *Here at the Centre of the World* is also related to living in a city like New York or like London, where so many corners of the world are colliding. In New York and London, I don't think it is possible ever to forget that the act of grounding one's identity is caught up with a process of collision. It seems to me that sometimes we call that cosmopolitanism, sometimes we call it urban nightmare, and now, in some ways, you're taking the two sides of that idea, of cosmopolitanism — we could be anywhere in the world, at home wherever we are, and also the idea that multiple differences in collision produce hell. You're taking that idea for a walk around the world.

JD Yes, it's like that.

NP I make that comment in a sense as a question rather than a description because I wonder whether you could have ever done that work in New York?

JD I think it might be perceived as romanticism in New York, because the melting pot and its insoluble problems are too loaded a metaphor there. There are too many stories in New York and the stories began to be gossip.

NP What is missing is a form of listening and response.

JD That's what I need, I need responses. Sometimes I need to know that I don't know, someone else knows it — not some one person, the knowledge is right around the corner in the sense of we are on the verge of desperately needing to know something — all of us, maybe — therefore we might learn it and therefore a piece of it might be in Yakutsk with somebody and they might tell me and I might have a little bit more knowledge than I did before.

NP In light of what you said earlier about revealing and concealing stories about home, I wonder whether this willingness to share has to do with the way other people listen. I often have this feeling, which comes when people ask me simple questions, like what I did this summer; and when they ask that question, I feel such weight that I just say, 'I saw my mum and dad for the first time'. I don't explain that this was the first time I had met them in Greece. I just can't be bothered and I feel such a weight and deadening force in the air that I can't tell them what it meant. I feel that weight and that negativity are to do with the fact that they want the story either as a bit of information that they can use, or as a bit of entertainment that will titillate them. For me there is always this fear that when you're telling something that you already know, each repetition is like a plane going over a piece of wood and you are frightened that if you tell it one more time that it will disappear.

JD That's perfectly the way it is!

NP Do you feel that the stories you are now writing are exercises in search of an audience?

JD Except then it becomes miraculous and horrible at the same moment. When I am in the process I find loaded non-things like the Linden Tree in Lisbon. I said to Maria Theresa, 'I must be the only one alive who knows so many things about linden trees'. First how to recognise that this is a linden tree and then the bark is good for this, the tea is good for this, etc. Knowledge is so specialised now. But I'm like a racoon. You have to be an omnivore because you starve to death if you're not an omnivore. I'm too intellectually poor to not be an omnivore so I have a wider sweep of knowledge, but no specialisation. Then when you find miraculous surprises of knowledge you already have, there's a responsibility. For instance, I can say, 'Here I am in Bohemia and I find a linden tree and it's just like the one that I've just found in Lisbon.' What does the world possibly need that knowledge for? Then you have to say is anything useful that I might be doing? If I put that question out as I intend to put it out to you, with a piece of the linden wood, hoping that you will either take it or send it to Greece .... I have it all as parts of a body and I am giving it to different people to take to different places and send back to me, so you are my Greek bearer! Then I'll take all that back, after it's been around the world and the story is still ridiculous, it still makes no sense, it's not really interesting as anything. Yet I think, well, I did find these linden

trees after all. I don't know what else to do so I might as well
... take some of this wood and fix it up and see if anybody is
interested.

NP Can you talk a little about the relationship between the political and the necessary in art?

JD Yes, even though I have no idea what might be necessary. I wish
I knew what necessary meant! When I first started doing the
work in New York, which was after I left the Indian Movement
and Maria Theresa ran away from home, we were living in New
Jersey and I was supposed to be writing a history of the Indian
Movement; the goal I set myself. But, it was too close and I
couldn't do it and I was still working with Paul Smith and we
were fighting and nothing was happening. I began doing art-
work again and I had done four or five pieces that were like
collages and assemblages, wall pieces which looked like paintings, but about specific situations, they explained our struggle.
One was about the horrible computerisation of life on the
Rosebud reservation. Maria Theresa had this friend, Juan
Sanchez, who was a political painter from Puerto Rico. She
invited him over because he was doing a show called *Beyond
Aesthetics*, she said, 'You should see my friend JD's work, he
doesn't have any aesthetics!'. He came over, liked the work and
said I'm going to put these three in the show that I'm doing.
That was my first show in New York, in 1980-1. The New York
art world liked them. People who saw the work said that it was
great work and I hadn't expected that response. I was still in the
movement, the response I expected was, 'That's happening now
on the Rosebud? Let's see what we can do! That's the response
I expected. Talk about naïve. Then when the work was appre-
ciated, but when people still didn't organise against controlled
data corporation, I said there's something about art that I don't
like. I'm going to do something else. But soon I'm in the art
world again because I'm popular and Juan Sanchez did another
show immediately afterwards and I was in that too. I changed
the idea in the second show, but not very much, I just added
some irony. I kind of accused them of not doing anything. They
liked that too, they thought that was also great. So, then I said,
I have to find a way to challenge what they think is not there to
be challenged, I have to challenge something that is unknown
as challengeable, because they already know everything that I'm

doing. So I don't have to say it, I can just say, 'What I already said!'. That's a thing that American blacks do and I like it very much. Some guy says something good and the other guy says, 'What he said!'. I don't want to live my life saying what I have already said and being applauded for it because that really is betrayal of your people, a betrayal of the struggle.

NP Can we return to the question of stereotypes and the techniques of 'passing'?

JD It gets very predictable. I know quite a bit about European history and Belgian history and I know much more about the local wildlife than they do, which is expected. They expect me just magically to know that. But people say things like, 'Your work seems to so much more European now', I say, 'In what way?'. They say, 'It doesn't seem to be so Indian-oriented now', and I say, 'What piece was Indian oriented?' 'Well, your work has always been ... ', it kind of goes like that. I'm having to try strategically to formulate responses that are fresh and spontaneous that say, 'I'm still as authentic as I used to be but I'm trying to speak to you about *here*, I'm trying to be here. Would you please allow me to be here at this moment and forget wherever we both might have been yesterday?' But it has to be articulated strategically and I haven't found a way to do it. I'll tell another story, another city, not Belgian. A very famous dealer/collector said, 'You seem so nice and last time I saw you, you were very mean and belligerent.' I hadn't' even remembered having met her. But I do remember having been mean and belligerent too many times in my life so I agreed with her and said, 'It's just because I'm trying to be civilised now. I'm living in Europe, I want to be part of civilisation. I like European civilisation as an idea and I want to participate in the project.' She liked that answer very much, she was pleased because I had struck a note between authenticity as a savage and enough intellectuality to talk about my savagery. I comforted her with that line. Then she said, 'Are you really full-blood Cherokee?' I said, 'Who knows if there is any such thing, but I'm not one'. And she said, 'But that would be nice wouldn't it — to be a full-blood Cherokee?' I said, 'I suppose it would — yes'. We were best buddies from that moment on. It's the point where I allayed all of her fears, I answered her accusations and I behaved in a way that made me trustworthy and not mean and belligerent any more even though she remembered having liked me *because* I was mean and belligerent — that's why I stood out in her memory!

NP When you really face art you are aghast for a long time. It takes a long time to find words. The 'tactile dialogue' you described earlier is a way of moving from symbols to metaphors, but it is also a way of facing the gaps and 'misfit' between different languages. Do you find the term 'hybridity' helpful for identifying this process?

JD I would like to answer your question in the broadest possible way and to do that I want to tell specific anecdotes. I want to make a framework of universality that says something about human nature, where we are as humans, to make it seem as if I know what I'm talking about with my specifics. If I imagine that the state of humanity is that we are oppressed by humanity then I say that our human purpose is to free ourselves from human oppression.

In Oklahoma, The Osage, they were quite militant and they beat the US army a few times and they captured the army bugles. They incorporated that music and that captured instrument into their traditional music and it's there now in anthropology. So here is an Osage song that everyone is singing and there are drums and in the middle of it, the guy comes up with the bugle and plays the same tune over and over again and that's all he has to play, he doesn't know another. He knows the tune that he heard just as he grabbed the bugle out of the mouth of the US army soldier! They did it celebratorialy in the beginning. They are saying here is our music and in the middle of this you tried to interrupt us and all you knew was this tune and we stole even your tune from you! That's what they were doing. Then twenty years later when they are defeated and they are still playing exactly the same thing for the anthropologists and it's recorded for anthropology, it's no longer a celebratory song, it's only a souvenir. Osage music, where is it now? It stopped at that point, there is no more Osage music.

The only American-Indian music that became viable came out of the Peyote cult that was Mexican and US. Everyone who was militant in the fifties was part of the Peyote cult, there was no other way to be militant. To be militant was to be what was called Pan-Indian. How to get away from your own little community struggle and universalise it for all Indians, which for us, meant US and Mexico, later it included Canada. It was the attempt to blend Mexican Catholicism, South-West Catholicism which had been put on us with the Peyote Cult that seemed like it might be the connection between those two things. It seemed like it might be the way for all of us to make ourselves Pan-Indian, become hybrid. I think people now misunderstand what that Peyote cult was. It was called the Native-American Church, then it became the American-Indian Church.

One of the first things I tried to do when I got to Geneva and I saw that all kinds of churches were there, I went and made friends with the secretary of the World Council of Churches and said, 'I'm part of the Native-American Church and perhaps you might like to invite our church into your World Council of Churches. He said, 'I didn't know you had such a thing — what's it like?' I said, 'Well we take Peyote and Peyote is the same as Jesus so ... ' Suddenly he lost interest. Peyote wasn't the same as Jesus, he already knew what Jesus was, it was wheat crackers — that was clear, what was not clear was why I wanted us to be part of his gang!

When you take Peyote in the church you remember all the Peyote songs that were ever sung. You can sing them even if you never heard them before. Nobody else is singing, you remember a song and start singing it. Everyone else remembers it. It has been recorded and in fact it is a song that has been sung before but you didn't know it at that moment because you'd never heard it before. We didn't need recorded anthropological proof to know that, we knew that. The priest who's called the Roadman, told us that. As we're going under, as we're taking our Peyote and chewing it, as he gives it to us out of his own mouth he is preaching and his preaching is always politics it's never religion in those days. Now it is only religion, I went back to the church in the eighties and the late seventies and it's only religion. It was only like Jesus if you believe in Peyote it will save you, he will save you. But in the early days it wasn't that way, from the turn of the century until the 1950s it was — we take this Peyote, we take this Jesus, we take this holy thing among us as long as we walk our Indian path which the Roadman told us to walk. As long as we support each other, as long as we sing our old songs and remember our history we can be free. That was the gist of every sermon with lots of embellishments and personal testimonies and that sort of churchy thing. The point was never faith in the something and then you will be free, it was we together will do our way together and then politically we will be free. In the sixties politics took over and the church went away, then the seventies, eighties, politics were defeated and the church came back as a regular Christian church. It came back in a bad way. Those are 'into the fray' remarks.

Everyone knows that one of the good definitions of the US is the music and the music is black music. The sound of the US is the sounds that black people make in their music whether it's blues, jazz or rock and roll, defined by the sound of music and that's black people that did that. It's celebrated as being a hybrid, as being what people do, blending in a new situation; that's a cliché of what's jazz, what's blues — that it is a hybrid thing. When I look at the same phenomenon; first, I'm jealous that we can't do it. That we're stuck with our anthropological bugle, we're stuck with a cute story that didn't develop into music. I say, 'Why didn't we? Why couldn't we? Why couldn't our sounds be part of the sound of the US and defeat defeatism that way; defeat the lack of hope by dancing and singing?' We try all the time, we dance and sing all the time, we do our stuff all the time and it goes nowhere. There's only the white and the black radio stations, there's no Indian music on the radio stations. If there were, most of us would still listen to Country and Western music because we identify with that. Nonsense, why do we identify with that? Why don't we identify with Miles Davis? Why don't we identify with the great blues guys? That's not even on the agenda, that's not even given to us. We can't even hear that on most radios in most Indian country, they only offer the white stuff. But, even the white stuff is a hybrid, it's a hybrid of Irish and black music and it makes it somehow speakable to much in the world, in the oppressed world. So then I go back to — what's the difference between Stan Getz and Louis Armstrong? What's the difference in the great old blues men and people like Hogey Carmichael and the white guys who cleaned up their music, ripped it off and got rich and famous?

When you listen to blacks doing black blues, you hear, whether or not you know that you're hearing it, their sublimated agenda. With great celebration and with great pain, a man sings a song 'My Baby Left Me' and the words don't go much beyond

that. He's not allowed to say or sing in his song in those days
that — my folks are being lynched and I don't have a job and
I'm afraid for my life. All he can sing is 'My Baby Left Me',
other words are taken away from him because he will be
lynched if he sings the other words. He finds a way to put those
other words in the song, in emotional and distorted ways that
you can't always pinpoint, is it that guitar note, or that note —
no, it's everything together. You hear it, you feel that pain and
that resistance to inhumanity. Not because you are taught to but
because you feel it, because it's there. Not because you know the
story, you feel it, you know it's there. When jazz comes along
and the white guys play jazz, they play it from a kind of 'formula', then you can judge it strictly as music. You can say Take
five is good, Take five is bad; this song is good, or this song
needs a little ... ; you can treat it strictly aesthetically. It doesn't
mean when Coltrane plays that you leave out the aesthetics, you
can do exactly the same thing but you can't deny a message that
Coltrane is giving through the music and I know I'm not being
romantic, I know that you can feel it because you can do the
same thing with Django Reinhardt. You can say, there's something in what he is playing that's not exactly there when ... he
was showing us his resistance in a celebratory way.

NP Hybrid becomes most poignant to you, it seems, when it can
be emancipatory, which is a reminder that, if hybrid is simply
the result of any form of exchange, then there also can be negative hybrids.

JD Take Mexico for example. You know my line on the difference
between the English and the Spanish? The Spanish saved Indian
lives because all they wanted was to rape, rob and enslave and
the English wanted to kill everyone and they almost did kill
everyone. The Spanish saved lives by raping and enslaving and
they even created more lives because they created little bastards
all over Mexico. But the little bastards weren't necessarily their
fathers' children, they were potentially free little bastards and
could at this very moment be free any time they choose indi-
vidually. So, you can say perfectly well humans are horribly bad
animals and that humans are very hopeful and miraculous
things. The hope and the miraculous only come from when we
resist the other side. Any spirit that might come from the hybrid
state comes from the resistance to this enslaver, the raper.

14.

THE 'ISLAND FEELING' IN A CHANGING WORLD

Do islands exist? Has the rising tide of globalisation submerged all borders? The boundaries of culture are not as stable as they once were, the networks of power are ever more complex and diffuse. Wealth, freedom and knowledge are not more forthcoming in the new configurations of trans-national corporations, the chaotic movements of migrants and the mediatised transferral of information, ideas, symbols, narratives and rules. The old hierarchies of inequality and exploitation may have collapsed but they have not disappeared, they have shift and diversified. We live in a world where the decisions that influence our everyday lives are made elsewhere. The nuclear disaster in Chernobyl affects the birth of lambs in Wales. Iraq invades Kuwait and the US respond with a multinational strikeforce. A fluctuation in oil prices affects everyone.

We have become more conscious of forces that operate on a global scale. We are increasingly aware that many problems are now too big for purely local responses. Different parts of the world are becoming more interconnected and the power of individual states to retain their sovereignty over the forms and structures of their economy, society and culture are diminishing. Cheap transport has stimulated the 'outsourcing' of labour intensive and low value-added commodity production. In the dependence on electronic modes of communication for substantial financial decisions and the development of significant social relationships, we have witnessed a revolution of time and space.[1]

Our sense of time and space becomes abstract, measurable and interchangeable. Both become quantifiable and can be controlled and disconnected from diffuse social networks and personal associations. The 'could be anywhere' feeling of holiday resorts and the fragmentation of work schedules into discrete and digitalised time units are banal examples of these transformations. In this 'world', are there any islands left? Has the distinction between island and mainland collapsed?

Questions of space have been overtaken by the calculations of time. With the deregulation of national economies and the electronic interface of the stock markets of New York, Tokyo and London, these places have now developed important information networks which are more dependent on each other than they are on their domestic spaces. These are places which have built 'bridges' of communication and transportation that interlink key nodal points, bypassing traditional borders and voiding space. Information moves at speeds which approach zero delay. Disconnected from fixed ties, seeking more favourable options, these new trading zones are not only dominating the global economy but are also disappearing from the horizon. They are becoming invisible — virtual islands of power. Decisions are now less informed from the perspective of proximity and involvement but on the basis of abstract calculations of possible futures and the relational effect of traded risks. The value of financial services has vastly outstripped the value of commodity trade. The major players in the global economy are no longer manufacturers like the Ford motor company but brokerage houses like Morgan Stanley. This has raised the spectre of 'restless capital' and the 'homeless subject' to a degree that was previously unimaginable, even by Marx.

In colonial literature, in particular that of the French and British Empires, the island was a place of adventure. The islands of the colonies were defined in opposition to the 'mother country'.

> The further afield Verne's works were to take the nineteenth-century reader — whether in the dark interior of the mysterious African continent, the cavernous depth of the Pacific Ocean, the uncharted shores of deserted islands or, indeed, amidst the working of scientific equations and formulae — the closer they came to a description of the civilised. The more unfamiliar the terrain the more readily it could assimilated and ascribed to the familiar.[2]

Their identity was to be conferred by the coloniser. We can only speak of their 'discovery' if we assume the perspective of the coloniser. The tales that followed, or in some cases preceded, such 'discoveries' reveal more of colonial fantasies than the histories and experiences of these other places. From Shakespeare's *The Tempest* to Stevenson's *Treasure Island*, the story of the island was related from beyond its shores.

The literature, popular discussion and political rhetoric on islands has been referred to as 'island discourse'. Islands were perceived as remote and exotic. Wild and fertile, open and deserted, lush and dark. The island provided the pretext for the dream of new forms of control and domination. A place inhabited by savages and beckoning civilisation. No matter what signs of life existed there, or how different and unknown was the landscape of the island, the surface was rendered like a *tabula rasa*, to be inscribed by the visions and technologies that had already given birth to the colonial venture. The island discourses were thus mapped not by the contours of the topos but by the tropes of desire and conquest. The myths of islands could often furnish dreams of manliness and social reinvention, rather than histories of disinheritance and the dispossession of indigenous peoples. The island became the idealised space upon which social experiments could be conducted, sexual codes inverted and the whole order of 'manliness' restaged. The island was deliverance to a place of rebirth and genesis.

> The island draws a line around a set of relationships which do not possess the normal political, social and cultural interference: a simplification of existing colonial problems and thus an ideological process of wish-fulfilment.[3]

The island is a metaphor for space in which the relationship between 'man' and nature could be recoded and islands therefore have the potential to be Utopian spaces. Their identity is fixed by a conjunction of the known and the imagined. These images helped fuel both an escapist and reclamationist fantasy of the home. The island was both a place where the past could be overcome and where the ideal life could be constructed. Yet this myth which energised and comforted the minds of the coloniser was the dystopic seed for the islanders. The classical tales of empire rendered the indigenous people mute, invisible and docile or as barbaric savages awaiting conquest and civilisation. What dominates 'island discourse' is the projection of fantasies and the exploitation of resources. The islands were seen as sites for transposing unfulfilled desires and the ruthless abuses of nature. Colonisation of the island is different from other forms of occupation, it presupposed not just the taking of the place but also the transformation of the space. Colonisers distinguished themselves not only for their inability to establish convivial forms of co-existence but in the fact that their subjugation of other people involved a reordering of social and economic priorities that reflect the interests of the 'mother country'. It was the coloniser's grip on technology that gave them a different claim and view of the island.

When it came to visual representation, similar dynamics and problems were evident. The artists who accompanied the explorers of the Pacific, in particular on Captain Cook's voyages, aspired to portray people, landscape, plants and animals with objectivity and clarity.[4] But their vision was framed by the conventions and ideologies of their time. The artists were the heirs of the Enlightenment and were working in the context of a guarded colonialism. Signs of conflict, resistance, futility or depravity were explicitly checked. One of Cook's most celebrated artists, John Webber, was explicitly instructed that 'nothing indecent' should appear in his books irrespective of 'whatever may happen to you as such'. His portrait of Poedua, which Jeanette Hoorn argues, was painted while she was being held hostage on board Cook's ship, depicts her with a *Mona Lisa* like smile, her body draped in white cloth, flowers in her hair and the background is set in a lush landscape. Only the dark clouds above give hint of her captivity. The most 'objective' work of these artists were the scientific drawings of the plants and animals. With precision and care, draughtsmen tried to render accurate impressions of unknown 'specimens'. They dissected and classified them according to first the Aristotelian principles and, when this failed, they adopted the Linnaean classification. The portraiture of native people that was executed by colonial draughtsmen also reflected the limitations of such quasi-scientific codes.

Bernard Smith has argued that the portrayal of the Pacific people was framed by two dominant conventions: the allegorical and ethnographic. The allegorical convention has roots that can be traced back to antiquity. The representation of place was constructed through archetypal figures. Hence, the maps which show the four continents of the world are personified by images of man and monster. Images of the other people at furthest points from the centre of these maps were defined not only in opposition to the normative self-images of the West, but were depicted as the 'natural production' of these remote locations. Allegories of people and place were clear expressions of the exotic aesthetic: the exotic was not only distant from the European mind, it was its polar opposite. By reference to the exotic the European could define itself all the more clearly: it was defined in opposition to the conventions of beauty, health and order. It also conflated the differences of the other into a singular homogenising form.

One of the earliest representations of the exotic was Cyclops, the one-eyed giant, cannibalistic and isolated island dweller who captured Odysseus. In *Barbaric Others*, the authors present a spirited manifesto against the cultural categories of colonialism in which they argue that Columbus and his successors were swayed by such figurations of other people. The significance of the Cyclops myth is thus measured not in the truth or falseness of its empirical accuracy but in the degree that it shaped the actions, encounters and interpretations of other travellers.

> The Greeks thus very early established the outer dimensions of what later became the European debate about human nature and anthropology.... It was the Greeks who introduced the pygmies; the *Kynokephaloi*, the dog-headed people; the *Skiapodes*, the shadow-footed people, the *Akephaloi*, the people with no head and with their eyes on their chest; as well as the Cyclops....Greek literature is replete with hybrid races: minotaurs, centaurs and satyrs. The monstrosity of Other Peoples the physical character of their being, is a direct corollary of the difference of their lifestyle and behaviour from the Greek norm. Together they define the barbarism without.[5]

It is clear from the accounts of Columbus's doctor Diego Alvares Chanca that these mythical traits of cannibalism were attributed to the people of the Caribbean,[6] but such conventions could not persist after encounters with the Pacific people. The ethnographic convention, as a practice of visual culture, was more directly related to the scientific and philosophical views of its time. However, the realism that emerged still drew on the vocabulary and forms of classicism. A Tahitian chieftain was playfully given the Greek name Lycurgus. A Polynesian chieftain whose sense of justice was admired was thus depicted as a Roman magistrate. As Bernard Smith observes, 'there is more than a touch of Rousseau' in the depiction of the Pacific people as noble savages. At times, the warm and fertile islands of antipode became a symbol of the grace from which the West had fallen.

Despite their intention to depict the landscape and people of the Pacific as objectively as possible, the artists echoed the forms of Arcadia most pleasing to the political directives of their masters. They were also guided by the norms of their own education. Europe's original 'primitivism', its elevation of Ancient Greece to the ideal cultural model, served as both the door and the barrier through which other 'civilisations' must pass. To understand the Pacific the reality of the people and their place had to be encountered and not just interpreted within the confines of prior classificatory schemes, even when in the sensory presence of these people the European's ability to perceive their difference was limited.

Not all the representations produced in the context of colonial expansion in the Pacific were purely ideological. Artists combined aesthetics and science to fit the preferences of Empire but, as Paul Carter has noted, the attempts to translate 'other' landscapes and cultures also produced significant disruption to the prevailing codes and conventions. To depict the indigenous fauna and flora as well as the landscape, the coloniser required a different sort of geographical knowledge. In Carter's view this understanding needed to be more 'open, mobile and fleeting'. Space was different and demanded to be understood in a different visual language. The detail could not be possessed and captured straightforwardly, the coloniser needed to bend and twist. Go-betweens and translators who could mix their styles and alternate their viewpoints created new hybrid visual forms. Carter has argued that this passage of styles was particularly evident in the use of watercolours for the 'uncanny' depiction of dreamlike coastlines and a 'babbling' ground.

> watercolour may have been sympathetic to 'seeing through' the linearism associated with imperial history's logic of causes and effects and its handmaiden, the majestically bounding line of representation, but it was the occasion of cross-cultural encounter that irresistibly showed the artificiality of these boundaries, the necessity to acknowledge a ground that could not be translated into linear enclosures.[7]

This attention to the failure of the Eurocentric models of classification and the hybrid formations that emerged from the encounters of different cultures helps break down the ideological polarities — high and low, pure and contaminated, primitive and modern — which frame much of the discussion of modernism and its boundaries. This perspective may also serve as a bridge contemporary art. Ian Webbe has argued that a number of artists in New Zealand (and Jacqueline Fraser is included) have utilised what he calls a knowing reappropriation of paradigms and a double consciousness of concepts that were once used to address the limits of European civilisation. In particular he seizes on the exhausted but shifting signifier of primitivism in modern art. From being a reference to fourteenth- and fifteenth-century Italian artists like Giotto, to the folkloric practices in the Balkans, and then as the master-concept for the crisis of metropolitan taste and sensibility that hits the West at the turn of the century, it finally reappears to describe both the artworks from the peripheral colonies and the practice of appropriation by Western artists like Picasso. Throughout this trajectory is the recurring narrative of nostalgia for lost innocence.

The most privileged port of longing in the European evocations of Arcadia is the island of Cythera, the small Greek island on the southern trip of the Peloponnese, which has become a romantic symbol of tarnished glory and profound melancholy. Here the sublime rested on rocky crags and nested in abandoned harbours. The icon of Cythera becomes the subject for a more theatrical staging of origin and loss in the work of the artists in New Zealand about whom Webbe so eloquently writes. He sees a new strategy which is both expressive of place and a critique of politics. The art world and the lingering consequences of colonialism are targeted equally. This is achieved by the way an inherited narrative of displacement is taken but then flattened out until its 'face value' can reveal different desires. A provincialised modernism thus seeks its revenge by taking the very images in which it was meant to remain bound to, and then usurping the depths and stretching the surfaces of the prior narrative. The moorings of Cythera are loosened from their connotations of serenity, innocence and harmony, as they are dragged into the 'morbid personifications of the secular, the art dealers, become demonic undertakers'.[8] This restaging of myth is also a critical intervention into the place of the artist. The nostalgia for reconciliation with our island of origin is reworked into a daily struggle with the streams of politics and power.

If Cythera was the longing symbol of early modernity, then Manhattan has become the icon of late modernity: an island of constant arrival and departure, where the activity of the port sets the tone for everything. On such a location John Berger saw a unique expression of recognition and accommodation in the paintings of Ralph Fasanella. New York is conventionally seen as the archetypal place of estrangement and anonymity. An eviscerated place where everything that exists runs out along the surface. All the immigrants' dreams are hung out of windows and along exterior walls. The city is a constant 'circuit of messages'. Yet despite this representation of restless traffic, Berger claims that the tone in Fasanella's paintings is not tragic, for neither are they haunted by despair, nor do they seek to offer respite from the tense rhythm they express. There is no judgment *against* others but only the painted condition *of* others. In Fasanella's paintings we see both a more consensual perspective and a convivial approach: 'The island of Manhattan is a gigantic metaphoric model of the compression of an immigrant ship that has moored and never left'.[9]

This representation of longing and belonging is seen in the photography of Bryndis Snaébjornsdottir, in particular her snowy landscapes of Iceland, *Vatnajokull* (1995). This sequence is almost entirely white: the horizon disappears as snow and clouds merge. Only the faint smudge of a distant house gives a sense of scale and position. This house beckons and stands alone. It remains isolated and only just returning my sense of position. I try to imagine the sound of this island: a few tuning forks being tapped at irregular intervals; the notes spreading further apart; sparse sounds full of resonance; an echo, a vibration, between two positions, a rebounding of low waves, a fragile stillness. 'Listening' to these incidental sounds, the wind, I realise that there can be no complete silence, just as there is no real emptiness.

Snaébjornsdottir's work often begins with the representation of a national symbol. Whether we recognise this symbol is not the central question. However, other questions do follow. Why do national symbols so often refer to the land? What is the link between culture and land? And, in turn, how are these symbolic links staged on the body of the citizen? Such questions gain poignancy when reflection starts on another island. This island need not be distant, its difference is sufficient to open up the *placings* of identity. In this case, the tension is found in the gestures that orient the symbol to the body. The depiction of a soft, curly hat has symbolic value to me only in the way it is grasped, clutched and cradled, not in what it is supposed to stand for. It is the portrayal of a relationship between the various shades of softness and whiteness with the body who holds it that directs us towards a subtle form of displacement. Here we sense both anguish and tenderness. In these images I hear voices, like sirens, beckoning, but then these calls also turn into reassurances and requests that the one who leaves may know how to return. This second voice is more mysterious and more banal. It is heard in ordinary conversation but it resonates across the seas. This voice also gives recognition to the distance between home and exile and that the one who travels in-between needs what we call in Greek, a *filakto*, a sort of offered protection. Whether it is taken is another matter, but it is the consideration which counts, for it is from there that the metaphors of journeying away and return come. It is by addressing the incongruence between the symbol and the physicality of her island that other spaces in between emerge, this attention is energised like an echo. People who live in mountains are aware of the subtle forces between avalanche and stillness, just as sailors know of the candle in the lighthouse.

The island of Cythera was a major port for the ships that traded between the Aegean and the Ionian seas. The cutting of the Corinth canal and changes in the scale of shipping effectively killed trade and meant an exodus of its people and, from being an island with over 40,000 people at the beginning of this century, it now barely holds 4,000. Cythera was the inspiration for Watteau and Baudelaire. The evocations of Cythera swayed John Conomos a Greek-Australian filmmaker with Cytherean forebears. Conomos completed a film, *Autumn Song*, in which he investigated his relationship to Cythera and his uncle. Growing up in the working-class and ethnic suburbs of Sydney, Conomos's academic and artistic bent was a sign of bemusement for his family. Where did this predisposition for literary optic to the world come from? To make sense of their son they constantly compared him to his Uncle Manolis. But this was also a kind of warning. The return to Cythera was a search for the distant place of origin and the uncle who had become a mythical reference point, his own original and doubled identity. Uncle Manolis proved to be a misanthropic, hermit-like figure with an encyclopaedic knowledge who had remained on the island playing endless games of backgammon in the local tavern. He was the author of numerous books.

The film *Autumn Song* is saturated in a melancholic mode. An island is surrounded by the sea and the horizon, an infinite line that separates two forms of blue, is full of ambivalence. The sea is work, it is pleasure, it is hope and threat. The *caiques* rot at the edges of the old harbour. The houses on the cliffs hear the low rumble of the passing super-tankers. Old men with white stubble are hunched over an unknowable destiny. Their curse spits out their outrage and respect before a submission to this marvellous blue. The winds can be as generous as they are capricious. A secret solidarity is expressed to this unfathomable and unpredictable deity. All who live on this island must constantly guess at its course.

The border between stability and change, like the coastline between sea and land, constantly shifts. When 'landmarks' are not fixed, one's sense of movement and return must remain open and attentive to change. This involves a more dynamic and interactive understanding of mapping, where the flows of memory and place combine to establish paths. Perhaps all movement and meaning requires this open frame and the 'island feeling' is a metaphor for living with a changing world.

NOTES

1. Scott Lash and John Urry, *Economies of Signs and Spaces*, Sage, London, 1994.
2. Diana Loxley, *Problematic Shores: The Literature of Islands*, Macmillan, London, 1990, p.21.
3. Ibid., p.3.
4. The following section is heavily indebted to the pioneering research conducted by Bernard Smith and Jeanette Hoorn. See Bernard Smith, *Imagining the Pacific*, Melbourne University Press, Melbourne, 1992.
5. Zia Sardar, Ashis Nandy and Meryl Wyn Davies, *Barbaric Others*, Pluto Press, London, 1993, p.28.
6. See also William Artens, *The Man Eating Myth*, Oxford University Press, Oxford, 1979 and Peter Mason, *Deconstructing America: Representations of the Other*, Routledge, London, 1990.
7. Paul Carter, 'Encounters', *Art & Cultural Difference: Hybrids and Clusters*, ed. Nikos Papastergiadis, Academy Group, London, 1995, p.59.
8. Ian Webbe, *How to be Nowhere*, Victoria University Press, Wellington, p.91.
9. John Berger, *About Looking*, Writers and Readers, London, 1980, p.96.

INDEX